WAR ECONOMIES IN A
REGIONAL CONTEXT

A project of the International Peace Academy

WAR ECONOMIES IN A REGIONAL CONTEXT

Challenges of Transformation

MICHAEL PUGH AND NEIL COOPER
WITH JONATHAN GOODHAND

LYNNE
RIENNER
PUBLISHERS

BOULDER
LONDON

Published in the United States of America in 2004 by
Lynne Rienner Publishers, Inc.
1800 30th Street, Boulder, Colorado 80301
www.rienner.com

and in the United Kingdom by
Lynne Rienner Publishers, Inc.
3 Henrietta Street, Covent Garden, London WC2E 8LU

Library of Congress Cataloging-in-Publication Data
Pugh, Michael C. (Michael Charles), 1944–
    War economies in a regional context : challenges of transformation
/ Michael Pugh and Neil Cooper with Jonathan Goodhand.
        p. cm. — (Project of the International Peace Academy)
    Includes bibliographical references and index.
    ISBN 1-58826-251-0 (hardcover : alk. paper) — ISBN 1-58826-211-1 (pbk. : alk. paper)
    1. Economic conversion—case studies.   2. War—Economic aspects—Case
studies.   3. Regional economics—Case studies.   4. War and society—Case
studies.   5. Peace—Case studies.   I. Cooper, Neil.   II. Goodhand,
Jonathan.   III. Title.   IV. Series.

HC79.D4P84   2003
330.9—dc22
                                                                    2003058573

British Cataloguing in Publication Data
A Cataloguing in Publication record for this book
is available from the British Library.

Printed and bound in the United States of America

The paper used in this publication meets the requirements
of the American National Standard for Permanence of
Paper for Printed Library Materials X39.48-1992.

5   4   3   2   1

For Gitte

Contents

Illustrations

Maps

Figure

Tables

Foreword

David M. Malone,
President, International Peace Academy

Until very recently, the economic dimensions of intrastate armed conflicts have been an underexplored aspect of conflict research and policy design. Through its Economic Agendas in Civil Wars program, the International Peace Academy has sought to fill this lacuna by bringing analysis of the political economy of armed conflict to bear upon policies of conflict prevention and conflict management. Early research led to the now widely cited volume *Greed and Grievance: Economic Agendas in Civil Wars,* which focused attention on this important area of conflict research and pointed to the need for both further empirical study and policy development. Subsequent research culminated in a volume of case studies, *The Political Economy of Armed Conflict: Beyond Greed and Grievance,* which extended empirical understanding of the varying ways that economic factors combine with political, strategic, and ideational factors to shape the onset, character, and duration of separatist and nonseparatist conflicts.

From the outset, one of the main objectives of this research has been to contribute to more effective policy approaches to assist transitions from protracted war to lasting peace. In this thought-provoking volume, Michael Pugh, Neil Cooper, and Jonathan Goodhand explore the regional dimensions of war economies and the challenges they pose for sustainable peace and development. As their analysis makes clear, not only has the political economy of regional conflict complexes been neglected by peacebuilders, but this neglect has left many war-torn states vulnerable to continued instability and poverty. In urging a more regionally sensitive approach to peacemaking and postconflict reconstruction, the authors also offer a trenchant critique of current efforts to regulate war economies by control policies of embargo and interdiction. More controversially, they offer a compelling indictment of neoliberal models of development as inherently unsuited to the needs and interests of vulnerable and war-torn societies.

Policymakers are beginning to understand the ramifications of ignoring economic agendas in war transformation, but find themselves with few practical tools to use in combating current or future strife. It is our hope that this volume will fill part of that gap by offering policy options for addressing the regional dimensions of war economies.

We at the International Peace Academy extend our deepest appreciation to our funders, who continue to support us in our research. In particular, we would like to express our gratitude to the Canadian Department of Foreign Affairs and International Trade, the Canadian International Development Agency, the government of Norway, the government of Switzerland, the government of Sweden, the Department for International Development of the United Kingdom, the Rockefeller Foundation, and the United Nations Foundation. We are also grateful to Lynne Rienner and her colleagues for their professionalism and forbearance in seeing this volume through the publication process.

Acknowledgments

This book has been the product of collaborative research under the auspices of an International Peace Academy (IPA) project on war economies. We would like to express deep appreciation to the IPA for making a generous grant available to conduct the research. We owe special thanks to Karen Ballentine and Karin Wermester for organizing the publication of the book and providing much useful editorial advice. We also thank Margaret Pugh, who labored tirelessly on the text at the preliminary copyediting stage.

We owe a debt of gratitude to the great many people who assisted in providing material and answering queries. In particular, Jonathan Goodhand expresses thanks to the UK Department for International Development and the Overseas Development Institute (ODI) for funding research in Afghanistan, and to David Hume, Michael Bhatia, Haneef Atmar, Adam Pain, and Mohammed Suleman, who worked on the ODI Afghanistan study. Michael Pugh expresses thanks to Annika Hansen, Graham Day, and Christopher Freeman, who facilitated a visit to Bosnia and Herzegovina. Also, the Office of the High Representative staff in Sarajevo, Andreas Niemann in Banja Luka, and Professors Rajko Tomaš and Dragoljub Stojanov were especially generous with their time and comments. Andreas and Dragoljub kindly permitted an adaptation of their tabular material for Chapter 5. Neil Cooper expresses thanks to Samantha Davis of the University of Plymouth, who kindly assisted with the design of figures and tables.

Finally, we owe a huge debt to our families, friends, and colleagues, who sympathetically accommodated our demands and demanding schedules. *C'est parce qu'ici ou là, dans un autre pays.*

—*Michael Pugh, Neil Cooper, and Jonathan Goodhand*

1

Introduction: Approaches to the Political Economy of Civil Wars

Both scholarly and policy approaches to contemporary civil conflicts have been dominated by concerns that focus on problems within states that experience such conflicts. Prominent among these concerns, for instance, has been the part played by identity issues, whether by analyses that emphasize primordial enmities, encapsulated by the phrase "ancient ethnic hatreds," or those that focus instead on elite manipulation of nationalist discourse, with the aim of sowing discord within a state. Another concern has been with the alleged erosion of moral and civilized virtues by what is seen as an upsurge of irrational, criminal behavior, if not of entire communities, then of social substrata who have taken control of them. Yet another focus of interest has been the failure of domestic politics and the inadequacy of governments, leading to endemic state weakness and collapse. Such concerns are reflected in strategies introduced to assist wartorn states in their recovery and development. Priorities in peacebuilding have included addressing ethnic hatreds by separating groups or impelling them to live together, redressing violent conflict by promoting rule of law and criminal justice, and building democratic institutions to substitute local rule with internationally guided good governance.

This book explores a rather different set of concerns. It emphasizes the role of economic factors in the conditions that lead to state collapse, give rise to and sustain conflict, and complicate peacebuilding. More than this, we contend that a fixation on factors occurring *within* conflict-prone states, whether economic or not, overlooks two dimensions vital to our understanding of civil conflicts and the challenges for postconflict transformation. First, the existing state-level focus tends to ignore the role of regional linkages in permitting and sustaining conflict and as obstacles to transformation. Chapter 2 elaborates on the conflict dynamics that arise from economic, military, political, and social networks within regions, which can create "regional conflict complexes." These are characterized by the cross-border spillover of violence, the empowerment of borderlands as sanctuaries for combatants and nurseries for recruits and also as centers of shadow economic activity, and the intraregional commercial and other connections that make for prolonged and intractable conflicts. Second, the focus on the dynamics of conflict in states of the developing world tends to artificially distance the outside, predominantly "Western" world from their genesis and evolution—treating these conflicts as if they were exclusively driven by indigenous factors rather than as a systemic feature of contemporary patterns of globalization.

This book is concerned with political economies of armed conflicts that not only have regional dimensions but also reflect the negative impact of globalization, particularly the efforts of the developed world and international financial institutions (IFIs) to reorder the global economic system according to neoliberal economic precepts. Since the neoliberal revolution of the 1980s, the political economy of transformation from conflict to peace has been predominantly conceptualized in terms of radical socioeconomic change—away from precapitalist, statist, or command economies and toward free markets open to penetration by the global capitalist system. The formula of fiscal discipline and monetarism, export-led growth and trade liberalization, open access to foreign direct investment (FDI) and global market integration, market deregulation, and diminution of the state as an economic actor was devised for Latin America in 1989 by the American economist John Williamson. Known as the "Washington consensus," it was adopted by the U.S. Treasury, the World Bank, and the International Monetary Fund (IMF). The original harshness of this model has been toned down with "poverty reduction strategies" and a belated acknowledgment by the IMF that FDI contributes to growth and employment only marginally, if at all, while increasing the vulnerability of developing countries to financial crisis.[1] Nevertheless, in promoting the "manifest destiny" of the free market, the ideology advances an idealized model of economic rationality in which everything is turned into a commercial commodity.[2] For regions where conflict is endemic or peace is fragile, this is an approach that increases vulnerability to poverty, "crime," and persistent social unrest.

The study of war economies in general is important for elucidating the motivations of prominent actors, the strategies developed by populations to survive through conflict, the economic mechanisms devised to perpetuate conflict, and the economic challenges for postconflict transformation. In regard to the last of these, in practice, peacebuilding has not neglected issues of political economy. But the economic agendas introduced on the coattails of international intervention have tended to disregard crucial aspects of war economies, especially their regional linkages and the functional aspects of shadow economic activity. The consequences of this neglect, it will be argued, are significant in several respects.

First, the difficulties of achieving peace settlements are often underestimated, because analysts and mediators approach conflicts as if these were confined within sovereign state borders. Neglect of the transnational and regional dynamics that feed conflict has resulted in partial settlements that remain fragile and easily disrupted or in interventions that do little to stop violence from shifting around a region. In particular, the disarmament and demobilization of combatants on a state basis can, as in West Africa, neglect the "revolving door" of mercenaries and the regional channels of arms smuggling that perpetuate and displace conflict to surrounding areas. Similarly, a failure to recognize the significance of conflict trade at regional levels can result in partial and "soft" controls on conflict goods that do little to mitigate the broader networks that feed conflict.

Second, a relapse into conflict can occur, as in Afghanistan and Kosovo-Macedonia, when the security of marginalized borderlands is neglected. These areas often serve as reservoirs of violent resistance to the reassertion of central state sovereignty or function as "no-go areas," marked by internecine warfare between armed factions.

Third, and equally problematic for delivering cease-fires and sustainable peace agreements, peace spoilers draw strength from sources that are often neglected by current policies: that is, from their direct control of or indirect access to regionally embedded economic power bases and from populations rendered dependent on shadow economies. These sources of finance and power enable combatants and war entrepreneurs to avoid the pressures for settlement that might otherwise arise from the exhaustion of highly localized resources, including manpower. In other words, "hurting stalemates" that might drive protagonists into mediation can be avoided longer, while commanders and war profiteers can seek common cause in championing resistance to peace agreements.

Fourth, the extent to which combatants have continued access to lucrative resources presents a significant challenge for transformation. Peacebuilders are torn between disregarding "economic criminals" on the one hand and co-opting them into state building on the other. For instance, the IMF and the World Bank either discount the significance of alternative economies in their calculations and prescriptions or they assume they can easily be formalized through appropriate licensing, usually at the national level.[3] At best, an inability to transform war economies perpetuates corruption, flawed governance, and tensions generated by competing patrimonies or ethnic groups, perhaps sustaining gang warfare. At worst, it can store up long-term problems that can lead to the recurrence of violent conflict.

Fifth, neglecting the functional role of shadow economies in a regional setting can jeopardize economic recovery and development. Simply increasing state surveillance and criminal policing in an attempt to eliminate shadow activities does not suffice. Moreover, there is a double jeopardy at work when, as is invariably the case, a neglect of the welfare benefits of shadow economies is accompanied by neoliberal policies that fail to provide viable alternatives for civilian livelihoods. The immediate consequences are that the poorest sections of the population continue to depend on aid and employment generated by the international presence, are driven to emigrate, or are forced into further reliance on shadow activities in order to survive. In the medium term, the implementation of neoliberal policies hampers the recovery of locally owned state institutions essential to economic development. In the long term, neoliberal policies can have adverse systemic consequences that could lead to renewed conflict—in particular, by increasing a developing society's vulnerability to globally triggered financial and economic crises. As elaborated in Chapter 6, mere neglect is damaging enough; introducing policies that heighten economic injustice is like rubbing salt into war wounds.

Research Agendas

The purpose of this study is to redress the current deficiencies in the existing research on war economies. We propose to examine the ways in which the political economy of specific conflicts have been represented and the influence this has had on policymaking; analyze the regional linkages that support the political economies of particular conflicts; consider the challenges involved in transforming war economies after peace has been established; and interrogate the efficacy of "liberal peace" strategies in establishing political economies of postconflict peace.

It is our intention to contribute to the existing academic and policy literature on the political economy of contemporary internal conflicts. This literature has grown considerably and has become increasingly significant in terms of its contribution to contemporary academic and policy debates on the nature and dynamics of these conflicts. Much of it has addressed particular conflict trades, such as diamonds, or particular actors, such as criminal gangs and mercenaries, or has dealt with particular countries rather than dealing with countries in their regions and the adverse impacts of externally induced economic change. As discussed in Chapter 2, there has also been a lively debate on the issue of what motivates participants in conflict: greed or social, economic, and political grievances that have brought economic issues to the forefront of violent contention. In part, the emphasis in this study contributes to the lesson that a political economy of grievance should be incorporated into the common understanding of internal conflicts. Apart from interrogating the greed and grievance debate, the main lessons of much of the research to date has been to expose the need for a more holistic approach to peacebuilding that more effectively addresses the political economy of conflict and its legacies. In particular, more attention needs to be paid to bolstering the capacities of public institutions in wartorn states establishing more effective forms for the responsible governance of lucrative natural resources and the regulation of conflict trades, tackling corruption and the distorting effects of vested economic interests on politics, and refining postconflict economic strategies to address the destabilizing relationship between poverty and conflict.

However, there are notable gaps in the literature, which this study aims to rectify. First, because studies have been directed at state-level dynamics and the way that local war economies intersect with actors at the global level, there is a dearth of research specifically examining the way that regional networks and their vested interests support specific war economies.[4] Yet as elaborated in both Chapter 2 and the following case studies, most conflict trade depends on some combination of regional kinship or communal ties, and/or transnational business or political linkages.

Second, the literature is predominantly concerned with the inception or duration of conflict rather than the challenges of corruption and crime and civilian reliance on shadow economic activities posed by war economies for postconflict peacebuilding. A notable exception is Mary Kaldor's work on "new wars." For Kaldor, while conflicts such as those in the former Yugoslavia may be dominated by warlords and mafiosi, they are also populated by citizens who form "islands of peace" that need to be protected and empowered by the international community. Indeed, she criticizes previous interventions—such as those in Bosnia—that legitimized warlords at the expense of ordinary citizens. In Kaldor's account, then, a political economy analysis produces an argument for both a benevolent and reconstituted form of external intervention that aims to defend the innocent from predation, to uphold human rights, and to rebuild functioning states able to deliver order and peace. Although this approach can be criticized as being simply another variant of Western interventionist strategies dressed up in universalist ethics, it nevertheless implies a more radical and bottom-up approach to peacebuilding than is currently being used.

Third, other research has focused either on the political economy of peacebuilding in specific countries[5] or on control agendas designed to inhibit the trade in conflict goods.[6] These studies have increased our understanding of specific state-bounded war economies and of the impacts of, and international responses to, trade and commerce that feed conflict. Nevertheless, as explained in Chapter 2, the ways in which economic agendas have been represented and the functions played by the emerging discourse on the trade in conflict goods are still underresearched issues. The most notable exception is, perhaps, Mark Duffield's work on global governance and the "new wars." Combining aspects of political economy, critical security studies, and postmodernism, Duffield fuses an analysis of the global and local economic networks that underpin contemporary internal wars with an awareness of the ways in which the aid and conflict resolution discourses have been successfully reinvented to legitimize a variety of external interventionist strategies. The latter he labels the "liberal peace" in world politics, an ideological mix of neoliberal concepts of democracy, market sovereignty, and conflict resolution that determine contemporary strategies of intervention.[7] The liberal peace is a paradigm that gives priority to the rule of law rather than social justice, to quick-fix elections rather than political accountability, to neoliberal economics rather than state direction (dirigisme) to increase purchasing power, and to widening external influences rather than strengthening autonomy in the undeveloped world. In this vision of world order, interventions are represented as the application of the natural laws of state creation, economic relations, and the ethical protection of human rights. From another perspective, "liberal peace" strategies are deliberately employed to protect liberalism from unruly parts of the world—while avoiding having to deal with the structural injustices in the international system that foster instability. The political economy of the "liberal peace" is a parody of Marxist fundamentalism, as the agenda assumes that economic motivations, structures, and processes determine the superstructure of politics and social life, and that a correct implementation of the principles of the free market will bring economic growth and resolve the contradictions of development.[8]

Duffield's analysis of these forces provides an innovative explanatory framework for understanding their effects in the poor countries, one that can be further developed by examining the impact of liberal interventionist strategies on postconflict political economies and on the emerging control agenda around conflict trade. In particular, we note the significance of alternative political economies in the margins of capitalism where the "norms" and "imperatives" of market economics are resisted or are beyond the institutional competence of state authorities to incorporate effectively. Controllers of black markets, for example, create employment and welfare structures that enable the destitute to cope or survive. The rationales of local elites and their dependents for participating in such activities tend to be overlooked in explanations based on the notion that shadow economic behavior represents a kind of "deviance" from a "norm" of economic rationality. Shadow economic activities may not seem rational from a conventional political economy perspective, because the benchmarks for rationality are constructed by market criteria in leading capitalist economies.

Moreover, shadow economic activities, often referred to as "criminality," are significantly related to the structuring of the global economy and the dominant neoliberal model of economic development. However, in the context of conflict and postconflict transformation, "illegal" markets are not, as Pino Arlacchi insists, produced by the *regulation* of capitalism—and therefore readily distinguishable from, and incompatible with, legal markets.[9] On the contrary, the relationship between market and mafia is one of opportunity and collaboration. Shadow activities live in the spaces created by the so-called free market as much as in the lucrative margins that surround state regulation and command economies. In postwar Lebanon, for example, economic transnationalism takes the form of the expatriation of ill-gotten gains to Western banks and subsequent reinvestment in Lebanon to control lucrative economic sectors, profiting from the paralysis of government as a consequence of the war.[10]

Critical of their representation as "abnormal" and "alien," Francesco Strazzari credits the mafiosi with providing a very effective nexus between the global market, capital formation, investment, and an institutionalized "criminality" that, in the context of Southeast Europe, he regards as integral to state building.[11] From the perspectives of groups and individuals—whether war profiteers engaged in violent plunder or those rendered destitute by conflict who resort to selling black market cigarettes, participation in the shadow economy is based on rational calculations about the probability of the risk of getting caught by the authorities or the mafia, the level of the penalties involved, and the costs of not taking risks.

As well, there is a great likelihood that many people are "beneficiaries" of war economies while being denied knowledge about the mechanisms and the principal operators of the shadow systems who reap the greatest benefits. In postconflict settings, even as mafia and "criminal" structures challenge sustainable peace and development, they yet provide an alternative political economy to the liberal agenda. They are beyond the control of the hegemonic institutions, and their relationship to economic factors subverts attempts to introduce competition. In short, mafia activity is the ideal market that escapes regulation by powerful institutions and the corporate world. It is a market in which no one has rights other than the right to victimize or reward people on the basis of economic value, the state is denied income and economic influence, prices are negotiated, and the profits are considerable.

A Note on Terminology: Combat, Shadow, and Coping Economies

In view of the dominant tendency to dismiss "criminality" as an abnormality in war economies and postconflict transformations, it is essential to specify key terms used in this study to designate patterns of economic activity. Commonly employed labels, such as "criminal," "illegal," or "unofficial," used in opposition to "authorized," "legal," and "official," suggest the existence of hard normative distinctions between legitimate and illegitimate types of economic behavior. Particularly in war-torn and postwar contexts where there is a legal vacuum,[12] these dichotomies may prove both conceptually false and have limited descriptive or analytical value. In some instances, so-called "illegal" economic activity is tolerated and even encouraged by officialdom, not only because it offers elites opportunities for self-enrichment, but also because, in conditions of chronic underdevelopment or conflict, it has positive social effects in enabling people to cope along the margins of a dysfunctional formal economy. This does not completely resolve the conceptual problems inherent in the use of labels in the absence of a shared vocabulary among researchers and policymakers. For example, the term "parallel," commonly used to describe the nationalist-dominated shadow economies in Bosnia and Herzegovina (BiH), suggests economic activities and networks that run alongside, and are completely independent of, state-regulated economic activity. Instead there is often a symbiotic or parasitic relationship between the two—for example, where state officials are actively involved in subverting state regulation or where state regulation creates incentives for unofficial trade.

For the purposes of this study, therefore, quotation marks are used to indicate that terms such as "illegal" reflect the dominant social construction of particular economic activities as illegitimate. Our preference is to employ terms that avoid such normative loading and that can assist in distinguishing the kinds of economic behavior that occur in war-torn settings. The term "war economy" is used to include all economic activities carried out in wartime: hence the title of this book. We also use three descriptors—the combat, shadow, and coping economies—that suggest varied motives for, and dynamics in, waging war, profiteering, and coping. Combat economies include both (1) the capture of control over production and economic resources to sustain a conflict and (2) economic strategies of war aimed at the disempowerment of specific groups.[13] Whereas the former is exploitive and involves the generation of resources to wage war, the latter is predatory and involves the destruction of resources to undermine the ability of opposing groups to wage war. The central economic agents are combatant parties (whether state militaries or nonstate armed groups), and their political backers who endeavor to exercise economic power on behalf of their constituencies. The term "shadow economy" refers to economic activities that are conducted outside state-regulated frameworks and are not audited by the state institutions. The key economic agents are those whose objectives may be economic rather than military, but whose rationales depend on economic problems and opportunities brought about by the erosion of state authority. These agents may range from entrepreneurial elites who seek to profit from the expanded opportunities for shadow trade and production made available by the conditions of war, to the poor who participate in the shadow economy out of necessity and for purposes of economic survival. The shadow economy may incorporate the "coping economy." This latter term refers to economic activity undertaken by population groups that are using their asset-base to more or less maintain basic living standards or surviving by utilizing a dwindling asset-base to maintain minimum or below-minimum living standards. These descriptors are conceptually useful as an aid to analysis. In practice, however, there is considerable overlap. For example, although the motives of entrepreneurial elites may be primarily economic rather than military, they are often closely linked by kinship, ethnicity, or economic self-interest to the political and military elites, and may indeed be licensed by them.

Outline of the Book

Chapter 2 begins with an overview of the dominant approaches to explaining contemporary internal conflicts. It then provides a review of the debate on the role of economic agendas of combatants and conflict exploiters in the inception and perpetuation of conflict. The chapter then considers the dynamics of regional conflict complexes that affect war in particular states and suggests that the regional aspects of many civil conflicts need to be incorporated more effectively into peacebuilding strategies.

The following three chapters constitute the main body of this book and include case studies of Afghanistan, Sierra Leone, and BiH, focusing in particular on their war economies, the regional dynamics that underpin them, and the legacies they have left for peacemaking. These three cases present an opportunity to assess whether generalizations can be drawn across varied contexts and whether contrasts between them indicate divergent challenges for transformation and the need for context-specific poli-cies. They have been chosen on the grounds that each case study presents a different political and cultural context: the first in Central Asia, the second in West Africa, and the third in Southeast Europe. Each reflects a political economy of conflict centered on specific resources, or at least has been represented as such in popular discourse: drugs and cross-border smuggling in Afghanistan, diamonds in Sierra Leone, and a diversified war economy in BiH.

There is also an evolutionary element involved in the ordering of cases, because each is also at a different stage of the peacebuilding process. In Afghanistan the war economy continues to play a key role in the absence of a durable peace. The emphasis, here, therefore, is on the continuing dynamics of the Central Asian conflict complex. The peace-building process has been established only since the fall of the Taliban in 2002, and is thus a case where attempts at transformation are in their infancy and arguably the most contested. Of the three cases, transforma-tion in Afghanistan should in theory also be informed by the contempo-rary debates on the role of war economies and, particularly, the need to address the issue of the Afghan and regional drug trade. Sierra Leone has been marked by a succession of failed peace agreements throughout the 1990s, which at least in part were undermined by the ability of the actors to fund their war through the trade in conflict diamonds. The conflict in Sierra Leone commenced in 1991, but analysis of the role of economic agendas in civil conflicts became increasingly prominent only from the mid-1990s. Sierra Leone thus straddles a period when concern about eco-nomic agendas moved from the margins to the mainstream of academic and policy debate. By contrast BiH offers an opportunity to assess the impact of peacebuilding at an advanced stage, and to emphasize the impact of transformation strategies. BiH has a more mature postconflict political economy than the other cases, and the impact of liberal economic intervention can be more readily evaluated. Peacebuilding got under way at a time when the dominant explanations for regional conflict in South-east Europe highlighted the role of ethnic grievances. Consequently, peacebuilding strategies initially ignored the role of local and regional shadow economies, focusing instead on conventional, neoliberal macro-economic reforms.

In Chapter 3, on Afghanistan in Central Asia, Jonathan Goodhand begins by noting the dearth of reliable data on Afghanistan's war economy and the limitations this imposes for the development of effective transfor-mation strategies. He also notes the failure of popular constructions and policy approaches to place Central Asian conflicts in a historical perspec-tive. Constructions of the Afghan civil war as a "greed" conflict sustained by the opium economy have served to internalize the conflict, rather than to encourage consideration of its regional dimensions. This kind of representation also ignores the political economy of the conflict. In addition, the "postconflict" tag is questionable. There has been no formal peace agreement and it is only the international presence that currently masks the internal conflicts and the external agendas of neighboring states. Moreover, the shadow economy continues to thrive in these conditions of uneven and fragile peace. The opium trade currently generates more revenue than is provided in international aid—a situation that favors the continued independence of warlord and clan factions that oppose Kabul and that poses serious challenges for sustainable peace and development. Finally, Goodhand argues that a precondition for transforming the war economy into a peace economy will be international support for the development of a strong state with a monopoly of violence. In the context of Afghanistan's severe political and economic fragmentation, donor fantasies of creating a minimalist and benign liberal state are not only naive but also demonstrate a lack of contemporary understanding.

In Chapter 4, on Sierra Leone in West Africa, we argue that while the narratives of conflict have recognized the role of economic agendas in the country's civil war, the particular representation of them has served to obscure understanding of the dynamics underpinning its descent into war. We also argue that explanations that focus only on internal factors, whether the predatory behavior of the rebels of the Revolutionary United Front or the role of top-down corruption and neopatrimonialism, in both the slide to war and its prosecution, are insufficient. Such analyses need to be supplemented with an awareness of the way in which the regional geography of regulation created incentives for the development of long-standing, prewar informal trade networks. These networks not only underpinned Sierra Leone's prewar "illicit" diamond economy, but were also readily adapted to sustain the conflict. Furthermore, while the current phase of peacebuilding in Sierra Leone has been more successful than earlier initiatives, there are also question marks over the durability of the peace that has been established. In particular, the policies of the international financial institutions and external donors echo many of the policies that contributed to conflict in the first place. Local and regional actors in the shadow economy appear to be adapting to, and indeed exploiting, the new, postconflict geography of regulation.

The experience of peacebuilding in BiH, discussed in Chapter 5, illustrates the dynamics of a transformation economy in the wider European context. Part of this context is a level of socioeconomic development that places Southeast Europe in the middle rank of the UN Development Programme's human development index. By contrast, both West Africa and

Central Asia are represented by states whose development is registered toward the bottom of the index. BiH also provides a contrasting case study because it was already part of an economic federation that itself had strong links with both Central and Western Europe. In large measure, BiH has been a microcosm of the regional political and economic disintegration and reconfiguration that pushed civilians and local elites further into shadow economies, capitalizing on the permeability of shifting and contested borders. Having undergone large-scale conflict during the first half of the 1990s, BiH has also now experienced a longer period of postconflict peacebuilding than of war. It has been a testing ground for post–Cold War international administration in war-torn countries. But this case also demonstrates that the legacies of the wartime economies are far from eclipsed, despite more than eight years of external aid and guidance. Significant changes have occurred at the formal level, notably in the introduction of a neoliberal model of political economy based on the "free market." In the context of BiH, when there was little external recognition of the importance of the war economy, macroeconomic reform has constituted the principle strategy for building a political economy of peace. Not only have these reforms made little difference to the lives of the bulk of the population in terms of their ability to take care of basic needs—if anything, their situation has worsened—but they have also done little to revive production or attract the level of foreign direct investment that external agencies have spuriously insisted is essential for long-term development. Moreover, the shadow and coping economies have proven extremely persistent, reflecting in part the interpretive construction of the wars in the former Yugoslavia as the consequence of ethnic hatred or political manipulation, rather than as a violent political and economic disintegration, in which donor pressures for economic liberalization played a significant role. In addition, the state-bounded approach to reconstructing the political economy of BiH, underpinned by a large international presence with vested interests in fulfilling a state-bounded mandate, means that the regional dynamics of political economy have been sidelined. Here, it is worth recalling that the Balkans Stability Pact, with its apparent recognition of the importance of fostering regional recovery and integration, was introduced as an afterthought, when the Kosovo crisis exposed the narrow focus of the Dayton Agreement. As seemingly befits an afterthought, the consideration given to the purpose and content of a regional approach to Southeast Europe has not advanced very far, nor is it clear, officially, what role regional integration is expected to play vis-à-vis association with, and eventual accession to, the European Union.

Not only do these cases provide a broad geographical representation of war-torn societies, but the choice of contrasting areas is a methodologically useful way to highlight common issues such as the relationship between economic structural adjustment and state collapse, the critical role of marginalized borderlands in war economies, and the interaction of shadow economies and neoliberal policies in complicating the transformation from war to relative peace.

Chapter 6 provides an analysis of the control agenda that is emerging as the dominant approach for dealing with conflict trade as well as with the wider political economy of armed conflict. We argue that this control agenda has been part of a broader set of strategies designed both to foster liberal peace in the developing world and to prevent transmission of the "virus of disorder" to the developed world. These strategies encompass governance initiatives, prophylactic controls, and control-lite measures. However, such approaches are at best ineffective, and at worst counterproductive. They fail to address the structures of a neoliberal economic system that creates the permissive conditions for the networked violence of contemporary war economies.

The concluding chapter outlines several recommendations designed to address the regional dynamics underpinning war economies and the challenges posed by war economies for transformation and peacebuilding. In particular, we draw attention to the practical limitations of current peacemaking and peacebuilding strategies that result from their state-centric orientation. Many of the organizations dealing with conflict appear to have an inherent bias against, or are institutionally unsuited to, the task of looking beyond the formal boundaries of a particular conflict.

Placing the political economy of conflict in its regional setting does not necessarily simplify the challenges of transformation. However, it does open up consideration of potential alternatives to the narrow orthodoxy of policy prescriptions that currently dominate approaches to peacemaking and peacebuilding. The dynamics of regional conflict complexes may necessitate a move away from the negotiation of separate and successive peace agreements as each state emerges from conflict. Often, dealing with regionalized conflict on a serial basis simply results in the displacement of conflict and shadow trade (arms, drugs, mercenaries) across borders. Acknowledgment of the transnational nature of conflict complexes implies the need to address issues in a holistic fashion. One approach is to pursue negotiation of regional settlements for durable peace. A comprehensive settlement would be very demanding but, we argue, worth attempting. Its core elements might include initiatives on economic development of borderlands, regional-level regulation of conflict and shadow trading, and measures to encourage incremental forms of economic harmonization of the kind that emerged in Western Europe after 1945 as a component in the lengthy process of postconflict transformation. Regional economic harmonization is especially important given that shadow economies take advantage of differential regulatory practices among separate states. In addition, a key aspect of settlements for durable peace might also address the interrelationship between the region and the global economy. Regionalism might alternatively be conceived as a device to protect postconflict economies from externally derived policies that have the effect of reinforcing dependence on shadow economic activity. Indeed, both domestic and regional policies might be developed to protect vulnerable economies, rather than opening them up to the free market. This entails an emphasis on building state institutions and reintroducing the state into economic activity.

Notes

1. "IMF Warns Liberalization Can Harm Poor Countries," UN Wire, March 19, 2003.

2. Of the extensive critical literature on this issue, see particularly Joseph Stiglitz, *Globalization and Its Discontents* (London: Penguin, 2002); Pierre Bourdieu, *Acts of Resistance: Against the Tyranny of the Market* (New York: New Press, 2002); Noam Chomsky, *Profit over People: Neo-liberalism and Global Order* (New York: Seven Stories Press, 1999); Amartya Sen, *Development as Freedom* (Oxford: Oxford University Press, 1999); and Andrew Herod, Gearóid O'Tuathail, and Susan Roberts, *Unruly World? Geography, Globalization, and Governance* (London: Routledge, 1998).

3. Mark Duffield, *Global Governance and the New Wars: The Merging of Development and Security* (London: Zed Books, 2001), p. 143.

4. An exception is the work of Barnett Rubin. See Barnett R. Rubin, "Regional Approaches to Conflict Management in Africa," presentation to a meeting for the UN Security Council, August 8, 2001, www.cic.nyu.edu/conflict.

5. Michael Pugh, "Protectorates and Spoils of Peace: Political Economy in South-East Europe," in Dietrich Jung, ed., *Shadow Globalization, Ethnic Conflicts, and New Wars: A Political Economy of Intra-State War* (London: Routledge, 2003), pp. 47–69.

6. Neil Cooper, "State Collapse as Business: The Role of Conflict Trade and the Emerging Control Agenda," *Development and Change* (Special Issue: "State Failure, Collapse, and Reconstruction") 33, no. 5 (November 2002): 935–955.

7. Duffield, *Global Governance and the New Wars*.

8. See, inter alia, Robert W. Cox, *The Political Economy of a Plural World: Critical Reflections on Power, Morals, and Civilization*, RIPE Series (London: Routledge, 2002), p. 33; and Roland Paris, *At War's End: Building Peace After Civil Conflict* (Cambridge: University of Cambridge Press, forthcoming).

9. Pino Arlacchi, "The Dynamics of Illegal Markets," *Transnational Organized Crime* 4, nos. 3–4 (Winter 1998): 7–8. Arlacchi was director of the UN Office for Drug Control and Crime Prevention.

10. Elizabeth Picard, "Liban: la matrice historique," in François Jean and Jean-Christophe Rufin, eds., *Economie des guerres civiles* (Paris: Hachette, Collection Pluriel, 1996), p. 103.

11. Francesco Strazzari, "Between Ethnic Collusion and Mafia Collusion: The 'Balkan Route' to State Making," in Jung, *Shadow Globalization*, p. 158.

12. C. Nordstrom, "Shadows and Sovereigns," *Theory, Culture, and Society* 17, no. 4 (2000): 35–54.

13. Philippe Le Billon, *The Political Economy of War: What Relief Workers Need to Know,* Humanitarian Practice Network Paper no. 33 (London: Overseas Development Institute, July 2000).

2

The Regional Dimensions
of Civil War Economies

This chapter examines the dominant explanations of contemporary civil conflicts and presents a brief overview of the literature that has emerged since the end of the Cold War on the political economy of such conflicts. It notes the absence of analysis of the regional economic dimensions of conflict and, in particular, of postconflict transformation. We then define the concept of regional conflict complexes and analyze its key aspects, employing a framework devised by Barnett Rubin. In examining the economic, political, military, and social linkages that characterize regional conflict complexes, we consider the permissive conditions that give rise to them, the dynamics that sustain them, and the legacies that complicate both peacemaking and postconflict transformation. Subsequent chapters provide detailed case studies of conflict complexes in Central Asia, West Africa, and Southeast Europe; here we draw illustrative examples from other conflict complexes, in order to convey the diversity of economic relations that underpin regional conflict complexes.

Dominant Explanations of Contemporary Civil Conflict

One of the features of the post–Cold War era has been the dominance of internal conflict as the primary form of warfare. Indeed, of the fifty-seven major armed conflicts that occurred between 1990 and 2001, all but three were internal.[1] More than just addressing the phenomenon of civil war, however, which is by no means novel, scholars have also focused on apparent changes in both the character and conduct of contemporary internal wars. Not only is international war in apparent decline, but so too are conventional civil conflicts fought by disciplined armies.[2] Instead, contemporary civil conflict is more commonly perceived as peopled by "the paramilitaries, guerrillas, militias, and warlords who are tearing up the failed states of the 1990s" and by "the barefoot boys with kalashnikovs, the paramilitaries in wraparound sunglasses [and] the turbaned zealots of the Taliban."[3]

Furthermore, the issues over which actors fight are deemed to have changed. In particular, it has become commonplace in commentary on contemporary civil war to note the decline of ideologically based conflict and its replacement with other forms.[4] Exactly what kind of war has emerged instead, and what its causes are, however, remain an issue of debate.

There are four approaches to understanding contemporary civil conflict that have dominated academic and policy discourse on the subject. The first is the "ancient ethnic hatreds" thesis. This characterizes civil war as a function of social cleavages centered on issues of identity (such as religion and ethnicity). In this characterization, ethnic differences previously contained by authoritarian regimes in the Cold War have "erupted onto the political scene."[5] This ancient ethnic hatreds perspective is typified by John Garnett, for whom contemporary civil wars are largely ones in which

> people are brutalised and killed not because of anything they have done, not even because of their politics, but simply because of who they are. . . . Tutsis in Rwanda, the Tamils in Sri Lanka, the Kurds in Iraq, the Muslims in Bosnia, and the Albanians in Kosovo. . . . [Such wars] are not about the pursuit of interests as normally understood. They are about malevolence and they are unrestrained by any legal or moral rules.[6]

An alternative identity argument is that elites, desperate to gain or maintain power, manipulate political discourse to maximize even relatively small distinctions between groups in order to mobilize support for armed conflict—a phenomenon that Michael Ignatieff describes as "the narcissism of minor difference."[7]

A second approach might be described as the "new barbarism" thesis. This explains contemporary civil war as populated by belligerents who are essentially irrational and motivated by primeval savagery. Such conflicts take place between "erratic primitives of shifting allegiances, habituated to violence, with no stake in civil order."[8] These are wars, such as those in the former Yugoslavia, Rwanda, or Somalia, that appear to defy rational explanation and that "happen for reasons that call no strategy master."[9]

Such wars are apparently populated by dope fiends and pot-heads, by the mad and the bad, and by hate and vengeance. These are wars where the veneer of civilization has been ripped away to reveal participants motivated not by the narcissism of difference, but by the narcissism of violence, where "torture is exciting, rape is fun, and looting is profitable."[10]

A third perspective emphasizes the role of poor governance in fomenting conflict. In part, this relates to the long-standing idea that authoritarian repression can ignite rebellion. However, an important aspect of current debates is the emphasis placed on the way a mixture of corruption, nepotism, and underdevelopment has created weak states with neither the legitimacy nor the institutional capacity to wield the monopoly of force required to maintain order, territorial integrity, and peace. Thus, for John Mueller, "[To] a very substantial degree, the amount of warfare that persists in the world—virtually all of it civil war—is a function of the degree to which inadequate government exists."[11] As contemporary internal war is primarily explained as a failure of governance and of politics, it is these elements that should be emphasized in peacebuilding. Thus, as Chetan Kumar notes, while long-term structural contributors to violence must be understood, peacebuilding efforts should "focus principally on a society's political capacity to manage tensions arising from these causes, rather than on redressing [them]."[12]

However, starting in the mid-1990s, a fourth and increasingly influential body of research has emerged that places particular emphasis on the role played by economic agendas and the exploitation of lucrative resources in the inception and perpetuation of internal conflicts.[13] Although warfare commonly leads to breakdowns in communication, the attenuation of production and trade, and the abandonment of contractual obligations and trust, conditions of war also present new commercial opportunities for the exploitation of assets, investment, services, marketing, and welfare. Indeed, French researchers have demonstrated that armed factions are remarkably adept at economic diversification and at seeking optimum gains in the changing contexts of their struggle.[14] Contemporary civil war economies are often penetrated by flows of external goods and services supplied by diasporas, private security firms, aid workers, and commodity markets, and are thus deeply interconnected with both regulated and unregulated global trade and financial flows. War entrepreneurs often begin by conducting predatory operations—looting and destroying property and goading population movement to accompany or counterbalance military power. They may also undertake a more systematic form of predation to sustain political and military campaigns by exacting tribute, including the taxation of diasporas—a technique that was used among Kosovo émigrés to fund the Kosova government in exile, the shadow government of Ibrahim Rugova, and the Kosovo Liberation Army (KLA).[15]

Greed and Grievance

In some academic and policy circles, economic explanations of internal conflict have supplanted perspectives on civil conflict that emphasize ancient ethnic hatreds, failures of governance, and "new barbarism." For instance, various studies have argued that the availability of easily lootable resources in a country (such as diamonds, timber, gold) or other funds (such as diaspora remittances) influences not only the likelihood of civil war but also its duration and form.[16] Philippe Le Billon, for instance, distinguishes between resources that are proximate or distant from the center of power and also between diffuse resources and point resources found in concentrated locations. How these variables interrelate influences whether conflicts are likely to take the form of warlordism, bids to control the state, secessionist struggles, or rebellion and rioting.[17]

Other research has concentrated on particular aspects of war economies. These include the role of specific lucrative natural resources, such as timber or oil, in sustaining conflict;[18] the impact of resource flows into conflict zones such as aid or diaspora remittances;[19] the role of particular economic actors such as the new corporate mercenary groups;[20] and country- or region-specific studies highlighting the economic agendas that influence the various factions and warlords.[21] Research in this field has not only been undertaken by academics but also by nongovernmental organizations (NGOs) such as Global Witness and Partnership Africa Canada and also by multilateral organizations such as the World Bank and the UN.

Of course, neither the pursuit of profit nor academic engagement with the idea of war as "economics by other means" is novel. Charles Tilly, for instance, has long emphasized the role of economic factors in war- and state-making in Europe.[22] Other work has emphasized the long tradition of mercenary activity stretching back to the Middle Ages. The significance of this more recent body of research lies in the fact that it specifically attempts to explain the dynamics of the "new wars" of the post–Cold War era.[23]

Moreover, the focus in this literature is not simply on the role of economic motivations but also on the ways that local actors use transnational trading networks to generate both arms and resources for internal conflicts. Thus, work on the political economy of conflict has potentially profound implications for how we understand the influence and nature of globalization, the role of the state in international relations, and the inter-relationships between peace in the developed world and endemic conflict in significant portions of the underdeveloped world. This is not to suggest that the literature in this field is either theoretically unified or devoid of disputes. Indeed, much of the literature has polarized around a debate on "greed versus grievance."

The parameters of this debate were established by Paul Collier and Anke Hoeffler in a series of influential articles on the causes of civil conflict.[24] It is useful to outline their thesis, as it neatly illustrates some of the key issues addressed in the literature. More significant for the purposes of this study, the way one understands the political economy of conflict has a bearing on how one conceptualizes the challenges involved in transforming war economies.

Using econometric analysis of civil wars over the 1965–1999 period, Collier and Hoeffler arrived at a number of controversial conclusions concerning the causes of civil conflict. First, they argued that traditional grievance-based explanations of conflict were unconvincing. Inequality, whether measured in terms of income or landownership, had no effect on the risk of civil conflict; repression had only ambiguous effects, with severe political repression less likely to result in civil conflict than partial democracy; and ethnic and religious fractionalization was found to actually reduce the risk of conflict.[25] Second, certain factors, especially a high level of dependence on primary commodity exports, significantly increased the risk of conflict.[26] This, it was argued, reflected the fact that for rebellions to occur, rebel organizations have to be financially viable, and "primary commodities are the most lootable of all economic activities."[27] Similarly, the presence of a large diaspora able to fund conflict through sending remittances back home also increases the risk of civil war. The policy recommendations that flowed from this analysis included the need to address the trade in conflict goods, to use development assistance to diversify economies to reduce dependence on primary commodity exports, and to establish full democratic rights.

However, a number of criticisms have been leveled at this analysis. In terms of methodology, the data set ignored the anticolonial insurgencies of the 1960s. It also neglected patterns of resource distribution, and hence inequality, within countries and between individuals and groups.[28] Indeed, using other data, Wayne Nafziger and Juha Auvinen conclude that "objective grievances of poverty and inequality [do] contribute to war and humanitarian emergencies."[29] The validity of the various proxies used by Collier and Hoeffler to illustrate "greed" has also been questioned. A heavy reliance on primary commodity exports could equally be treated as an index of underdevelopment and hence a measure of grievance,[30] and large diasporas could be a function of conflict rather than a cause.[31] The focus on rebel greed also ignores the way that ruling elites manipulate conflict for profit and power. Discourses of grievance deployed by rebel groups are neatly dismissed by inverting the Marxist concept of false consciousness to come up with a newly minted World Bank version. The Marxist notion that social and ideational processes serve to obscure the proletariat's proper consciousness of oppression is simply reversed: "it is the rebel supporters who have the false consciousness: they are gulled into believing the discourse which self-interested rebel leaders promote."[32] However, if the original Marxist concept of false consciousness is reintroduced, this may be equally adept at explaining why apparently objective measures of grievance fail to explain the incidence of rebellion. Indeed, using false consciousness in its original meaning suggests that rather than examining objective economic data, World Bank studies should be examining ideational processes.[33]

It is also worth noting the points of convergence within the political economy school of civil conflict. In 2001, Collier and Hoeffler modified their argument to downplay the notion of rebel greed in favor of an emphasis on the *opportunities* for conflict provided by factors such as natural resources and diaspora financing. Moreover, while they contend that opportunity provides more explanatory power than grievance, they not only acknowledge the importance of the *perception* of grievance, but are also more equivocal about the relationship between opportunity and grievance, noting that a combined model is superior.[34] Overall, the debate has not been between a position that highlights the salience of economic agendas and one that does not. Rather, it has been between a perspective concerned exclusively with a political economy of rebel greed and one that seeks also to incorporate a political economy of grievance. Nafziger and Auvinen argue, for instance, that the increase in conflict in Africa is linked to its negative per capita growth in the 1970s and 1980s and stagnation in the 1990s.[35] Macartan Humphreys also emphasizes the role of endemic poverty, noting that differences in income between countries in conflict and those at peace is becoming greater. In a similar vein, Francis Stewart's research suggests that while inequality between individuals may not matter for conflict, inequality between ethnic groups or between regions certainly does.[36]

Other approaches view resource wars not as a function of the opportunities for predation, but either as distributional conflict over scarce resources or as a response to structural adjustment. For example, William Reno emphasizes the role of neopatrimonial rulers, especially their pursuit of private profit and power, initially sustained by flexible adaptation to the demands of international financial institutions (IFIs), but which ultimately undermines the state and creates the conditions for conflict.[37] This thesis bears similarity to explanations that emphasize the role of bad governance. However, in Reno's analysis, poor governance is not simply a function of bad rulers; it also arises out of the policies advocated by external creditors. Of direct relevance to our observations regarding the "liberal peace" in Chapter 1, the greed approach has been criticized as a remarkably convenient alibi for institutions promoting neoliberal policy approaches that exacerbate inequality and social stresses. Thus Duffield notes that "the argument and the evidence used . . . are a powerful means of delegitimation and a good excuse for the World Bank and others to pay little attention to critical voices from the South."[38]

From the perspective of this study, a common deficiency of the political economy literature is that the regional dimensions of local conflicts are poorly articulated, if at all. Regional dimensions hardly figure in the greed versus grievance debate, even though issues of local predation, distribution, opportunities for resource exploitation, and borderland poverty and crime cannot be divorced from cross-border activities. However, there has been little attempt to incorporate the regional level in analyses of conflict—and even less in analyses of postconflict transformation. In the cartography of the political economy of internal wars, maps tend to be drawn at two levels: the national and the global. At the national level, analysis is bounded by the external frontiers of the fragmented state. At the global level the contours of research fall into two parts. First, global studies have increased our understanding of how factions trade commodities through world networks, launder proceeds through the international banking system, and mobilize and tax diasporas. Second, analysts have been interested in the global controls on conflict goods and the proceeds of trade. Generally missing from this mapping, with the notable exception of the work of Barnett Rubin, is a depiction of any regional terrain. In practice, regional dimensions are often addressed at the level of high politics in arranging cease-fires and peace settlements, as in the approach in 1984 toward the Central American complex involving El Salvador, Nicaragua, and Honduras by the "Contadora" group of states. But the regional dimension to policy often seems to evaporate at the level of economic intervention and postconflict transformation. This may be partly because much of development and postconflict reconstruction policy is focused on a statist model of delivery that underestimates the interconnections across borders in the formal and particularly the informal economies that underpin many conflicts.

Consequently, policy analysis predominantly reflects the same concerns with the bounded state. For example, as we demonstrate later in this study, conflict trade controls have tended to be state-centric or global, rather than regional. The major IFIs have traditionally organized their strategies for postconflict reconstruction around country-based studies, programs, and policy reviews.[39] A central danger in ignoring regional linkages is that peacebuilding can lead to displacement effects whereby the creation of a regulatory framework in one state can have the unintended effect of shifting problems such as trafficking, weapons proliferation, and even conflict across borders. Another consequence of ignoring regional aspects is the underestimation of the obduracy and complexity of armed conflict.

Regional Conflict Complexes

Regional approaches to international relations generally were rather neglected in the Cold War security literature, with notable exceptions such as Karl Deutsch's work on "security communities" and Joseph Nye's work on "islands of peace"—where military conflict is ruled out as a dynamic in interstate relations.[40] But by the 1990s, the importance to security studies of including a regional level of analysis was rediscovered, particularly in the work of European academics who developed a theory of "security complexes" to reflect a growing post–Cold War interest in multipolarity and the emergence of integrated regional economic blocs.[41]

The term "region" is far from precise in spatial terms and can have seemingly little value in areas such as Central Asia, where regionalism has not been formally institutionalized. However, in functional terms, "region" can be used to denote a configuration of authority and networking that occupies a space between national and global levels. It signifies that interactions between units within a constellation are stronger and more frequent, whether hostile or benign, than those beyond it, though this certainly does not deny the existence of connections to global political and economic networks. These regional links are sufficiently close that the securities of states cannot be considered separately.[42]

Where closely interconnected conflicts occur, we can refer to a "regional conflict complex," the term borrowed from Peter Wallensteen and Margareta Sollenberg that we use in this study.[43] Of the 103 conflicts analyzed by Wallensteen and Sollenberg for the period from 1989 to 1997, strong regional dynamics and spillover were noted in 55 percent. Of the fourteen major conflicts that were in progress in 2000, ten directly affected neighboring states.[44] Although Rubin has subsequently used another term, "regional conflict formation," he defines the concept in much the same way as Wallensteen and Sollenberg: that is, as "transnational conflicts that form mutually reinforcing linkages with each other throughout a region, making for more protracted and obdurate conflicts."[45] The eruption of initially localized hostilities can generate substate movements and territorial claims that are fueled transnationally, sustained by the proceeds of regional trade, interconnected with other regional conflicts, or as in West Africa and the Democratic Republic of Congo (DRC), directly spill over into neighboring states and embroil regional actors. In West Africa, for example, an internal conflict spread from Liberia to Sierra Leone, back to Liberia, and subsequently to Côte d'Ivoire.

Regional conflict complexes pose particular challenges to the management of conflict and, by extension, to peacebuilding. On the one hand, although regional parties have local knowledge and are not so time-bound by exit strategies as external agencies, they may be ill suited to manage transformation because they exhibit dissension, are partial, or lack organizational competence. For example, in the case of the conflict complex of the African Great Lakes region, potentially relevant subregional organizations are weak and small, while the African Union is too large and cumbersome to provide effective conflict management. In the Central Asia complex, examined in Chapter 3, "there is no effective regional organization with . . . appropriate geographical scope and membership."[46]

On the other hand, extraregional agencies engaged in conflict management and peacebuilding have tended to focus on state-bounded diagnostics and cures, with elements of international administration operating territorially within the borders established by peace agreements, as in Bosnia-Herzegovina. Alternatively, extraregional states may have little interest in engaging in long-term conflict management activities. The United States under President George W. Bush has left peacebuilding in Afghanistan to its "allies," and neither the United States nor Europe has a particular appetite for engagement in nation building in Africa, despite a joint Anglo-French development initiative in 2000.

Regional Elements of Conflict Complexes

Military invasion and incursion are not the only forms of cross-border interaction that characterize such complexes. A whole range of connections, including population movements, transnational solidarity within identity groups, smuggling, and political links, underpin hostilities and complicate the task of resolving conflict. In Rubin's conception, regional conflict complexes are characterized by four types of networks: economic, military, political, and social. This provides a convenient framework to illustrate transnational links that affect the dynamics of conflict complexes and peacebuilding. However, the dynamics underpinning specific conflicts are not easily demarcated because they frequently overlap, and specific cases of conflict trade, for example, may reflect more than one element. This section discusses these elements, illustrating how economic, military, political, and social networks refer back to, and facilitate, regional economic exchanges and pose difficulties for postconflict transformation.

Economic Networks

Three ways in which economic networks add complexity to regional conflict are illustrated here: the outlets for trade in conflict goods; tax farming and avoidance; and the phenomenon of displacement. First, neighboring states may derive revenue or other rewards from allowing themselves to act as a country of provenance for conflict goods traded by nonstate groups. For instance, there has been extensive two-way trade in diamonds between Angola and the DRC. Dealers in the Congo have purchased illicit diamonds from both the Union for the Total Independence of Angola (UNITA) and non-UNITA sources in Angola and mixed them with diamonds from the DRC, which is then declared as the country of provenance. As a result, it is reasonable to assume that of the U.S.\$513 million worth of Congolese diamonds imported into Belgium between January and August 2000 (representing almost 10 percent of all diamonds imported into that country during this period), a significant proportion would have originated from UNITA in Angola.[47] The extensive trade in diamonds from the DRC thus amounted to a "double whammy," funding the war economies of both the DRC and Angola.

The extent to which regional channels can serve as outlets for conflict goods is amply illustrated by the transfer of the DRC's own conflict diamonds and a range of other goods, including timber and coltan, to neighboring countries.[48] Neither Rwanda nor Uganda has diamond production, yet diamond exports from Rwanda increased by almost 150 percent between 1997 and 2000, while exports from Uganda grew by over 500 percent, coinciding with Uganda's occupation of the eastern DRC (see Table 2.1).

A thriving mining and export trade in coltan, the mineral used in mobile phones and computing equipment, is a particularly striking outcome of the conflict in the DRC and its occupation by Ugandan and Rwandese soldiers. As shown in Figure 2.1, the interlocking factors of occupation, forced labor, mining, looting, financial flows, transport, processing, manufacture, arms dealing, and imports of mobile phones exhibit strong regional as well as global linkages. It is also worth noting the way in which the complexity of regional and global supply chains serves to obscure the

Table 2.1 Ugandan and Rwandan Diamond Exports, 1997–2000 (U.S.$)

	1997	1998	1999	2000	Increase 1997–2000	Increase over 1997 (%)	Total Exports, 1997–2000
Uganda	198,302	1,440,000	1,813,500	1,263,385	1,065,083	537.1	4,715,187
Rwanda	720,425	16,606	439,347	1,788,036	1,067,611	148.2	2,964,414
Total	918,727	1,456,606	2,252,847	3,051,421	2,132,694	232.1	7,679,601

Sources: Figures taken from United Nations, *Report of the Panel of Experts on the Illegal Exploitation of Natural Resources and Other Forms of Wealth of the Democratic Republic of the Congo*, S/2001/357, p. 21, tab. 2, and p. 25, tab. 5. UN Expert Panel figures are based on data from the Diamond High Council.

Figure 2.1 The Coltan Supply Chain

Mining

Prisoners from Rwanda used to dig coltan in return for reduction in sentence.
Child labor (estimated 30 percent of children in northeastern Congo dig for coltan).
Local Congolese.
Soldiers of factions (e.g., Ugandan soldiers).
Enemies sometimes cooperate with each other (e.g., Interahamwe cooperate with Rwandan military in mining coltan; Maï Maï do business with RPA coltan dealers).
But Rwandan army sometimes attack Maï Maï when coltan is bagged for extraction.
In mid-April 2001, over 9,000 people were forcibly displaced from Masisis by Rwandan army wanting to mine coltan.

Looting

The mining company SOMINKI had seven years' worth of coltan stocked in various areas. Rwandan forces and their allies organized its removal to Kigali. From November 1998 to April 1999, 2,000–3,000 tons of cassiterite and 1,000–1,500 tons of coltan were removed from the DRC.

Companies in the DRC

Wide variety of companies in the DRC deal in coltan (e.g., the Kotecha group of companies, based in Bukavu, at peak earned U.S.$700,000–800,000 per month, and by spring 2001 earned U.S.$200,000–300,000 per month.

Global Mineral: Purchases coltan in Bukavu and Goma. Part-owned by senior Rwandan officer Colonel James Kabarebe.

Rwandan army companies: Rwandan Metals, Grand Lacs Metals. In an eighteen-month period in 1999–2000, the RPA estimated to have earned U.S.$250 million.

RCD: Up to October 31, 2000, the RCD estimated to have exported U.S.$3.5–6.6 million of coltan.
In November 2000, SOMIGL obtained monopoly on coltan exports from the RCD for payment of U.S.$1 million per month. In Bukavu, the cigarette factory of Aziza Kulsum Gulamali, head of SIMOGL, was initially used as a cover for illicit coltan exports.
But monopoly encouraged smuggling by other traders. When monopoly ended April 2001, firms were instead required to pay an annual mining fee of U.S.$40,000 and an export tax of U.S.$6 per kilo.

SOMIKUVU: Owned by a German national who obtained a preferential loan of U.S.$500,000 from Germany to establish the company. Guarded by RCD-Goma soldiers.

Coltan Microeconomy

Miners taxed by armed factions or by SOMIGL.
Miners pay prostitutes in coltan (e.g., one kilo to purchase a "wife" for the duration of their mining stay).
Miners pay in coltan for treatment of sexually transmitted diseases (e.g., a tomato tin of coltan for antibiotics to treat gonorrhea).

Financial Arrangements

Money from SOMIGL was to be used to pay back a U.S.$1 million loan from the BCDI (a bank in Kigali) to Sonex, a company founded in Rwanda by RCD-Goma. The loan was to pay fuel bills to the airline Jambo Safari, which was involved in flying goods and equipment into and out of the DRC.
The UN panel of experts described the owner of Jambo Safari as a known figure in the entourage of President Kagame of Rwanda.

Uganda/Rwanda by Trading Companies

UN panel of experts lists large number of companies involved in the import of coltan from Rwanda, for example: Cogecom and Cogea—main agents in Brussels for SOMIGL.
Coltan imported into Belgium, Germany, India, Kenya, Malaysia, the Netherlands, the Russian Federation, Switzerland, and the UK.

A&M Minerals and Metals, UK, imports three tons per month of tantalum-bearing ore from Uganda. Supplies H. C. Starck, the largest coltan processing company.

Possible Arms-for-Coltan Route

Coltan traded in Butembo in the DRC purchased by buyers from the FSU. Fifty tons per month sold to Germany, South Africa, and Kazakhstan.
The company in Kazakhstan dealing with coltan is Ulba. The agent for Ulba in Kigali is Fin Mining, which is believed to be involved in arms dealing.

Processing Companies

These extract tantalum from the coltan.

H. C. Starck and Cabot account for 90 percent of the coltan processing market.
H. C. Starck purchases from both trading companies and direct from large mines and local traders.
UN report on the DRC identifies the company as a customer of Aziza Kulsum Gulamali, head of SOMIGL in the DRC.

These firms sell refined tantalum powder.

Transportation

From the DRC:
Dealers come in cars protected by the Rwandan army.
Rwandan army helicopters ship coltan directly to Kigali.
Victor Bout (a well-known arms dealer), has leased an Ilyushin 76 to carry coltan from the DRC to Kigali for Colonel James Kabarebe of the RPA, who is also part-owner of Global Mineral.

From Kigali:
Sabena Cargo of Belgium flew twice weekly from Kigali to Europe, but has now stopped these flights.
SDV of the Bollore Group: Main destinations by air are Brussels, Ostend, Amsterdam, Germany, and South Africa.
Coltan also shipped via Dar es Salaam in Tanzania and ports in Kenya.

In the United States:
Transported throughout the country by American Airlines (in partnership with Sabena).

Tantalum Capacitor Manufacturers

For example:
Kemet (world's largest tantalum capacitor manufacturer), Epcos AVX, Hitachi, NEC, Vishay, Daewoo.

High-Tech Companies

Capacitors used in manufacture of mobile phones, computers, game consoles (e.g., worldwide shortage of PlayStation 2 over Christmas 2000 was partly a function of a world shortage of coltan).
Companies using capacitors include Nokia, Hewlett-Packard, IBM, Lucent, Alcatel, Dell, Ericksson, Intel, Motorola.

Completing the Circle

Motorola mobile phones used by the AliR faction (comprising Interahamwe and former FAR members) in the DRC to communicate with each other.

original source of goods. Thus, whether by design or default, firms further down the supply chain can claim ignorance, often quite reasonably, when presented with evidence of complicity in the trade in conflict goods. Even when economic actors know their suppliers, the complexity of the chain allows them to maintain a moral distance from the conflict trade.

Unlicensed tax collection and tax avoidance also have regional dimensions that add complexity to conflict. During the wars in the former Yugoslavia, rival enclaves would each "take a cut" from goods in transit through their territories, including humanitarian relief supplies. As will be shown in the case studies that follow, smuggling of all kinds of goods for tax avoidance purposes remains endemic today in West Africa, northern Afghanistan, and Bosnia and Herzegovina (BiH), often facilitated by inadequately resourced or corrupt police and customs services. This not only deprives governments of needed revenue for postwar recovery, but also undermines efforts at peacebuilding on a national basis.

Where policing and controls are effective or pricing structures change, the phenomenon of displacement can occur, affecting key dynamics of conflict and war economies. As a consequence of a crackdown on opium production by the Taliban in 1999, for example, displacement occurred with poppy-growing increases in Burma and in the Northern Alliance–controlled areas of Afghanistan. Similarly, counternarcotics operations in Columbia have displaced drug cultivation to neighboring states where there is no conflict. Displacement is not only a function of regulation, however, as shadow economic activity can spontaneously generate dynamics that give rise to displacement. For example, during the war in BiH, tax farming increased the price of transiting goods through war-torn areas and thus encouraged traders to seek opportunities for cheaper routes and services, shifting the channels of shadow trade into neighboring territories, including Kosovo and Macedonia.

Military Networks

Two military factors are particularly significant to the political economy of regional conflict complexes: regional arms networks and regional mercenary networks. In large measure, these factors are significant because the availability of arms and mercenaries affects the opportunity costs of conflict: the wider availability of the means of war, the easier and cheaper it is to undertake. For instance, it has become a cliché to note that in some parts of West Africa an AK-47 can be exchanged for the price of a chicken.

The nature of the global arms market is such that localized conflicts are typically supplied with arms that originate from outside the region. However, regional arms networks can also play a significant role in supplying local conflicts. For example, Ethiopia, Eritrea, Yemen, and Djibouti are among the sources supplying the arms market in Somalia, in contravention of a UN arms embargo, according to a recent report of the UN Expert Panel on Somalia.[49] To the extent that regional arms networks play a significant role in supplying local conflicts, they both reflect and reinforce dynamics that influence the structure of regional conflict complexes. This occurs in a variety of ways.

First, regional arms networks become particularly important when direct or licensed supplies from producing countries to belligerent parties are problematic. Indeed, it is often the case that either the supplier or recipient has an interest in ensuring that arms deals are conducted covertly when a recipient state is under an arms embargo or has such an appalling human rights record that suppliers prefer to mask their association. In such cases, *indirect* supply via a neighboring state or states has obvious advantages — it hides the ultimate destination and also provides deniability to the supplier. In addition, the physical location of particular factions may make direct supply via a country's main ports and airports more problematic than indirect supply via neighboring states.

Second, the various political alliances in a regional conflict formation can influence the structure of regional arms networks. The way in which both physical location and the structure of political alliances can shape the direction of regional arms networks is neatly illustrated by the example of Iranian arms supplies to the Northern Alliance in Afghanistan. In one instance, 700 tons of arms were shipped to the Northern Alliance. However, the geography of regional alliances and territorial control in Afghanistan meant that the arms were shipped by rail via Turkmenistan and Uzbekistan and then by road through Tajikistan. Although the shipment was covert (it was labeled as "humanitarian aid"), the governments of the territories it traversed appear to have been complicit in the transfer. At one point, the shipment was impounded by officials in Kyrgyzstan, but the officials concerned were subsequently dismissed and, according to a report by Human Rights Watch, the arms ultimately reached their destination.[50]

Third, the dynamics of conflict in one state can create displacement effects that have implications for arms supplies to other regional actors. For example, where a peace settlement in one country is coupled with flawed disarmament, a supply of surplus weaponry can become available at knockdown rates to actual or potential combatants in neighboring states. A further example stems from the way in which conflict and state collapse in a particular state can contribute to the regional proliferation of arms. For instance, the arms channels established by the U.S. Central Intelligence Agency (CIA) to supply the mujahidin in Afghanistan suffered extensive leakage, contributing both to the domestic proliferation of arms within Pakistan and the supply of arms to conflicts such as that in Kashmir. Likewise, the complete breakdown of state control in Albania in 1997 resulted in looters seizing several hundred thousand weapons and 20,000 tons of ammunition.[51] This, in turn, transformed the political economy of revolt in neighboring Kosovo. Until this point, attempts by Kosovar Albanian militants to train and prepare for armed conflict in the 1980s and 1990s had not only been foiled by Serb police but were equally constrained by the difficulties involved in acquiring arms. Notably, Kosovo's position as a landlocked region and Albania's reluctance to jeopardize aid from the West or invite reprisals from Serbia placed a constraint on the acquisition of weaponry on the scale required for insurgency.[52] After 1997, however, large numbers of Kalashnikovs were suddenly available to the KLA for as little as U.S.$10 each, making the ensuing escalation of violence possible.[53]

The availability of regionally based mercenary forces represents a further dimension of the military aspect of regional conflict complexes. There is a popular conception of mercenary groups as either archetypal "dogs of war" hired from all around the world or as extraregional corporate mercenary companies such as Sandline in the UK or Military Professional Resources Inc. in the United States. However, some of the latter, most notably the now defunct South African firm Executive Outcomes, have worked regionally, for instance in Angola. In addition, just as peace may result in the displacement of arms to neighboring countries, it can also release former combatants available for hire—particularly where peace is accompanied by flawed demobilization and reintegration processes. This has occurred most notably in West Africa, where former Revolutionary United Front (RUF) combatants from the conflict in Sierra Leone have been hired to fight in conflicts in Liberia and Guinea.

Political Networks

Formal military alliances between governments and political leaders in neighboring states can both reflect and reinforce regional economic links. For instance, the political alliance between the late DRC leader Laurent Kabila and Zimbabwean president Robert Mugabe during the civil war in the DRC was underpinned through a variety of "legal" and "illicit" commercial deals. Thus, Zimbabwe Defense Industries provided arms and munitions to the Kabila government. In return, the Zimbabwean mining company Ridgepoint took over the management of the DRC state mining company Gecamines and received a 37.5 percent share of the company. Moreover, between 20 and 30 percent of the DRC's share of Gecamines's profits were used to fund the Zimbabwean war effort on behalf of the

DRC.[54] The operation produced cobalt estimated to be worth U.S.$6 million a month, with some of the proceeds reportedly used to pay bonuses to the Zimbabwean soldiers. There has also been lingering speculation that much of the money was being siphoned off for the personal benefit of senior military and political officials involved in the venture.[55]

Lucrative commodities, usually precious and semiprecious stones, may also be used instead of cash to buy or reward favors from allies. In some respects, this form of exchange was also a feature of the relationship between Kabila and Mugabe. A further example was the payment of diamonds by UNITA to win and maintain regional allies who, among other forms of reciprocation, facilitated the provision of arms and training to UNITA forces. Diamonds were supplied to Mobutu Seso Seko, president of what was then Zaire, as well as to the presidents of both Burkina Faso and Togo. However, like all business relationships, these were not devoid of tensions. For example, on one occasion President Gnassingbe Eyadema refused to allow the release of a missile system being shipped via Togo when UNITA's leader, Jonas Savimbi, refused to pay the required fee.[56]

Linkages between political associates across borders have also generated other forms of shadow economic activity. A remarkable case came to light in Southeast Europe in 2001 concerning a regionwide cigarette racket. Montenegrin president Milo Đukanović was investigated in Italy for smuggling. Documents alleged that Đukanović cooperated with Stanko Subotic-Cane, a former Yugoslav Security Service officer, and Zoran Djindić, then an opposition leader in Belgrade and later murdered by a mafia clan in March 2003, in a massive cigarette smuggling operation that underpinned other shadow activities.[57] Similarly, the notorious Serb warlord Zeljko Raznatović (Arkan), who skillfully exploited his connections with the Slobodan Milošević regime in Belgrade and Montenegro to build a lucrative criminal enterprise, was active in regional oil and cigarette smuggling.[58]

These political linkages may persist into the postconflict phase, as they did, for example, between the Croatian military and the hard-line Croat nationalists based in Mostar in BiH. The main effect seems to be to give succor to peace spoilers and anti-reformists in their resistance to external programs of neoliberal reform. The embedding of shadow economies with cross-border "political protection," therefore, requires a regional approach to address those links with neighboring governments, such as offering incentives to boost participation in regulated regional trade.

Social Networks

The social networks that underpin regional conflict complexes are defined by occupational, familial, and diaspora affiliations that actively transcend national borders. Occupational networks are particularly significant in both Southeast Europe and Central Asia, where lorry drivers were key participants in conflict trade. For example, a hub for drug and people trafficking in Plovdiv, Bulgaria, was found in 1999 to be controlled by an Albanian godfather from Kosovo, Nazim Delegu, whose trucking network extended from Italy to Albania and throughout the former Yugoslavia.[59] Where these shipments crossed several "tax" zones, they became a source of revenue for local militias. Hauliers who traded through Iran, Afghanistan, and Pakistan helped to sustain the Taliban government through its levies on goods and transport.[60] The Taliban imposed duties on trucks entering Afghanistan from Pakistan, many of which were involved in a large-scale smuggling operation that skillfully took advantage of the 1950 Afghan Transit Trade Agreement. Under this agreement, sealed trucks carrying imported goods to Afghanistan could transit through Pakistan duty-free. However, once entering Afghanistan, many trucks simply turned around and sold the goods in markets back in Pakistan—a practice that cost the latter U.S.$800 million in lost customs revenues between 1992 and 1995.[61] In contrast, the Taliban raised an estimated U.S.$75 million a year from taxing this trade, its most important official source of income.[62] Moreover, when the Taliban first emerged, it quickly gained the support of Pakistan's trucking cartels, which sought to secure their trade routes previously contested by various Afghan warlords. Indeed, these traders actually paid contributions to the madrasas where the Taliban were trained. Needless to say, these same routes and carriers have also been used to transport drugs and arms, the movement of which is equally aided by the conditions of the 1950 trade agreement; arms arriving by ship at the port of Karachi were then moved, in sealed trucks and uninspected, to Afghanistan.[63] Such activities have provided significant employment opportunities and have created alternative trade structures that have become an integral part of regional shadow economies and the livelihoods of borderland communities.

Family and clan networks play a critical role in ensuring economic survival in impoverished societies. The heads of these networks, usually patriarchs, provide loans or handouts, employment opportunities, and other useful services such as facilitating access to higher education or migration abroad. As the Afghan and Bosnian cases indicate, the demand for these forms of social support increases as state authority weakens, while informal and traditional social networks can play a crucial role in shadow economies in organizing the distribution of scarce goods. Sarajevo, for example, is noted for its famous families who exercise a preponderant influence in its political economy.

Diasporas influence their home countries and regions, not only politically but also economically. In one of the few investigations into the economic influence of diasporas, Aline Angoustures and Valérie Pascal emphasize that geographical proximity is not an essential feature of diaspora economic influence over a homeland—as illustrated by the sustained support for Croatia in its war against Yugoslavia from Croats in North America, Latin America, and Australia.[64] Nevertheless, regional diasporas can perform important functions, such as the provision of sanctuary, the physical movement of goods, and the maintenance of shadow economies in neighboring countries and borderlands. This is particularly true where peripheries are economically marginalized and borders are poorly monitored. For example, for the Pashtuns of the Afghanistan-Pakistan borderland, poverty and remoteness have created incentives that foster "emigration, smuggling, drug trafficking and recruitment to militant groups in territories where the Pakistan and Afghan states have been either unwilling or unable to maintain firm control."[65] Extraregional diasporas can also play a significant role. The Lebanese diaspora in Sierra Leone played an important role in sustaining both the peacetime shadow diamond economy and the war economy that emerged from it. Networks of Lebanese merchants have purchased rough diamonds from all factions, smuggled them out of the country, often drawing on wider Lebanese networks, and brought in consumer items and other scarce commodities.

Permissive Conditions, Sustainability, and Postconflict Resistance

Informal and established networks create permissive conditions for the development of shadow economies that sustain conflict.[66] Informal economies not only deny official authorities control over resources but also maintain an alternative socioeconomic system of employment and trade that, in turn, generates vested interests in its continuity. Also, as will be shown in the following case studies, the phenomenon of complicity between combatants on opposing sides is common and can fuel conflict by ensuring that they do not exhaust their supplies and reach a stalemate that would herald a cease-fire. In Sierra Leone, Nigerian peacekeepers were accused of trading with members of the Revolutionary United Front and of taking bribes from them in exchange for allowing the RUF to continue its exploitation of the country's shadow diamond trade. Interaction between government and insurgent forces in Sierra Leone was also marked by the "sobel" phenomenon of "soldiers by day, rebels by night."

A shadow economy operating alongside a state-controlled one does not prevent interaction between the two. This is apparent from the way that Pakistani intelligence agencies and their allies have used smugglers of drugs and other contraband to help ship arms throughout the region, in return for which the smugglers have been allowed to go about their own business unimpeded.[67] The collusion of government officials in the shadow and combat economies undermines the functions of the state, perpetuates immunity from prosecution, and enables insurgent commanders to continue their business with a degree of official connivance. The three cases in this book indicate that state regimes often forge symbiotic relationships with underworld gangs or warlords who may operate on a regional and transnational basis. The symbiosis has been observed in Lebanon, where militiamen have become "legitimate" reconstruction racketeers, dealers, and directors, taking advantage of an ultraliberal, unregulated economic environment and the marginalization of the state. As Francesco Strazzari comments, mafiosi in Southeast Europe "have emerged principally from the clientelistic degeneration of the state" and the peripheral character of the region, making it especially exposed to shadow trades and regional economic transactions in which corrupt political regimes are often deeply implicated.[68] As is discussed in Chapter 3, the current situation in Afghanistan raises the issue of the need to create incentives to bring these powerful economic actors into a productive form of engagement with the state and to invest in authorized enterprise, in short, to legitimize their "ill-gotten" gains. Otherwise, those who operate cartels and shadow infrastructures can be expected to resist efforts at peacemaking and postconflict transformation.

From the elements discussed above, and from our investigations into the economic factors in conflict, we can draw preliminary conclusions about the permissive conditions that allow regional conflict complexes to develop, to be sustained, and to resist resolution and transformation. Regional complexes may become more conflictual than cooperative where certain conditions exist. First, the prevailing economic order creates permissive conditions for conflict trade and the regionalization of war economies. In particular, where adjacent territories undergo rapid but differential impoverishment or structural adjustment, as demanded by IFIs, grievances over access to and the distribution of resources can weaken central state control. This occurs because the content of neoliberal policies weakens state capacity to generate, distribute, and regulate wealth effectively. Indeed, neoliberal policies require the state to withdraw from a formative role in the economy. Often the result is a reduction in the state's capacity to engage in strategic planning and to protect and nurture essential public goods, including the institutional and economic infrastructures necessary to bind the state together. Moreover, the focus of the IFIs on intervention in states separately rather than regionally, exacerbates regulatory differentiation between states, thereby providing an additional incentive for cross-border shadow trade. In more general terms, the free market order also facilitates direct access for provincial elites and guerrilla leaders to global and regional markets and networks at the expense of links to the central state.

Second, the economic marginalization of border areas from formal state economies is also a common permissive condition of regional conflict complexes. Paradoxically, however, borderlands are at the same time empowered by the key role they play in shadow economies. Borderlands may have existing traditions of economic resistance to central authority, as is evident in the interstices of empires in Southeast Europe, which are readily adapted to provide economic survival in situations of violent conflict. Economic disempowerment of the state exacerbates differential growth between parts of a national territory and opens up opportunities for borderlands to form nodes of shadow commerce and political and military resistance. The borderlands of Afghanistan—including the Pashtun territories and the Ferghana Valley in Tajikistan, Uzbekistan, and Kyrgyzstan—exemplify this deprivation of state peripheries of public infrastructure, social services, and other benefits of participation in the "official" economy. Acknowledging this, the World Bank has proposed earmarking part of the Afghanistan trust fund for borderland development in its Afghanistan Border States Development Framework.[69]

When the potential for shadow commerce in marginalized borderlands leads to fierce competition, it produces "neuralgia spots" of conflict between rival gangs and factions. The latter is exemplified by the Presevo Valley in southern Serbia, which has been attacked by an offshoot of the KLA. Sanctuaries and support bases across borders, used by refugees and militias, can provide opportunities to prosecute conflict beyond the reach of national governmental forces, and to provide a safe corridor for the continued supply of war matériel, rebel recruits, and mercenaries. A notorious example was the use of refugee camps by Hutu militias in Zaire to prepare armed attacks on Rwanda, but the use of cross-border supplies and mercenaries has also been a notable feature of the conflicts in West Africa. In sum, weak central institutions that are unable to effectively police or claim the allegiance of borderlands are a common feature of regional conflict complexes, enabling cross-border activities to further undermine the claims of sovereignty in more than one state entity.

Third, the absence of regional military security organizations or other fora of regional security cooperation that could rein in conflict is a notable feature of most contemporary conflict complexes. Strong regional organizations can provide a framework for cooperation to achieve peace and stability. By contrast, the absence of regional security mechanisms or the existence of regional bodies that lack capacity or are fettered by internal political divisions can also create the permissive conditions for conflict. Likewise, a lack of cooperative economic regimes and their enforcement at the regional level makes cross-border shadow trade feasible, thereby enhancing borderland capacity and incentives to resist incorporation into the official state economy. As the intertrading arrangements in the former Yugoslavia collapsed with the introduction of tariffs against other republics by Serbia, customs evasion became more attractive, if not essential, and, for example, official trade was reduced by 50–75 percent between Croatia and Slovenia.

In addition to these permissive conditions, the economic dynamics that sustain the regionalization of conflict include the access to conflict goods, taxation, diaspora remittances, predation, and shadow networks, already noted in the previous discussion of the elements of conflict complexes. Additionally, the use of modern technology by combatant elites and entrepreneurs during conflict facilitates information exchange and the transfer of money and resources across borders. The ability of displaced Hutu genocidaires to use laptop computers in their refugee camps to plan further campaigns of violence, and the widespread use by combatants of mobile phones to coordinate their military and commercial activities, have been frequently noted. Finally, opportunities for regional displacement in the production of conflict goods can also perpetuate and spread conflict by opening up alternative sources of economic supply, where local ground or resources have been lost.

From the perspective of conflict settlement and economic transformation, regional resistance can present considerable challenges. First, as Rubin notes, participants in regional economic networks can reduce incentives to reach a peace, partly because the larger number of interested actors makes resolution more difficult, and partly because combatant elites may become more interested in perpetuating profits than in pursuing political compromise.[70] To the extent that they have access to lucrative sources of finance, these elites may more easily ignore the war weariness of local populations, the battle fatigue of rank-and-file soldiers, and external diplomatic pressures that may be exerted on local politicians to reach peace agreements. Peace spoilers may be motivated by threats to their economic empires, which spread across borders and beyond the state-centric focus of mediators and peacebuilders.

Second, the legacies of regional war economies endure beyond the formal end of conflict because vested interests have local knowledge and experience, which is lacking in external agencies. The challenge for post-conflict transformation is to co-opt or subvert these interests in ways that will strengthen public institutions and provide for human needs. Third, even where there is prolonged and intrusive administration by representatives of the "international community," as in Southeast Europe, the local regional and global networks forged by shadow economic activities are able to adapt to new regulations and controls. Fourth, in the few cases where conflict trade controls have been imposed, they have been directed narrowly against the local sources of supply of conflict goods rather than against the freedom of first world consumers to demand. Local elites can either continue to circumvent domestic regulation using wartime cross-border channels of trade or they can negotiate with, even capture, the free market infrastructures introduced by IFI programs and adapt them for private rather than public gain. Because the economic agenda of the liberal peace places a high priority on the redistribution of socially owned assets among entrepreneurs, and because privatization exposes already economically vulnerable populations to new risks of unemployment, there is little incentive or opportunity for the majority of the population to participate in the new economic order. Transformation is further hobbled by the lack of policy attention to poverty and unmet social needs other than in providing short-term aid and relief. Where poverty persists after a cease-fire or peace settlement, the incentive to engage in shadow economic activities remains strong in the absence of alternative means of economic survival. If political fragmentation is left unattended or frozen into peace deals, as in the Dayton Accord, the state remains weak and unable to protect the population economically from the added stresses of market-based policies.

Conclusion

The concept of regional conflict complexes is a useful one that accords with the transnational character of many contemporary conflicts, which have usually, and perhaps misleadingly, been designated as "internal." The concept also encourages academics and policy practitioners to consider the prospects of promoting postconflict transformation on a regional basis. Displacement strategies inevitably require a regional approach. As a June 2002 conference on Afghanistan and its neighbors concluded: "Earmarking funds for regional cooperation and investing now in the transport, energy and communications infrastructure needed to connect the countries of the region to each other and to the world, will make any other investments in reconstruction more fruitful and sustainable."[71] Special provision for securing the economic future of borderlands is crucial because, paradoxically in view of their significance for national security, they are particularly vulnerable to "criminality" and prone to neglect by central governments. Borderlands are often difficult to secure and administer, are problematic to integrate into a national economy because of access and distance, and have populations with varied political allegiance.

Finally, ways should be sought to attract predatory networks and war-fueling diasporas to use their social capital for peaceful regional development. The ability of networks to delay peace processes and spoil agreements, in part *because* they often perform a social function and contribute to coping mechanisms, should be treated as a serious issue requiring innovative economic incentives if they are to be co-opted into transformation strategies.

Notes

1. Stockholm International Peace Research Institute, *SIPRI Yearbook 2002: Armaments, Disarmament, and International Security* (Oxford: Oxford University Press, 2002), p. 63.

2. John Mueller, "Thugs as Residual Combatants," paper presented at the International Studies Association annual convention, New Orleans, March 24–27, 2002.

3. Michael Ignatieff, *The Warrior's Honour: Ethnic War and the Modern Conscience* (New York: Henry Holt, 1997), pp. 3, 5–6.

4. Mary Kaldor, *New and Old Wars: Organized Violence in a Global Era* (Oxford: Polity Press, 1999).

5. John Garnett, "The Causes of War and the Conditions of Peace," in John Baylis, James Wirtz, Eliot Cohen, and Colin S. Gray, eds., *Strategy in the Contemporary World: An Introduction to Strategic Studies* (Oxford: Oxford University Press, 2002), p. 83.

6. Ibid.

7. Michael Ignatieff, "The Narcissism of Minor Difference," in Ignatieff, *Warrior's Honour,* pp. 34–71.

8. Ralph Peters, "The New Warrior Class," *Parameters* 24, no. 2 (Summer 1994): 16–26.

9. Colin S. Gray, *Modern Strategy* (Oxford: Oxford University Press, 1999), p. 277.

10. Ibid.

11. Mueller, "Thugs as Residual Combatants," p. 29.

12. Chetan Kumar, "Conclusion," in Elisabeth M. Cousens, Chetan Kumar, and Karin Wermester, *Peacebuilding as Politics: Cultivating Peace in Fragile Societies* (Boulder, CO: Lynne Rienner, 2001), p. 185.

13. For instance, François Jean and Jean-Christophe Rufin, eds., *Economie des guerres civiles* (Paris: Hachette, Collection Pluriel, 1996); Mats Berdal and David Keen, "Violence and Economic Agendas in Civil Wars: Some Policy Implications for Outside Intervention," *Millennium: Journal of International Studies* 26, no. 3 (1997): 795–818; William Reno, *Warlord Politics and African States* (Boulder, CO: Lynne Rienner, 1999); David Keen, *The Economic Functions of*

Violence in Civil Wars, Adelphi Paper no. 320 (Oxford: Oxford University Press for the International Institute of Strategic Studies, 1998); and Mats Berdal and David M. Malone, eds., *Greed and Grievance: Economic Agendas in Civil Wars,* International Peace Academy Occasional Paper Series (Boulder, CO: Lynne Rienner, 2000).

14. Jean and Rufin, *Economie des guerres civiles,* p. 13.

15. Jean-Christophe Rufin, "Les Economies de guerre dans les conflits internes," in Jean and Rufin, *Economie des guerres civiles,* pp. 36–42. A feature of the Kosovo war was the activity of the Albanian diaspora in Switzerland (headquarters of the Homeland Calling Fund), Austria, Germany, Sweden, and the UK in supporting the KLA, which in turn established links to NATO. See Tim Judah, *Kosovo: War and Revenge* (New Haven, CT: Yale University Press, 2000), pp. 127–129; and Alexandros Yannis, "Kosovo: The Political Economy of Conflict and Peacebuilding," in Karen Ballentine and Jake Sherman, eds., *The Political Economy of Conflict: Beyond Greed and Grievance,* International Peace Academy Occasional Paper Series (Boulder, CO: Lynne Rienner, 2003), pp. 167–197.

16. Macartan Humphreys, "Economics and Violent Conflict," August 2002, www.preventconflict.org/portal/economics; Michael Ross, "How Does Natural Resource Wealth Influence War?" working paper, University of California at Los Angeles, 2002; Michael Ross, "Oil, Drugs and Diamonds: The Varying Roles of Natural Resources in Civil War," in Ballentine and Sherman, *Political Economy of Armed Conflict,* pp. 47–73; Karen Ballentine, "Beyond Greed and Grievance: Reconsidering the Economic Dynamics of Armed Conflict," in Ballentine and Sherman, *Political Economy of Armed Conflict,* pp. 259–283; Paul Collier, "Economic Causes of Civil Conflict and Their Implications for Policy," World Bank, June 15, 2000, www.globalpolicy.org/security/issues/diamond/wb.htm; Indra de Soysa, "The Resource Curse: Are Civil Wars Driven by Rapacity or Paucity?" in Berdal and Malone, *Greed and Grievance,* pp. 113–135.

17. Philippe Le Billon, "The Political Ecology of War: Natural Resources and Armed Conflicts," *Political Geography* no. 20 (2001): 561–584. See also Ross, "How Does Natural Resource Wealth Influence War?"

18. For instance, Global Witness, *Taylor-Made: The Pivotal Role of Liberia's Forests in Regional Conflict,* September 2001; and Global Witness, *All the President's Men: The Devastating Story of Oil and Banking in Angola's Privatised War,* March 2002. These and other Global Witness publications are available at www.globalwitness.org.

19. Phillippe Le Billon, "The Political Economy of War: What Relief Workers Need to Know," paper no. 3 (London: Overseas Development Institute, 2000); Aline Angoustures and Valérie Pascal, "Diasporas et financement des conflits," in Jean and Rufin, *Economie des guerres civiles,* pp. 36–42.

20. Abdel-Fatau Musah and J. 'Kayode Fayemi, eds., *Mercenaries: An African Security Dilemma* (London: Pluto Press, 2000).

21. For instance, Reno, *Warlord Politics and African States;* John L. Hirsch, *Sierra Leone: Diamonds and the Struggle for Democracy,* International Peace Academy Occasional Paper Series (Boulder, CO: Lynne Rienner, 2001); Ian Smillie, Lansana Gberie, and Ralph Hazleton, *The Heart of the Matter: Sierra Leone, Diamonds, and Human Security* (Ottawa: Partnership Africa Canada, 2000); and Ballentine and Sherman, *Political Economy of Armed Conflict.*

22. Charles Tilly, *Coercion, Capital, and European States,* A.D. *900–1992,* rev. ed. (Oxford: Blackwell, 1990).

23. Mary Kaldor, *New and Old Wars: Organized Violence in a Global Era* (Oxford: Polity Press, 1999).

24. Available at www.econ.worldbank.org/programs/conflict.

25. Paul Collier, "Doing Well Out of War," in Berdal and Malone, *Greed and Grievance,* p. 97.

26. Ibid.

27. Collier, "Economic Causes of Civil Conflict."

28. João Gomes Porto, "Contemporary Conflict Analysis in Perspective," in Jeremy Lind and Kathryn Sturman, eds., *Scarcity and Surfeit: The Ecology of Africa's Conflicts* (Pretoria: African Centre for Technology Studies and Institute for Security Studies, 2002), p. 13.

29. E. Wayne Nafziger and Juha Auvinen, "Economic Development, Inequality, War, and State Violence," *World Development* 30, no. 2 (2002): 156.

30. David Keen, "A Response to Paul Collier's 'Doing Well Out of War' and Other Thoughts," presentation to the CODEP conference, June 18–20, 2001, School of Oriental and African Studies, University of London.

31. Humphreys, "Economics and Violent Conflict," p. 12.

32. Collier, "Economic Causes of Civil Conflict," p. 4.

33. Neil Cooper, "Conflict Goods: The Challenges for Peacekeeping and Conflict Prevention," *International Peacekeeping* 8, no. 3 (Autumn 2001): 21–38.

34. Paul Collier and Anke Hoeffler, "Greed and Grievance in Civil War," October 21, 2001, www.worldbank.org/research/conflict/papers/greedandgrievance.htm.

35. Nafziger and Auvinen, "Economic Development," pp. 153–163.

36. Humphreys, "Economics and Violent Conflict," p. 3; Francis Stewart, "Horizontal Inequalities as a Source of Conflict," in Fen Osler Hampson and David M. Malone, eds., *From Reaction to Conflict Prevention: Opportunities for the UN System* (Boulder, CO: Lynne Rienner, 2002), pp. 105–136.

37. Reno, *Warlord Politics and African States.*

38. Mark Duffield, *Global Governance and the New Wars: The Merging of Development and Security* (London: Zed Books, 2001), p. 132.

39. See World Bank Operations Evaluation Department, "Post-Conflict Reconstruction," *Précis* no. 169 (Summer 1998).

40. Karl W. Deutsch et al., *Political Community and the North Atlantic Area* (Princeton: Princeton University Press, 1957); Joseph Nye, *Peace in Parts* (Boston: Little, Brown, 1971), chap. 5.

41. Barry Buzan, Øle Waever, and Jaap de Wilde, eds., *Security: A New Framework for Analysis* (Boulder, CO: Lynne Rienner, 1998).

42. Ibid.

43. Peter Wallensteen and Margareta Sollenberg, "Armed Conflict and Regional Conflict Complexes, 1989–97," *Journal of Peace Research* 35, no. 5 (September 1998): 621–634.

44. Ibid., p. 624; Stockholm International Peace Research Institute, *SIPRI Yearbook 2001: Disarmament and International Security* (Oxford: Oxford University Press, 2001), p. 16.

45. Definition from the Center on International Cooperation, New York University, www.cic.nyu.edu/conflict.

46. Barnett R. Rubin, "Regional Approaches to Conflict Management in Africa," presentation to UN Security Council meeting, August 8, 2001, www.cic.nyu.edu/conflict.

47. See Diamond High Council information on conflict diamonds available at www.conflictdiamonds.com/pages/Interface/reportframe.html.

48. Christian Dietrich, *Hard Currency: The Criminalized Diamond Economy of the Democratic Republic of the Congo and Its Neighbours,* Partnership Africa Canada, Diamonds and Human Security Project, Occasional Paper no. 4, June 2002, www.partnershipafricacanada.org.

49. "Experts Recommend UN Sanctions for Violators of Arms Embargo in Somalia," UN News Center, April 3, 2003, www.un.org.

50. Human Rights Watch, *Afghanistan: Crisis of Impunity—The Role of Pakistan, Russia, and Iran in Fueling the Civil War,* July 2001, app. 1, "Case Study: Supplying the United Front: Iranian and CIS cooperation," www.hrw.org/reports98/publctns.htm.

51. Richard Williams, "Helping Albania Manage Munitions," *NATO Review* 48 (Summer–Autumn 2000), p. 26.

52. Neil Cooper, "Security Sector (Lack of) Transformation in Kosovo," in Keith Krause and Fred Tanner, eds., *Arms Control and Contemporary Conflicts: Challenges and Responses,* PSIS Special Studies no. 5 (Geneva: Programme for Strategic and International Security Studies and Geneva Centre for Security Policy, 2001), pp. 65–127.

53. Michael MccGwire, "Why Did We Bomb Belgrade?" *International Affairs* 76, no. 1 (January 2000): 4.

54. International Crisis Group (ICG), *Scramble for the Congo: Anatomy of an Ugly War* (Nairobi and Brussels: ICG, December 20, 2000), p. 61.

55. Global Witness, *Zimbabwe's Resource Colonialism in the DRC: A Briefing Document by Global Witness* (London: Global Witness, August 26, 2001), p. 11.

56. United Nations, *Report of the Panel of Experts on Violations of Security Council Sanctions Against UNITA, Established by the Security Council Pursuant to Resolution 1237 (1999), Concerning the Situation in Angola,* S/2000/203, March 10, 2000, p. 25, par. 101.

57. Christopher Corpora, "Boxing with Shadows: Understanding and Addressing the Global Asymmetric Threat Complex," paper presented at the George C. Marshall Center conference "Countering Terrorism in Southeast Europe: Future Directions in SEDM Cooperation," Garmisch, December 7–12, 2002.

58. Francesco Strazzari, "Between Ethnic Collusion and Mafia Collusion: The 'Balkan Route' to State Making," in Dietrich Jung, ed., *Shadow Globalization, Ethnic Conflicts, and New Wars: A Political Economy of Intra-State War* (London: Routledge, 2003), p. 152.

59. Ibid., p. 146.

60. Rubin, "Regional Approaches to Conflict Management."

61. Human Rights Watch, *Afghanistan,* p. 25.

62. Ibid., p. 25.

63. Ibid., p. 31.

64. Angoustures and Pascal, "Diasporas et financement des conflits," p. 512.

65. Report of the conference "Regional Approaches to the Reconstruction of Afghanistan," Istanbul, June 3–5, 2002 (Barnett R. Rubin, rapporteur), www.cic.nyu.edu/conflict.

66. On the connections between informal and war economies, see Ballentine, "Beyond Greed and Grievance," pp. 259–283.

67. Tara Kartha, "Controlling the Black and Gray Markets in Small Arms in South Asia," in Jeffrey Boutwell and Michael T. Klare, eds., *Light Weapons and Civil Conflict: Controlling the Tools of Violence* (Lanham, MD: Rowman & Littlefield, 1999), p. 53.

68. Quoted in ibid., p. 158.

69. Report of the conference "Regional Approaches to the Reconstruction of Afghanistan," pp. 14–15.

70. Rubin, "Regional Approaches to Conflict Management."

71. Report of the conference "Regional Approaches to the Reconstruction of Afghanistan."

3

Afghanistan in Central Asia

Jonathan Goodhand

This chapter examines the factors that have contributed to the development of the war economy and the implications for current efforts to build peace in Afghanistan.[1] The domestic, regional, and international dimensions of the Afghan war economy are analyzed from an historical and political economy perspective. It is argued that analysis needs to go beyond the simplistic "warlords and greedy profiteers" type of discourse that has influenced past and present policies toward Afghanistan. Recognizing the variety of actors and activities involved in the political economy of contemporary Afghanistan and combining a "fine-grained" analysis of micro-level processes with an appreciation of macro-level dynamics are essential to an accurate understanding of the policy challenges and to designing well-informed policy responses. In no small part, "winning the peace" will depend on how well international and domestic efforts effectively transform the war economy into a peace economy.

While the starting point is an analysis of the causes and dynamics of the war economy *within* Afghanistan, these cannot be understood in isolation from the regional context. Afghanistan is part of a *regional conflict complex*—in other words, a "bad neighborhood" that connects other latent and open conflicts within the region, including Kashmir, Tajikistan, and the Ferghana Valley. According to Peter Wallensteen, the Central Asia conflict complex is one of sixteen regionalized violent conflicts to have occurred since the Cold War.[2] The outer borders of this complex are unclear. For instance, following Wallensteen's categorization of regional complexes, "Central Asia" merges in the east with the "South Asia, West" complex and to the west with the "Caucasus" complex. Stakeholders in

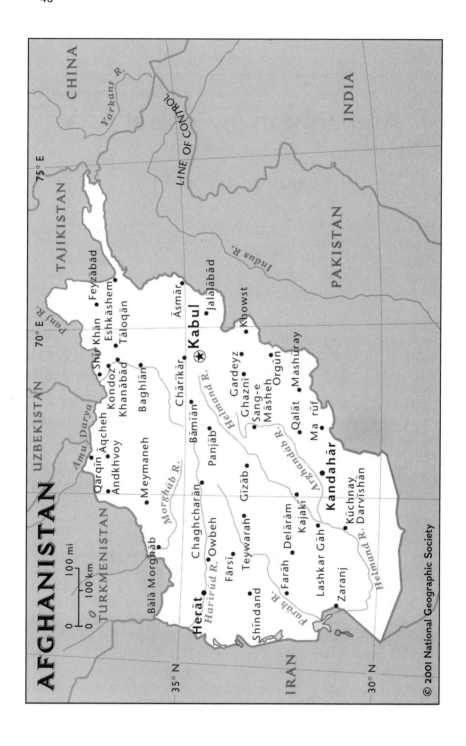

© 2001 National Geographic Society

the Central Asia complex extend well beyond the region itself, including, for example, drug dealers in Moscow and London and radical Islamic groups in Chechnya and the Philippines.

For the purpose of this study, the core Central Asian regional conflict complex is defined as Afghanistan, its neighboring countries Pakistan and Iran, and the Central Asian states Tajikistan, Uzbekistan, Turkmenistan, Kyrgyzstan, and Kazakhstan. While the last two states do not share a common border with Afghanistan, strong transnational linkages with Afghanistan developed during the course of the conflict in the late 1990s, primarily as a result of the drug trade. The region encompasses close to 300 million people. Beyond this core, China, India, Kashmir, the Caucasus, and the Middle East, particularly Saudi Arabia, are also significant players in the wider conflict complex, as political, religious, and socioeconomic networks connect them with various conflict stakeholders inside Afghanistan.

As Afghanistan's fate cannot be disentangled from the Central Asian regional conflict complex, a state-centered approach to peacebuilding is insufficient to meet the more fundamental challenge of transforming interstate and nonstate relations, institutions, and economic structures at the regional level that have contributed to repeated cycles of conflict and instability in Afghanistan. Indeed, a neglect of the regional dimensions of the conflict is one of the main weaknesses of the peace process set in motion by the Bonn Agreement of December 2001.

This chapter is structured around the following key themes:

• Afghanistan has been an "orphaned conflict" for more than a decade—this applies not only to earlier international attempts to contain rather than resolve the conflict, but also to the lack of serious research inside the country.[3] The rural economy remains to a large extent statistically unknown.[4] The paucity of quantitative and qualitative data on the war economy has held back efforts to respond to the problem, as policies have frequently been based on limited data and questionable assumptions. There is an urgent need to "skill up" in terms of improving understanding through an investment in research and analysis.

• International representations of conflict in Afghanistan have tended to be ahistorical. While the contemporary dynamics of the Afghan war economy are the product of long-term historical processes, international policy has tended to treat the country as a blank slate. This is particularly true in the post–September 11, 2001, context, in which many new external actors are entering the fray with limited experience or knowledge of the country. While the war has brought about profound transformations, there are also important continuities with the past. Afghanistan represents an opportunity to avoid repeating past mistakes in peacebuilding—particularly the neglect of the regional and economic dimensions of peacebuilding.

• Despite the signing of the Bonn Agreement in 2001, the extent to which Afghanistan has entered a postconflict phase remains questionable. The political basis for peace remains highly uncertain, as large sections of the population, particularly ethnic Pashtuns, and powerful regional leaders feel sidelined by the post-Taliban order. The interim and transitional administrations, established with the support of the international community, face significant challenges in expanding the remit of the government's power and influence beyond the capital.

• Many elements of the combat and shadow economies continue to thrive in Afghanistan. Despite pledges of international assistance by Western governments and statements from Afghan leaders declaring a "war on drugs," Afghan farmers have resumed large-scale poppy cultivation. Indeed, the opium-heroin drug trade generated close to U.S.$1.2 billion for the Afghan shadow economy in 2002, a figure that exceeds the amount of international aid for that year. Given the allure of high returns of engaging in these activities, and the web of social relations that underpin them, those who benefit from the opium trade have powerful incentives to resist central interference and control. Efforts to curtail these activities will achieve little progress in the absence of a comprehensive program for creating alternative livelihoods.

• Many of Afghanistan's neighbors continue to pursue political, economic, and other interests in Afghanistan that are antithetical to the consolidation of stability and peace. While efforts have been made to develop "friendly neighbor" agreements and practices, significant challenges and contradictions remain. It will be impossible to build peace in Afghanistan without also tackling the sources of conflict—including their economic dimensions—that persist at a regional level.

• Afghanistan faces a triple transition from war to peace (security transition), from "rogue state" to a legitimate, functioning state (political transition), and from a war economy to a peace economy (socioeconomic transition). The persistence of the war economy can only be tackled as part of a wider peacebuilding framework that simultaneously tackles the three interrelated transitions.

• The challenge of "winning the peace" is ineluctably a political one involving the creation of institutions that transform incentive systems. A precondition for transforming the war economy into a peace economy will be international support for the development of a strong state with a monopoly of the use of force. Far from criminalizing the profiteers, attempts will need to be made to encourage them to invest their accumulated profits in the licit economy. Similarly, a more nuanced analysis of warlords, their capacities, and their incentives systems is required. Opportunities at forging constructive political relationships will be missed if the warlords are uniformly castigated as conflict entrepreneurs or economic criminals.

The Evolution of the Political Economy of War in Afghanistan

This section charts the evolution of the political economy of Afghanistan in relation to the processes of war-making, state building, and state collapse that have characterized the history of that country. The contemporary war economy is partly an outcome and partly a cause of these processes. Over the last two decades, the various conditions of war created a context in which illicit activities could thrive, which in turn created a self-sustaining war economy. As the conditions of state fragmentation, external interference, and extreme underdevelopment that gave rise to Afghanistan's war economy remain, so too do powerful incentives to resist current efforts at building peace through the centralization of political authority.

Historical Background

In the sixteenth century, Central Asia was a nexus of long-distance trade, travel, and transmission of ideas and culture between the civilizations of Europe, the Middle East, and South and East Asia.[5] Afghanistan emerged as a tribal confederacy in the second half of the eighteenth century, located in the interstices of the powerful empires of Iran, the Indian subcontinent, and Central Asia. By the middle of the eighteenth century, with British imperial control in India and an expanding czarist empire to the north, the imperial powers together demarcated the territory of Afghanistan in order to make it an effective buffer state. The drawing of the Durrand Line in 1893, the border between British India and Afghanistan, was to become an ongoing point of contention and conflict, as it divided the Pashtuns and left them straddling the border.

The state was dependent for its support and legitimacy on external largesse—first from British and subsequently from Russians subsidies. Rentier incomes were used to develop means of coercion and social control, allowing the domestic elite to rule without being domestically accountable. In the 1960s, Afghanistan depended for nearly half of its budget on foreign aid, primarily from the Soviet Union.[6] There was limited interaction between the state apparatus and citizens. In addition, the state administration was too weak to alter traditional patterns of authority and economy in rural areas. In parts of the east, for example, taxation and conscription were resisted—the price for tribal support in the civil war of 1929 was the favorable treatment of landed interests by the state.[7]

Development aid played an important role in regime legitimization and maintenance strategies, although the insufficiency and irregularity of external flows caused continual instability. Projects such as the Helmand Valley Authority (HVA), a dam-building/irrigation project funded by the United States, were one means by which the state sought to legitimize dominance over unruly groups. To U.S. and Afghan royal government officials, the project was a means of dealing with a floating population of Pashtun nomads whose disregard for laws, taxes, and borders symbolized the country's backwardness.[8] The HVA was a classic state-led response to the problem of borderlands—although it aimed to create a secure political base, bring populations within reach of modernization, and reduce transborder flows, it proved difficult to entice the Ghilzai Pashtun to become ordinary farmers.[9] By the outbreak of war in 1978, after almost three decades of support, the project had more or less ground to a halt. Ironically, by 2000 the Helmand Valley produced 39 percent of the world's heroin.[10]

During the 1970s, Afghan-Pakistani trucking merchants became a growing economic force. A smuggling economy developed, encouraged by the Afghan Transit Trade Agreement (ATTA), signed with Pakistan, which enabled landlocked Afghanistan to import selected commodities duty-free. Goods were then smuggled back across the border and sold in Pakistan's markets. Timber was also smuggled across the Pakistani border.[11] The trade was controlled by the Pashtun tribes (primarily the Afridi clan) who straddled the border between Pakistan and Afghanistan. Road construction in the 1970s and investment in heavy trucks with the help of West German credit further facilitated this development.[12] Poppy cultivation also increased during this period as opium crops in the Golden Triangle countries declined. By the late 1970s, poppy was being cultivated in over half of Afghanistan's twenty-eight provinces, annually producing 250 metric tons of opium for export.[13]

Political liberalization led to growing instability and competition between communist and Islamist parties. A communist coup in 1978 (the Saur Revolution) sparked rural resistance and ultimately the 1979 Soviet invasion.

The Cold War Conflict, 1979–1992

External engagement in the 1980s gradually eroded the primary functions of the state, including its monopoly of the use of force, as the mujahidin opposition increasingly controlled the countryside. Further, the Soviet invasion was accompanied by deliberate efforts to terrorize rural populations and destroy infrastructure. This led to a drop by almost two-thirds in food production. It also caused widespread internal and external displacement, resulting in rapid urbanization, and the development of "warrior refugee" communities in Iran and Pakistan. Financial and humanitarian assistance during this period also contributed to the economy's rapid monetization.[14]

The Cold War also brought with it politically motivated resource flows that transformed Afghan governance and economic structures. On the one hand, from 1979 to 1992, the regime depended on Soviet financial and military support and revenue from gas sales. On the other hand, a logistic support system arranged by the U.S. Central Intelligence Agency (CIA) and the Pakistani Inter-Services Intelligence (ISI)—the so-called CIA/ISI pipeline—delivered massive military and financial support to the anticommunist opposition. Further, political parties in Pakistan and Iran served as logistical conduits between the external Afghan resistance commanders and internal "fronts." Saudi Arabia and China were also significant suppliers of arms to the resistance. U.S.$6–8 billion worth of arms were sent through the Afghan pipeline. The supply of arms and ammunition became a political currency by which external parties bought influence.[15]

The arms pipeline and the system of brokerage that underpinned it laid the foundations for the regionalized combat and shadow economies of the 1990s. Profits accumulated by commanders and traders were reinvested in the drug and cross-border smuggling economies. Already by the mid-1980s, there was an arms pipeline going into, and a drugs pipeline coming out of, Afghanistan. According to John K. Cooley, the drug trade was encouraged by proxy backers of the mujahidin as a "weapon of war" to destabilize Soviet-controlled Afghanistan and the Central Asian republics. In 1989 the seven major mujahidin groups were responsible for a total production of over 800 metric tons of opium.[16] Pakistan also became a major opium producer and by 1989 was producing a similar quantity.[17] An immense narcotics trade developed under the CIA/ISI umbrella that went to the heart of the Pakistani state. It involved collusion between the mujahidin, Pakistani drug dealers, and elements of the Pakistan military. The U.S. Drug Enforcement Agency (DEA) identified forty major heroin syndicates, including some headed by top government officers in Pakistan.[18]

Fragmentation and Warlordism, 1992–1994

The breakup of the Soviet Union and the emergence of the newly independent Central Asian states meant that Afghanistan lost the strategic position it had previously enjoyed as a buffer state, reverting to some extent to its previous position as a transmission zone with open borders crossed by trade routes. In the early 1990s it became increasingly misleading to talk about "the Afghan conflict." There were multiple conflicts that together formed a regional conflict system of interconnected zones of instability including Kashmir, Tajikistan, and the Ferghana Valley. With the decline of superpower patronage, warlords were forced to develop internal revenue sources. Politically, the fragmentation of central power—reversing the state-building processes of the preceding century—went hand in hand with the emergence of regionalized politico-military groups backed by neighboring powers. The minting of different currencies by opposing factions symbolized the de facto fragmentation of sovereignty.

In these circumstances, the shadow economy was able to expand rapidly. Between 1992 and 1995, Afghanistan produced 2,200–2,400 metric tons of opium per year, rivaling Burma as the world's largest producer of raw opium.[19] Drawing upon its geographical comparative advantage as a de facto free trade zone and established social networks, Afghanistan became a marketing corridor for an expanding "illicit" economy. Internally, the impact was the intensification of centrifugal pressures on the Afghan state, whereby growing integration of the economies of provincial cities with neighboring countries, combined with interfactional fighting and wide-scale destruction in and around the capital, rendered Kabul an economic backwater. Arguably, provincial warlords had few incentives to put the state back together. Violence became a means of controlling markets and creating a monopoly on predation. The fragmenting of authority became one of the main obstacles to a political settlement. The carrots and sticks of traditional interstate diplomacy had limited influence on the motivations and actions of the freewheeling, powerful, nonstate actors that increasingly ruled Afghanistan.

Talibanization, 1994–2001

The emergence in 1994 of an assertive Islamic traditionalism in the form of the Taliban marked the next phase of conflict in and around Afghanistan. "Taliban" is derived from the Arabic word *Talib,* meaning "religious student." The movement rapidly became the preeminent politico-military force, controlling approximately 90 percent of the country from 1996 onward. By 1998 the Taliban had taken control of most of the key airports and border crossings, which enabled it to establish a virtual monopoly of predation.

International and regional dimensions. The consolidation of the Taliban regime was closely linked to state and nonstate interests in Pakistan.

First, powerful elites in Pakistan saw the Taliban as a means of furthering its pursuit of "strategic depth" in relation to its confrontation with India. The stability brought by a pliant regime in Afghanistan would also enable Pakistan to establish an economic bridgehead—through transport, communications, and pipelines—with Central Asia. Pakistan's aid included bankrolling Taliban operations, providing diplomatic support as the Taliban's virtual emissaries abroad, arranging training for Taliban fighters, recruiting skilled and unskilled manpower to serve in Taliban armies, planning and directing offensives, providing and facilitating shipments of ammunition and fuel, and on several occasions, providing direct combat support.[20]

Second, the Taliban enjoyed the backing of the Afghan-Pakistan transport sector, whose economic interests had been damaged by the rampant warlordism of the early 1990s. The Taliban brought a modicum of security and stability, which enabled cross-border trade to flourish once more. As one haulier reported: "You can drive from one end of the country to the other even at night with a car full of gold and no-one will disturb you."[21] The licit economy also benefited from the stability of Taliban rule; agricultural production increased substantially during this period, although after 1997 it was adversely affected by drought.[22]

Radical Islamic groups in the region, particularly those based in Pakistan, were a third constituency supporting the Taliban.[23] This period saw the consolidation of transnational political and religious networks, with groups such as Al-Qaida, the Islamic Movement for Uzbekistan (IMU), and various Kashmiri separatists, outlawed Pakistani groups, Chinese Uighurs, and Chechen militants establishing bases in the country. According to Ahmed Rashid, between 1994 and 1999, an estimated 80,000–100,000 Pakistanis trained and fought in Afghanistan.[24] Becoming a safe haven and training ground for "stateless" internationalist Muslim fighters[25] ensured Afghanistan's continued international isolation as well as destabilizing neighboring countries, particularly Pakistan and Uzbekistan. Although the empirical evidence is limited, during the late 1990s the networks of the Islamic groups, the drugs and cross-border trading mafia, and the Taliban appeared to become increasingly entwined.

Finally, Saudi Arabia also provided funds and heavily subsidized fuel supplies to the Taliban. Although official Saudi aid stopped due to U.S. pressure, nonstate support continued in the form of private contributions, including support for the Taliban regime's Ministry of Enforcement of Virtue and Suppression of Vice.

The anti-Taliban forces of the United Front (UF)[26] were also the recipients of external aid. Hizb-i Wahdat, one of the parties within the UF alliance, received support from Iran including weapons, munitions, and training. Russia also supported the UF with the aim of preventing the spread of "fundamentalism" to the Central Asian republics. In addition to securing regional cooperation among the Central Asian countries by facilitating the supply of arms to UF forces, Russia provided direct assistance in the form of personnel and matériel.[27]

Two additional sets of international actors played a significant role in influencing the incentive systems and affecting the capacities of Afghanistan combatants and other domestic actors. These were the oil companies and the international diplomatic and donor communities. As Rashid argues, Afghanistan became a significant fulcrum for the "new Great Game" in Central Asia, as great powers competed for access to the energy reserves of the Caspian Sea basin and the routing of pipelines out of the region.[28] When it first appeared that the Taliban would bring security to Afghanistan, there was growing competition between U.S. and Argentine oil companies, Unocal and Bridas respectively, for the contract to build a pipeline from Turkmenistan transiting across Afghanistan to South Asia. As Rashid argues, the initial "romancing" of the Taliban by Unocal was closely linked to U.S. policy on Afghanistan—it would not construct the pipeline or discuss commercial terms with the Taliban until there was a recognized government in Kabul so that the World Bank and others could lend money for the project.[29] The question of international recognition was therefore one of the few bargaining chips that the international community had in relation to the Taliban, as this would have enabled access to international finance and major development projects including oil and gas pipelines. Ultimately talks broke down due to a hardening in the U.S. attitude toward the Taliban, attributable in large part to the sheltering of Osama bin Laden and pressure from the U.S.-based group Feminist Majority over Taliban human rights abuses.

Arguably a paradoxical combination of international action and inaction contributed to the development of the combat economy and militant safe havens during this period. To a considerable extent, the flourishing of Afghanistan's war economy was a function of an international political economy of neglect. While the shift toward the 6 + 2 negotiating framework (the six neighboring countries plus the United States and Russia) signaled a recognition of the regional and international dimensions of the conflict, the lack of robust and sustained support by the major powers meant that the leverage of the UN was extremely limited. Indeed, Afghanistan became a "graveyard" for UN negotiators.[30] The UN Security Council's imposition of one-sided sanctions in 1999 and 2000 aimed to isolate and weaken the Taliban, but arguably strengthened the position of hard-liners within the movement and pushed the Taliban into a closer relationship with radical Islamic groups. As the political track faltered, growing conditionalities were tied to humanitarian aid through the UN-led strategic framework in an attempt to build peace and induce behavioral change within the Taliban with regard to humanitarian and human rights principles. In this sense, Afghanistan is illustrative of what Mark Duffield has described as "the growing securitization of aid," that is, the use of development and humanitarian assistance as a tool for peacebuilding.[31] However, in this case, the approach involved unrealistic assumptions about the importance of humanitarian aid in relation to other resource flows driving the war economy. If one compares, for example, the value of aid to Afghanistan (roughly U.S.$300 million per annum at this time) with the U.S.$2.5 billion generated in 1997 alone through cross-border trade between Afghanistan and Pakistan, it is clear why threatening to turn off the aid tap had a limited effect.[32]

Internal dimensions. Although international attention has tended to focus on the narcotics trade, cross-border smuggling has generated the most revenue for Afghanistan's combat and shadow economies. At its peak in 1996–1997, the cross-border transit trade between Pakistan and Afghanistan produced approximately U.S.$2.5 billion,[33] with the Taliban generating an estimated U.S.$75 million through taxing this trade.[34] The Taliban placed a tax of 6 percent on each item imported into Afghanistan. "The consignments range from Japanese camcorders to English underwear and 'Earl Grey' tea, Chinese silk to American computer parts, Afghan heroin to Pakistani wheat and sugar, East European Kalashnikovs to Iranian petroleum."[35] Consumer goods from Dubai were imported by air to Kandahar and Jalalabad. Fuel from Iran, where oil products are heavily subsidized, entered Afghanistan via Herat. From Turkmenistan, a range of manufactured goods such as automobile spare parts were imported. Most of these goods were bound for Pakistan. The Taliban controlled all six of Afghanistan's major airfields, which gave it a military advantage over the UF, which lacked easy supply lines, and also enabled it to maximize revenue from the smuggling trade. The UF's ability to generate revenue internally was more limited. It controlled mining operations and the export of precious stones (lapis lazuli and emeralds) from the Panjshir Valley, an industry that generated moderate incomes of U.S.$7–10 million per annum. It also controlled a monopoly on the production and sale of salt and import of gasoline and diesel fuel.

While smuggling may have been the primary source of internally generated revenue for the Taliban, clearly the opium economy was also important. The opium trade in Afghanistan reportedly generated approximately U.S.$30 million per year for the Taliban, which controlled 96 percent of the areas under opium cultivation. Related to the illicit trade were a range of connected service industries including fuel stations, shops, and tea houses. In 1999 the northeastern region of Afghanistan, controlled by the UF, produced only 3 percent of the country's opium, for a total of about 60 tons. Russian organized criminal groups sold arms to Ahmad Shah Massoud, a Jamiat commander of the UF forces, and purchased heroin from traders.[36]

The Taliban's policy toward the cultivation, production, and trafficking of drugs was marked by a curious mixture of religious principles, ambiguity, and expediency.[37] During their early years, policy appeared to be largely dictated by expediency, and production rose rapidly. In Kandahar, for example, production of opium in 1996 increased from 79 to 120 tons over the previous year. In 1997–1998 the total production of opium for Afghanistan was 2,700 tons, which represented a 43 percent increase from 1996. Poppy cultivation had also begun to spread to new areas, including territories outside the control of the Taliban in the north and northeast. In 1999, production reached its peak of 4,500 tons, representing 75 percent of world supply.[38] However, in 2000 it fell back to 3,600 tons. The decline in production is most often attributed to a decree issued in August 1999 by Taliban leader Mullah Omar to reduce cultivation by one-third, although poor weather conditions were likely also a factor. A second edict, passed on July 27, 2000, was more rigidly enforced and declared the cultivation of opium poppy as "un-Islamic," or *haram*. That year, production in Taliban-controlled areas was brought down to a mere 74 tons.[39] As a result of displacement dynamics, poppy growing increased in non-Taliban-controlled areas. In Badakhshan, for instance, the area of land planted reportedly increased from 2,458 hectares in 2000 to 6,341 hectares in 2002.[40]

The reasons for the Taliban's bans on poppy cultivation are unclear; there are a number of competing theories. According to one explanation, the Taliban may have seen a crackdown on drug production and export as a bargaining chip in negotiations with the international community. By eradicating poppy production, the Taliban perhaps expected to be "rewarded" with the international recognition that had long eluded it. Another theory is that the Taliban sought to reduce production in order to bring up prices of its own opium stockpiles. Because of overproduction in previous years, farmgate prices for opium declined from U.S.$60 per kilo in 1998 to U.S.$20 per kilo in 2000. Following the ban, there was a tenfold increase in prices. The edict may also have been motivated on religious grounds, and the mullahs certainly played an important role in promulgating the ban.[41]

Before the opium edict, poppies were grown in 40 percent of the districts in Afghanistan. The structure of the opium trade differed from area to area. For instance, in the south, there was a relatively free market structure, while production in the eastern region was more tightly organized and controlled by larger traders. In the east, the quality of poppy was higher, and consequently so were prices. Helmond and Nangahar dominated supply, accounting for three-quarters of the total amount of land planted with opium between 1993 and 2000. Opium was typically exported as a morphine base, which was attractive to traders because of its less bulky form and less noticeable odor. There is limited information on the network of laboratories located along Afghanistan's northern and southern borders. Some Afghan labs are reportedly capable of producing high-grade heroin—tailor-made for Western markets.[42] Acetic anhydride, which is required for processing, is imported through neighboring countries; China, for instance, has seized 5,670 tons of the chemical hidden in carpets destined for Afghanistan.[43]

It is thought that 85 percent of all heroin seized in the UK is produced from Afghan opium. International routes have varied, as traders are quick to adjust to the changing political situation. The northern route through Central Asia has increased in significance due to stronger border controls on the Iranian and Pakistani frontiers. Some 50 percent of Afghanistan's opium is consumed within the region. Traffickers are often paid for their services in kind.

While in Afghan terms, the opium trade is a lucrative one, it is estimated that only 1 percent of total profits have gone to farmers, with 2.5 percent remaining in Afghanistan and Pakistan in the hands of dealers. Some 5 percent of profits are spent in countries through which the heroin passes en route, while the rest of the profits accrue to dealers in Europe and the United States.[44] The trade is marked by a lack of vertical integration, with traders generally selling only at the border. While some traders travel as far as the Persian Gulf, none is involved in the lucrative Western retail markets. A by-product of the opium trade also appears to be the growing problem of drug addiction within the region, with an estimated 1.5 million addicts in Pakistan and 1.2 million in Iran.

Post-Taliban: Contemporary Dimensions
of the Afghan Political Economy

The attacks on the World Trade Center and the Pentagon on September 11, 2001, marked the start of a new phase of the Afghan conflict. The U.S.-led campaign against Al-Qaida in Afghanistan resulted in the rapid collapse of the Taliban regime. In December 2001, the UN-sponsored "Agreement on Provisional Arrangements in Afghanistan Pending the Re-establishment of Permanent Government Institutions," commonly known as the Bonn Agreement, provided for the creation of an Afghan interim administration and the convening within six months of an emergency Loya Jirga (Great Council) to decide the composition of an Afghan transitional authority.[45] A constitutional Loya Jirga was then to be held within eighteen months in order to adopt a new constitution. Finally, elections were to occur no later than two years after the emergency Loya Jirga.[46]

Both the continued U.S. military presence and the International Security Assistance Force (ISAF), established to provide security in and around Kabul as part of the Bonn Agreement, have been able to maintain a tenuous peace since the agreement was signed. However, underlying tensions remain. Regional warlords have been jockeying for positions and control of markets. There is growing resentment, particularly in the Pashtun areas of the south and east, toward the interim and transitional governments and the nascent institutions that surround them, for their failure to deliver palpable peace dividends and for what many perceive to be their lack of representativeness. Remnants of Al-Qaida and Taliban forces are reported to be regrouping in the tribal areas of Pakistan on the Afghan border as well as in the eastern provinces of Afghanistan proper. Although a regional noninterference treaty was signed by some of Afghanistan's neighbors on December 22, 2002, it was not signed by Russia, India, or Saudi Arabia, and there are further indications that regional players are once again backing proxy powers within Afghanistan. Moreover, the CIA has spent U.S.$70 million financing local commanders in the war against Al-Qaida and the Taliban.[47] These "Pentagon-created warlords" are having a destabilizing effect and are likely to resist attempts by the central government to establish a monopoly of force. There are concerns that the war in Iraq in March–April 2003 and its aftermath could lead to a possible scaling down of the international presence in the region and to renewed violent conflict across the country.

Combat, Shadow, and Coping Economies in Afghanistan

As described in Chapter 1, analysis of the political economy of conflict in Afghanistan is facilitated by a distinction between combat, shadow, and coping economies. While empirically they overlap, each encompasses a distinct set of key actors, motivations, and economic activities that have qualitatively different implications for peacebuilding. Table 3.1 presents characteristics of the three economy types as applied to Afghanistan.

The opium trade in Afghanistan cuts across all three economy types. The opium economy is a classic example of the growth of transborder trade in zones of conflict and instability. Mark Duffield characterizes such transborder trade as a mercantilist activity that is largely uninterested in long-term productive investment, involved with the control and apportionment of wealth, dependent on maintaining differences and discrete forms of control for profit, and likely to encourage informal protectionism.[48] In many respects, this sort of trade has illiberal, quasi-feudal tendencies. It is important to emphasize that the transformation from war to peace threatens to disrupt established systems of production and exchange that provide such warlords and their followers with livelihoods.

The combat, shadow, and coping economies have persisted into the post-Taliban order. As the Taliban regime was collapsing in November 2001, farmers quickly resumed planting their fields with poppies. In part, this was driven by economic necessity. The ban of the previous year had increased rural destitution, pushing poor farmers into greater indebtedness. During this period, lenders monetized loans that were originally to be repaid in opium, but this conversion was based on the then *current* cash value of the amount of opium on which the advance was originally obtained. With a significant increase in the prices of opium in the 2000–2001 growing season, this monetization of advances had the effect of charging interest at 1,000–15,000 percent.[49] Farmers and dealers also calculated, rightly, that regime change would leave a power vacuum and that any new administration would lack the power to enforce a ban.[50] Although the Afghan transitional authority has staged a number of high-profile crop destructions, it has had insufficient resources, has been too compromised,[51] and has had limited leverage over regional warlords to enforce a drug eradication program. In the eastern province of Jalalabad, for instance, the government was offering U.S.$350 per hectare for farmers to destroy their crops, while local residents were demanding U.S.$3,000 per hectare. As one Afghan farmer remarked: "They should provide jobs for our young people. We will cultivate poppies for another 5 years until we are sure our people will have permanent jobs."[52]

In addition, many of the international and regional dimensions of the Afghan shadow political economy are still present. The absence of an effective state with sufficient capacity and authority for economic regulation accentuates this global and regional "connectivity." Profiteers tend to reap the lion's share of benefits, while communities engaged in subsistence and survival become increasingly vulnerable as they are exposed to

Table 3.1   Afghanistan: Economies, Actors, Motives, and Activities

	The Combat Economy	The Shadow Economy	The Coping Economy
Who? Key Actors	Commanders, "conflict entrepreneurs," fighters, suppliers of arms, munitions, equipment.	Profiteers, transport sector, businessmen, drug traffickers, "downstream" actors (truck drivers, poppy farmers).	Poor families and communities— the Afghan majority.
Why? Motivations and Incentives for War or Peace	To fund the war effort or achieve military objectives. Peace may not be in their interest as it may lead to decreased power, status, and wealth. Fighters may have an interest in peace if there are alternative sources of livelihood.	To make a profit on the margins of the conflict. Entrepreneurs profit from the lack of a strong state and a highly liberal economy. Peace could be in their interest if it encourages long-term investment and licit entrepreneurial activity. Peace requires alternatives to the shadow economy; otherwise a criminalized war economy will become a criminalized peace economy.	To cope and maintain asset bases through low-risk activities, or to survive through asset erosion. Peace could enable families to move beyond subsistence.
How? Key Activities and Commodities	Taxation of licit and illicit economic activities (opium, smuggled consumer goods, lapis and emeralds, wheat, land tax). Money, arms, equipment, and fuel from external state and nonstate actors. Printing money. Economic blockades of dissenting areas. Destruction of means of economic support. Asset stripping and looting. Aid manipulation.	Opium economy. Cross-border smuggling under ATTA agreement. Mass extraction of natural resources (timber, marble). Smuggling of high-value commodities (emeralds, lapis, antiquities, rare fauna). Hawalla (currency order and exchange system). Aid manipulation.	Employ diverse livelihood strategies to spread risk. Subsistence agriculture. Petty trade and small businesses. On-farm and off-farm wage labor. Labor migration and remittances. Redistribution through family networks. Humanitarian and rehabilitation assistance.

continues

the turbulence of regional and international markets. The overall picture is one of growing opportunities for the few and growing risks and vulnerability for the majority. At the same time, there are also important continuities with the past. The current political economy builds upon much older patterns of human organization and interaction. For instance, the drug,

Table 3.1 continued

	The Combat Economy	The Shadow Economy	The Coping Economy
What Effects? Impacts	Disruption of markets and destruction of asset bases. Violent redistribution of resources and entitlements. Impoverishment of politically vulnerable groups. Outmigration of educated. Political instability in neighboring countries (e.g., circulation of small arms, growth of militarized groups).	Concentrates power and wealth. Inflationary effects. Undermines patron-client relationships, increasing vulnerability. Smuggling circumvents Pakistan's customs duty and sales tax, impacting revenue collection and undercutting local producers. Increased drug use.	Coping may reinforce social networks, but survival may lead to negative or regressive coping strategies. Lack of long-term investment. Long-term effects on human and social capital—lowering levels of health, education, strain on social networks, and the like.

Source: Adapted from Adam Pain and Jonathan Goodhand, "Afghanistan: Current Employment and Socio-Economic Situation and Prospects," International Labour Organization, Infocus program on crisis response and reconstruction, Working Paper no. 8, March 2002, p. 2.

smuggling, and religious networks draw upon prewar social networks based on *qawm* and tribal loyalties.[53] Warlords and profiteers play new games by old rules, mobilizing the "economy of affection," just as other rulers have throughout Afghan history.

In part as a result of these complex and interrelated factors, Afghanistan is reverting to the pattern of governance of the early 1990s, with regional warlords reestablishing control over personal fiefdoms. While warlords control the smuggling and drugs trades, which in turn generate funding for their own private militias, they have few incentives for engaging with the embryonic central state, whose remit did not stretch much beyond Kabul more than one year after the signing of the Bonn Agreement. As a senior European aid official noted in June 2002, "The warlords with income are stronger now than they were last December when the Taliban fell. They can defy the central government and the international community at will."[54]

The Combat Economy

While international attention has tended to focus on drugs in relation to the war economy, it is important to remember that external resource flows including arms, ammunition, fuel and financial support from state and nonstate actors in the region have probably been more significant than internally generated revenue. During the 1980s, Afghanistan received more than 3 million tons of military supplies, making the country the world's largest per capita arms recipient. There are at least 10 million small arms and light weapons (SALW) currently in circulation, with a total value of U.S.$8 million.[55]

Clearly, then, the war economy needs to be located within a global and regional framework. Strategies of reproduction adopted by states play themselves out beyond national borders. Pakistan's pursuit of strategic depth in relation to India, for instance, has had profound implications in terms of Afghanistan's political economy. There have also been regional "blow-back" effects, most seriously in Uzbekistan, where the Islamic Movement for Uzbekistan challenges the legitimacy of the state, and in Pakistan, where armed proto-Taliban groups have caused growing instability and may threaten the long-term security of the state.[56]

The regional dimensions of the combat economy appear to be deeply entrenched and have persisted beyond the Taliban phase of the conflict. In addition, warring groups continue to develop and utilize extremely sophisticated ways of operating in and exploiting regional and global economies—Duffield's description of warlords who "act locally, but think globally" is an apt one.[57] These conflict entrepreneurs have developed their "asset portfolios" by building up a command over the means of violence and developing links to global markets. As a result, warlords have access to sophisticated weaponry and lootable resources while fighters can be recruited for one meal a day.

As highlighted above, warring groups have always depended on external support from international and regional actors and few have ever been purely self-financing. For instance, a close protection unit seconded from the Special Forces of Uzbekistan is currently guarding General Rashid Dostam, a UF commander based in Mazar-e-Sharif. There are indications that elements within Pakistan's ISI are supporting Hekmatiya's Hezb-i Islami and Taliban forces. Russia continues to provide arms to the Shuri-nizar in the northeast.[58]

In addition, a range of strategies have been utilized to generate resources internally, including pillage; protection money; controlling trade, land, and markets; appropriating aid; and the smuggling of goods, people, and drugs. Moreover, various economic strategies of war have been pursued, including the economic blockade of Hazarajat by the Taliban, their scorched earth tactics on the Shamoli Plains, the deliberate destruction of rural infrastructure by the Soviets, and more random and opportunistic forms of violence and criminality (as occurred in Kabul and Kandahar during the early 1990s). While both organized and random violence led to processes of dispossession and the violent redistribution of entitlements, "roving" rather than "stationary" bandits have had the most damaging effects on infrastructure and markets. The loss of a monopoly on the use of force in a particular locale creates incentives for more predatory behavior. For instance, in 1998, when fighting between Dostam and a rival general broke out in Mazar-e-Sharif, trade with Uzbekistan was disrupted, leading to greater militia extortion of the rural population.[59] There was hoarding of food by the army and increased looting and selling of booty in Central Asian markets.

The opium economy also continues to play an important role in sustaining the war economy. During the Taliban era, reports suggested that Talibs became dealers or used their relatives as middlemen in the drug trade.[60] Preferential access was given to trading networks and licensing based on tribal connections. Taxation of the opium economy took two forms: *ushr* (10 percent tax on farm products), which was used for local expenses amounting to U.S.$15 million in 1999, and *zakat* (20 percent tax levied on traders). It is estimated that the Taliban received up to U.S.$30 million through taxing the cultivation, production, and trade of opium per year.[61] These taxes, however, were not collected uniformly throughout Afghanistan.

During the post-Taliban period, reports suggest that in Kandahar, customs revenues generate around U.S.$18 million per annum while as much as U.S.$50 million is generated in Herat.[62] Not surprisingly, many current struggles between warlords are thought by observers to be related to control over trade routes and markets. For instance, clashes between Ismael Khan and Gul Afgha in the west are at least partly over control of lucrative trade routes coming through that part of the country. In Nangarhar, clashes in the wake of the July 2002 assassination of Abdul Qadir, one of the vice presidents of the transitional administration, have been linked to control of trade routes for smuggling heroin and other goods into Pakistan.[63]

According to Johnson and colleagues, one year after the signing of the Bonn Agreement there remained around 70,000 men in regular forces and another 100,000 irregular militia members.[64] There are still strong bottom-up incentives to engage in violence. The demand for protection and the lack of alternative livelihoods remain powerful motivations to join military groups. As Jack Hirshleifer notes, the poor may have a comparative advantage in violence as they have less to lose.[65] Given the strong demand for security, warlords will likely continue to play an important role.

The Shadow Economy

While the interests of the conflict entrepreneur and the war profiteer have often coincided, this has not always been the case. For instance, while transport merchants may have had extremely close links to the Taliban, their interests did not always coincide with those of the frontline commanders. In fact, at certain moments, their objectives have been diametrically opposed. For example, profiteers undermined the Taliban's economic blockade of Hazarajat by keeping trading networks open. Similarly, in 1995, against the advice of Pakistani military advisers, Pakistani traders looking to capture the trade routes and markets in the West[66] bankrolled the Taliban offensive on Herat.

Clearly, access to markets and profits are a function of access to political power and the means of violence. While in the 1950s the Afghan merchant class was politically weak and heavily taxed, by the 1980s and 1990s the transport sectors in the Pakistani cities of Peshawar and Quetta were an important political force, due largely to their close ties with military groups. Markets in the East have become increasingly articulated toward Pakistan. Borders have become areas of high-risk but high-opportunity economic activity where deals have been cut between profiteers and conflict entrepreneurs. As poppy moves from farmers' fields to the borders, there is a fivefold increase in price. The largest profits are made through cross-border smuggling, a trade that is controlled in the south by specialized Baluchi traffickers with Afghan, Iranian, and Pakistani passports. Beyond borders, prices increase again. For instance, in the Tehran wholesale market there is a sixfold increase in prices from Pakistan's border areas. Opiate trafficking profits in the countries neighboring Afghanistan amounted to some U.S.$4 billion in 2002, of which U.S.$2.2 billion went to criminal groups in Central Asia.[67]

The shadow economy has led to a growing socioeconomic differentiation among population groups. For example, farmers with land and capital lease out their land for poppy cultivation and are able to accumulate assets, while landless farmers who have no other sources of credit are pushed further into debt.[68] There were approximately 15,000 opium traders in the country in the late 1990s (about one trader per thirteen farmers). Profits from the trade have been invested in conspicuous consumption and have had inflationary impacts in core growing areas.[69] Violent conflict has destroyed some markets while creating others. In Badakshan, for example, the livestock trade with Kabul was decimated due to insecurity, but the opium trade with Tajikistan has flourished. The informal economy also plays an important role in shaping formal economies; transborder trade has undermined the economies of Pakistan and other neighboring states. Moreover, while the shadow trade has helped mitigate some of the negative impacts of drought, it is not productive activity, as it provides no long-term investment in infrastructure or industries. Entrepreneurs gravitate toward quick-return activities and most of the profits have been accumulated outside the country. Without a strong state and a legal framework to protect property rights and enforce contracts, there are few incentives for entrepreneurs to make the shift toward longer-term productive activities. The shadow economy has led to the reconfiguring of regional networks and has entailed considerable costs for neighboring states. Criminal organizations have become embedded in the region and the shadow economy undermines the formal economies of surrounding countries. The open trade regime of Afghanistan compared to the restrictive trade regimes of neighboring countries creates powerful incentives for smuggling. Cross-border smuggling circumvents Pakistan's customs duties and sales tax with its consequent impacts on revenue collection and the undercutting of local producers. In 1992, the loss in customs revenues to Pakistan was U.S.$87.5 million, which rose to U.S.$500 million in 1995.[70] The shadow economy is based upon social solidarity networks within the region. Particularly important have been Pashtun diaspora communities in Dubai and Karachi with their links to Quetta and Kandahar.

Historical experience shows that wartime capital accumulation is brutal and war is the most common contemporary form of primitive accumulation. Asset portfolios are built upon oppressive working conditions, fear, and force. However, the shadow economy may also support processes of actually existing development, something that Mark Chingono describes in Mozambique as being a "barefoot economy" or a vibrant capitalism from below.[71] Research in Badakshan has revealed that, in some respects, the opium economy has had some positive developmental outcomes, although the benefits have been unevenly distributed.[72] There is evidence of accumulation and investment back into the Badakshan village economy, and this appears to have reinforced rather than eroded food security. Moreover, young men who might otherwise have left the area have remained because of the opium trade. On the other hand, the opium economy has created new tensions within the village in terms of how wealth is produced and distributed, by creating a nouveau riche of the young men involved in the opium trade and the commanders who tax and control it. Women in Deh Dehi village, Argu district, Badakshan, reported to me in 1998: "Some of our relatives have become rich through trade and smuggling and their lives have changed. My husband is old and he can't do these things. Some of them were our shepherds but now they won't even invite us to social occasions because we are so poor."

The Coping Economy

Overall, civilian vulnerability has grown with the gradual erosion of asset bases among all groups. Families have either retreated into subsistence or are adversely incorporated into the market through, for instance, laboring in poppy fields or sending their children to work in the carpet industry. Labor has become one of Afghanistan's primary exports. Remittances are central to the Afghan economy, as well as to Afghans living in neighboring countries. Social obligations fuel the remittance economy. Diaspora remittances also increase social differentiation—in general, families with relatives in Europe or the Gulf are able to accumulate, while the remittance economy in Pakistan and Iran is more commonly associated with survival. Therefore, Afghan households have tended to "stretch" themselves over several countries in the region and mobility has been a key component of coping or survival.[73]

There is a tendency to assume that those who have been involved in poppy farming or the opium trade are either "greedy" entrepreneurs or profit-maximizing farmers. In fact, for the majority, involvement in the opium economy is motivated by the need to cope or survive in adverse circumstances. Afghan families seek to spread risks by diversifying entitlement portfolios—sons migrate to Pakistan, some women and children work in the carpet industry, fathers enter sharecropping arrangements to gain access to land to grow poppy and subsistence crops, and the remaining women and children play an important role in tending the crop since poppy is extremely labor-intensive.[74] While only about 2.6 percent of agricultural land is used for cultivation of poppy, by the end of the 1990s, between 3 and 4 million people (about 20 percent of the population) were dependent on poppy for their livelihoods.[75]

In Afghanistan, there are a number of incentives for growing poppy. Farmers grow poppy, first, because of its comparative advantages and multifunctional role in relation to other crops, and second, because it provides access to land and credit. The comparative advantages of poppy are several. It is highly resistant to natural disease, its residue provides fuel for the winter,[76] its oil is used for cooking and oil cake for winter fodder, and it has medicinal value. In addition, the opium resin has high value, has a long shelf life, and is easily transportable—an important factor in Afghanistan, considering the state of most roads. Because poppy growing is also labor-intensive, it provides an important source of labor for those without land.

The second incentive to grow poppy is the access it provides Afghan farmers to land and credit.[77] The profitability of poppy is determined by the resource endowments of those involved in its cultivation. Those with land, water, and credit can profit, while those with few assets merely survive. For instance, a landowner may get a net return of U.S.$1,957 for every hectare cultivated, while a sharecropper receives U.S.$212 per hectare.[78] In many areas, opium production has become entrenched in local agricultural systems and has become a medium of exchange between the resource rich and the resource poor. Land rent, for example, is calculated on the basis of potential yield of opium the land can produce. Although landholdings in Afghanistan are more equitably distributed than in Pakistan and India, this varies from area to area, and with population growth landlessness has increased. In many places, poppy has become the main way of gaining access to land or to seasonal employment.[79] For the landless, leasing is the preferred arrangement but requires agricultural inputs. More commonly, then, the poor enter into sharecropping arrangements where their labor is the only contribution. The share of the final opium crop varies from area to area. For instance, in the east it may be fifty-fifty, but in the south, where there is a greater level of landlessness, the landowner gets two-thirds of the crop. Itinerant laborers can receive between a fifth and a quarter of total yield produced.

Poppy cultivation therefore gives sharecroppers access to land on which they can also cultivate food crops. In addition, through the salaam system, they gain access to credit. Typically, this involves an advance payment on a fixed amount of agricultural production, with opium being the crop favored by moneylenders. The resource poor typically sell their entire crop prior to harvest in return for an advance payment, with the price agreed in advance as half the current market price of opium. The system facilitates distress sales that allow traders to acquire opium at prices significantly less than harvest price, but for the poor this option may provide their only source of credit during the winter months, when food shortages are most acute. The salaam system locks the poor into a patron-client relationship with local traders. In 1997–1998 a poor harvest led to the rescheduling of payments, which in turn ensured the lender a future supply of opium while co-opting the borrower into further poppy cultivation.

Clearly, poppy cultivation provides disproportionate gains to those with land and capital. A landowner can retain a share of the crop and sell in the winter months, when the prices can increase by as much as 100 percent.[80] For the resource poor, poppy cultivation is purely about survival. Tellingly, the poppy bans imposed by the Taliban in the late 1990s, combined with famine during that period, had a major impact on the survival strategies of the poor. The monetization of loans forced many into deeper debt, leading to the distress sales of livestock[81] or emigration to Pakistan in search of wage labor. This, however, happened at a time when there were restrictive border controls and increased pressure on refugees in Pakistan to return to Afghanistan.

The control agenda in relation to opium tends to be asymmetrical in the way it appears to place a priority on protecting first world interests and underplay the responsibilities of Western governments to address the question of demand. Drug policies toward Afghanistan have in the main been driven by technical specialists with the consequent risk that drugs are "separated out" and treated as a technical rather than a political and economic issue. A greater appreciation of the historical roots of the opium economy might encourage policymakers to move beyond the one- or two-year project time frames common in Afghanistan. It took fifteen years, for example, to eradicate poppy cultivation from Dir district in Pakistan.

Research conducted in 2003 showed a renewed and growing dependency on poppy as a means of survival.[82] Poppy growing has had an inflationary impact and increased the levels of land rents, marriage costs, and interest rates on loans. People have been taking increasingly desperate measures to repay debts, including absconding, the sale or leasing of long-term productive assets, and the early marriage of daughters. Creditors have also been using more authoritarian tactics to ensure repayment, including kidnapping daughters, confiscation of domestic possessions, and compulsory land purchases. Failure to repay debts has become a major source of conflict. An average accumulated debt of U.S.$1,835 per capita was recorded in the areas researched, and in Helmond the average debt was U.S.$3,010 per capita. Farmers anticipated paying off debts within a two- to six-year period. Therefore, many are locked into the opium economy for several years into the future.

Although agricultural harvests in 2002 improved by as much as 80 percent, the growth in production has been uneven. Furthermore, the return of almost 2 million refugees is likely to have a significant impact on livelihoods and competition for scarce resources.[83] There are reports of conflicts in the north as a result of Pashtun returnees.

The Linkages Among Combat, Shadow, and Coping Economies

The typology of combat, shadow, and coping economies evidently simplifies reality. In practice, there are no clear boundaries among these three economies, and networks have developed with complex overlapping connections. Incentive systems vary at different levels of the commodity chain. For a resource-poor farmer, poppy is part of the coping or survival economy, for the landowner leasing his land or for the opium trader it is part of the shadow economy; and for commanders who tax poppy it is part of the combat economy. Opium is simultaneously a conflict good, an "illicit" commodity, and a means of survival. Different commodities—such as weapons, money, drugs, consumer goods, or food—may travel along the same routes. The *sarafi,* or money changer, is an important node in these networks and his services are used by warlords, profiteers, communities, and aid agencies.

Conflict resolution approaches tend to assume a clear division between pro-war and pro-peace constituencies or between a criminalized war economy and a licit peace economy. But network war dissolves the conventional distinctions between people, army, and government.[84] The shadow and coping networks that support war cannot easily be separated out and criminalized in relation to the networks that characterize peace. Attempts by the United States to clamp down on the *hawalla* system of informal banking, for instance, would have a negative effect not only on the revenues available to warlords and profiteers, but also, and more critically, on the livelihoods of the bulk of the population.

In border areas, this intermingling and overlapping of various "licit" and "illicit" flows—of arms, drugs, and smuggled luxury goods along with wheat, watermelons, and refugees—is most apparent, though not always visible. These borders are places of opportunity and exploitation.[85] Borderlands are also places of constant flux, as the geography of the conflict ebbs and flows and the policies of neighboring countries change. In Nuristan, for example, a new infrastructure of roads, hotels, and bazaars developed during the 1980s from the need to secure supply routes for the resistance.[86] Opium laboratories tend to be located close to borders.

The shadow economy may well promote processes of development— they link remote rural areas to major commercial centers, both regionally and globally, though the benefits of this development are unevenly distributed. The benefits of the drug economy can be seen in the reconstruction of the villages around Kandahar.[87] These economies also involve complex sociocultural and political as well as economic organization, in networks of exchange and association. These networks are governed by rules of exchange, codes of conduct, and hierarchies of deference and power,[88] and are reinforced through a series of strategies, including interfamilial marriage (wife-givers and wife-takers), gifts, and partnerships (with family members presenting claims for profit, involvement, and opportunity). They are not anarchic and do not depend purely on coercion. Trust and social cohesion are critical. Counterintuitively, it may be the *absence* of a state and of predictable social relations that engenders greater trust and solidarity at the local level.[89] Interestingly, many Pakistanis use the *sarafi* system even though there is a functioning formal banking sector; evidently, the informal system provides the reliability and predictability lacking in the official economy. It may also be more "propoor" in the sense that the poor are considered by the formal sector to be too risky.

International assistance interacts in various ways with these three economies. Development assistance in prewar Afghanistan contributed to the growth of a rentier state as well as to the structural tensions that contributed to the outbreak of war. During the 1980s, humanitarian assistance was the nonlethal component of support to the mujahidin and much of it fed directly into the war economy, with donors being prepared to accept "wastage levels" of up to 40 percent. Aid has also been a significant factor in the coping and survival economy, as the second largest sector of the "illicit" economy after agriculture. Before September 11, 2001, about 25,000 Afghans were employed with aid agencies. The Swedish Committee for Afghanistan, an international solidarity nongovernmental organization (NGO), was the largest single employer in the country. In urban areas, particularly Kabul, where there is a large aid-dependent population, humanitarian assistance has been critical to survival. Finally, aid interacts with the shadow economy, particularly in the current context in which the relatively large injections of resources into Kabul have created a parasitic "bubble economy." The U.S. dollar increasingly dominates the money exchanges in the cities, whereas the countryside remains in the Afghani or Pakistani rupee zone.[90] There is an obvious danger of history repeating itself, with international assistance exacerbating the underlying tensions and disparities between countryside and city.

There should perhaps be an additional economy in our schema and this might be termed the "emotional economy." Although it has been rightly argued that war cannot be fought on hopes and hatreds alone, the contention that war is purely about interests rather than passions can be questioned.[91] The ideas and meanings that people attach to events, institutions, policies, leaders, and their motives are important. To an important extent, the madrasas from which the Taliban emerged responded to a hunger for social identity among an earlier generation of marginalized and traumatized Afghanistani refugees. Again, aid interventions can have an important impact on this emotional economy by influencing ideas, relationships, social energy, and individual leadership. Education programs and media initiatives, such as the British Broadcasting Corporation's "New Home, New Life" program, are positive examples of how aid may engage in the battle for ideas. The perceived legitimacy of aid actors depends to a great extent on how sensitive they are to this "emotional economy."

In this analysis of key aspects of Afghanistan's combat, shadow, and coping economies, I have attempted to highlight the nexus between global markets, capital formation, investment, and criminality. In Afghanistan, there have been a variety of processes of systematic adaptation by elites to changing international and regional conditions. Rather than seeing the emergence of combat and shadow economies as purely a *reaction* to state failure, one could alternatively conceptualize state collapse as something that is *actively sought after* by elites living on the periphery.[92] Wartime economic activities have involved processes of brutal primitive accumulation that, in Afghanistan and elsewhere, have extended beyond the formal end of the fighting. When left alone, a common response of wartime entrepreneurs after a peace settlement has been to shift capital abroad or to continue primitive and predatory forms of accumulation, by exploiting "illicit" activities or high-rent market opportunities with little state regulation. Arguably, an assertive central authority is needed to break up violent primitive accumulation, to protect the interests of the poorest, and to bring about structural transformation that supports both political stability and socioeconomic development. Simply attempting to fence in and criminalize the shadow and combat economies is likely to have perverse effects. For example, a complete closure of the border between Afghanistan and Pakistan and the cessation of illegal trade would likely create the conditions for a social explosion in several regions of Pakistan, as cross-border trade is central to the coping and survival strategies of border communities. Similarly, in the past, drug-control policies have tended to put a higher priority on establishing a "security belt" around Afghanistan rather than investing significant resources inside the country to create alternative livelihoods and transform governance structures. Arguably, there has been an asymmetrical focus on regulating the supply side of the narcotics market rather than addressing the demand in Western countries. With the right combination of (dis)incentives, wartime entrepreneurs who have historically been labeled profiteers, economic criminals, or greedy warlords may perhaps also become builders of a basis of longer-term, more legitimate economic success.

Policy Implications

For the first time in recent history, states with an interest in and influence on Afghanistan and the Central Asian region are potentially following compatible strategies. However, as already mentioned, it would be premature to label Afghanistan as a "postconflict" state. To date, no comprehensive peace settlement has been achieved, and what fragile peace there is exists at the mercy of U.S. forces and the ISAF.

Key policy challenges in relation to the "triple transition" faced by Afghanistan in the post-Taliban era include the following: from war to peace (security transition), from "rogue state" to a legitimate, functioning state (political transition), and from a society and economy ready for war to a society and economy prepared for peace (socioeconomic transition). Before discussing these challenges, however, four general points that stand out as guiding principles for improved international policy should be addressed.

First, as already highlighted, the lack of historical and contextual understanding on the part of international actors, which has often been a constraint in the past, is likely to be even more of a hindrance now, given the influx of new actors with no track record in the country. Afghanistan has fallen off the research map for more than two decades and, to an extent, understanding is stuck at prewar levels. Given Afghanistan's diversity—every mountain valley has its own microclimate—the need for "fine-grained" analysis to inform policy should be emphasized. There is a need to make an investment in developing indigenous research and analytical capacity. In the long run, this means supporting the state in areas where it was always weakly developed—such as data collection and census-making—in order to make society more "legible" and therefore more governable.

Second, international policy toward the reconstruction of Afghanistan needs to be consistently informed by a regional perspective. As Clare Short, then UK minister for international development, stressed, ensuring the security of Afghanistan will require a long-term, sustained engagement with Pakistan, India, and the Central Asian republics.[93] Conflict resolution in Kashmir, for example, is critical to stability within the region as a whole. International governments and development donors concerned primarily with conflict prevention and peacebuilding in Afghanistan will have to think more carefully about the coherence of their policies toward Afghanistan's neighbors. Currently, the evidence suggests that this issue is not being sufficiently considered. For example, unconditional U.S. and Russian military support for Central Asian regimes is likely to exacerbate the dynamics of conflict in the region, which has led to the creation of movements like the IMU. Similarly, international financial institution (IFI) models of economic transition contribute to growing structural tensions.[94] Further, states in the region continue to pursue policies that create new incentives for the perpetuation of the combat and shadow economies—including a tightening of borders that prevents legal cross-border trade, the repression of Islamic groups, human rights abuses, and the reduction of public services and development programs. In spite of their common history, infrastructure, and culture, the states of Central Asia have been moving away from regional integration, creating new tensions over resources, trade, immigration, and security policies.

Understandably, the Bonn Agreement is a state-centric "road map" for peace, focusing on political, economic, and security questions within Afghanistan. However, the "postconflict" tag will remain only an aspiration if the regional dimensions of the conflict are ignored. A much bolder and ultimately more sustainable approach to peacebuilding would be to conceptualize it as a process of regional transformation rather than simply a case of putting Afghanistan "back on its feet." Particularly since the breakup of the Soviet Union, regional organizations in Central Asia have been weak. International actors can play a role in promoting and supporting mechanisms for sustained regional cooperation in areas such as security, infrastructure, trade, and development cooperation.

Third, another lesson from the past is that international neglect has been a significant factor in the development and expansion of Afghanistan's shadow economy, thereby offering easy opportunities for the reemergence of a war economy. The obvious point to be made here is that there needs to be the right sort of engagement over an extended period of time from the international community. Without an international guarantor—in effect, a strong U.S. backing for the United Nations—the negative dynamics of the shadow economy will continue, keeping open both the opportunity and the incentive for disaffected but powerful warlords to spoil the peace. With international concern now shifted to Iraq, there is a real possibility that Afghanistan's needs again will be neglected, with all the danger this implies for regional peace and development.

Fourth, I have emphasized that to address the continuing legacies and possible resurgence of its war economy, Afghanistan needs a credible and effective state. A strong state is required to accelerate economic development and poverty reduction, to consolidate peace, to reduce the scope for extreme brutality and the predatory exploitation of social relations, and to withstand the intrusive interests of regional powers.[95] The danger of a "back to the future" scenario with a return to the depredations of the warlord period is very real. Despite the visible support given to Hamid Karzai's transitional administration, there is still a critical need to develop coherent and complementary strategies that support the emergence of a legitimate state with the capacity to provide security, wealth, and welfare. Already, short-term imperatives, particularly the arming of militias by the United States in the fight against terrorism, and distrustful donors circumventing the state and relying on a host of international NGOs and subcontractors to implement their own "pet projects," threaten to undermine this long-term objective. It is also important to note that there is support from the Afghan population as a whole for a strong and effective centralized state.[96]

Security Transition

As Clare Short noted, development thinking has failed to take sufficiently into account the importance of the state in retaining its monopoly of violence. The remit of the Afghanistan state has always been shaky because of its inability to establish a monopoly of force. The collapse of the state was part cause and part consequence of the proliferation of violence and predation after 1992. In a 2003 report by the UK Parliament's International Development Committee (IDC), it was noted that the international community has lacked the collective will to create security on the ground. In fact, as already mentioned, the arming of local militias by the United States to pursue the war against Al-Qaida works against the long-term objective of creating a state with a monopoly of force. Military air cover and the ISAF security umbrella of Kabul are holding things together tenuously. However, attempts to establish a national army and police force and implement a disarmament, demobilization, and reintegration (DDR) program have been fraught with difficulties. Under the Bonn Agreement, the warlords, armed forces, and militia groups were to come under the control of the transitional administration. However, the transitional administration lacks the power to challenge the warlords directly, many of whom, for a variety of security, ethnic, political, and economic reasons, have shunned being part of the national army.

The United States has been charged with the development of a national army, but this embryonic force has been dominated by a faction led by Afghanistan's defense minister, General Mohammed Fahim, the former deputy to assassinated commander Massoud. There are concerns that programs to build a national army will merely provide warlords with an opportunity to exploit access to better-trained and better-equipped personal forces. Furthermore, there are indications that Pashtun frustrations are being channeled into renewed support for the Taliban and Hizb-i Islami. A lesson from Bosnia and Herzegovina is that halfhearted or symbolic military action may be as bad or worse than none at all. The continued failure to extend the ISAF beyond Kabul may come to be viewed as a costly and fateful mistake. Clearly, establishing security on the periphery is a priority, particularly in border areas, where Kabul currently has little control over customs and other revenues.

Afghan rulers have traditionally used a mixture of capital and coercion to establish their rule and manage opposition. In the absence of a robust national strategy of security and governance, they will deploy similar strategies today. The IDC report stresses that security is the primary concern, but security cannot be developed in isolation from other, economic policies of peacebuilding—for example, if Karzai's transitional administration is not able to deliver at least some of the benefits that were promised, commanders will continue to rely on more traditional methods of promoting their own and their constituents' interests, strategies that will certainly be at odds with Kabul's project of state building.[97]

The question of security must also be tackled at the regional level. Al-Qaida and Taliban groups continue to operate in the tribal areas of Pakistan. The IMU is also thought to be regrouping, while proto-Taliban groups threaten stability in Pakistan. A regional arms embargo is required to put a stop to the continued military support of different factions by neighboring countries. The recent inclusion of Afghanistan in the Organization for Security and Cooperation in Europe (OSCE) may be a positive step, if it presages greater regional cooperation in areas such as security and human rights. Peace in Afghanistan would represent a regional public good. But for this to be sustained, there needs to be much more robust and coherent international support for conflict prevention and peacebuilding in the region as a whole. As long as the Kashmir question remains unresolved, for example, there is likely to be ongoing instability in India and Pakistan that will have implications for peacebuilding in Afghanistan.

Political Transition

A number of key dilemmas can be highlighted in relation to the political transition, none of which lend themselves to easy prescriptions. First, an important dilemma for the UN in the transition period remains the gap between the legitimacy conferred on the interim and transitional Afghan administrations—first through the Bonn Agreement and then the emergency Loya Jirga—and the reality of its narrow political base and continued resistance to meaningful power-sharing with a wider range of actors.[98] The longer the current incumbents remain in power, and the more aid they control, the more they are likely to resist sharing power. While declared a success by the international community, the Loya Jirga was marked by violence and by the intimidation and harassment of delegates. It also resulted in the appointment of several prominent warlords to key cabinet posts.[99]

Second, and in apparent contradiction to the first point, the limited power and remit of the interim and transitional administrations is a significant constraint. There is a major disjunction between formal power and practical influence.[100] As one international donor commented in Kabul: "we are supporting the creation of the appearance of authority in the hope that it leads to the creation of actual authority."[101] The state's ability to disrupt the warlords' patron-client relationships depends to a critical extent on the resources it has at its disposal. However, as highlighted in the next section, the lion's share of international reconstruction funding has bypassed the state. Donors complain that the state lacks the capacity to absorb funds or spend them effectively. To an extent, however, donors have created a self-fulfilling prophecy, since with neither funding nor control over policy at the macro level, the state has little chance of building the requisite capacity.

Third, and relatedly, the international response to date has contributed to the creation of a protected enclave in Kabul, which in turn is likely to produce an Afghan leadership that is more responsive to the international community than to society as a whole. In the past, reliance on international funding has typically encouraged versions of the Afghan state that have foregone the evolution of reciprocal relations with the variety of interest groups in the country. As the state did not need to mobilize resources for its own reproduction from within those groups, it had little incentive to deliver reciprocal benefits, public goods, or development.

The central policy challenge is therefore to contribute to the development of a strong but accountable state and to avoid replicating the rentier state of the past. The fiscal, regulatory, and allocative decisions of the state will be affected by a complex set of incentives and disincentives for peace. Institutions of governance need to be developed in the context of Afghan history and social relations rather than simply implanted from off-the-peg models of liberal democracy. Elections, for example, should not be viewed as the be-all and end-all of good governance and the visible consolidation of peace. In a number of postconflict settings, the precipitous holding of elections has proven to be destabilizing and counterproductive. Decentralized or federal systems may sound attractive, particularly given the size and ethnic and regional heterogeneity of Afghanistan. But they are likely to lead to massive tensions in Afghanistan between the center and regions and to be inherently destabilizing, since they may simply serve to ratify the extreme de facto fragmentation that prevails today. Not surprisingly, a number of the regional warlords favor a federal system, as this will allow them to preserve their fiefdoms at Kabul's expense. However, in general, the expectations and preferences that ordinary Afghans have for the state have been changed by the war and the experience of warlordism. Most Afghans, it appears, favor a strong, centralized state.[102] Without a state that can provide a legal framework and stable environment, a criminalized war economy will simply become a criminalized peace economy. This does not discount the need for some form of decentralization that can allow conditions for meaningful public participation in political processes. But careful thought must be given to the question as to which powers are to be devolved and to the sequencing of such a process.

Also important with respect to ensuring an effective political transition are the state-building strategies of neighboring countries. Warlordism is intimately connected to foreign interests and backing. Neighboring states should be monitored and held accountable to agreements already made in the regional noninterference treaty.[103]

Socioeconomic Transition

As President Hamid Karzai has noted, security and development are two sides of the same coin. However, peace agreements often pay limited attention to the question of economic security. In a country where, according to the World Food Program, more than 6 million people remained vulnerable one year after the fall of the Taliban, this is an important question.[104] A significant, palpable peace dividend is urgently required. But if it only rewards a small, powerful group of "shareholders," the spoils of peace may end up legitimizing the spoils of war.

In spite of this, an evaluation in 2003 of the establishment of the UN Assistance Mission in Afghanistan (UNAMA),[105] whose mandate is to support the political transition in Afghanistan through an integrated approach addressing political, development, and humanitarian issues, found that there had been limited interaction between the political and reconstruction tracks of the peace process.[106] Recent reports have further argued that the aid effort has been too little, too fragmented, and tied to too many vested institutional interests.[107] At the meeting of aid donors in Tokyo in February 2002, U.S.$4.5 billion was pledged over a five-year period. This was less than half of what preliminary estimates suggested were needed—a joint assessment by the World Bank, the UN Development Programme, and the Asian Development Bank estimated that U.S.$14.6 billion would be required over the next ten years.[108] Furthermore, only a few of the pledges from Tokyo covered a period of more than two years, and much of it was geared toward primarily humanitarian types of activities (for example, two-thirds of UK aid is spent on relief).[109] In addition, donors have front-loaded funding so that a disproportionate amount is spent in the first year, in spite of international experience highlighting the need for increased funding after two years or more, when absorptive capacities have been developed.[110] While international comparisons should be made with care, donors have been less generous toward Afghanistan than toward many other "postconflict" countries. Based on pledges made, per capita donor spending on Afghanistan was U.S.$75 for the first year, compared to U.S.$288 for Kosovo and U.S.$175 for East Timor.[111] In addition, the transitional administration's recurrent government budget projection of a mere U.S.$483 million is likely to fall far short of its needs and thus further undermine its already limited credibility.[112]

One of the main challenges with regard to efforts to support the political transition through international assistance is the tension between the desire to support Afghan-led development and the need to channel resources where there is the capacity to spend them. In terms of relief and reconstruction, the main source of capacity is the international NGO and

UN system, which is estimated to employ approximately 40,000 Afghans. According to the minister for rural development, over 90 percent of external aid entering Afghanistan has been channeled through nonstate entities.[113] As has happened elsewhere, the salaries and working conditions offered by international agencies have tended to attract the best-qualified Afghans and in a sense have actively decapacitated Afghan institutions.

Another and related challenge is the tension between the need for quick-impact programs that meet humanitarian needs and counteract the immediate bottom-up incentives to engage in the combat and shadow economies, and the need for longer-term support that builds the capacity of the state. Both have to be pursued simultaneously and in a coordinated fashion. However, as with the security transition, short-term imperatives should not undermine longer-term goals. Again, a regional frame of reference is required. The return of about 2 million refugees within the first year of the signing of the Bonn Agreement strained resources and infrastructure, and in many respects hijacked the development agenda in Afghanistan as resources were allocated to emergency assistance.[114] A regionally informed analysis might have led development agencies to think more carefully about the sequencing of return and continuing support for refugees in neighboring countries.

As Michael Von der Schulenberg argues, it is not that international donors are underinvesting in Afghanistan, but that they are misinvesting. Here, the challenge is largely about how to do more with less. Although the UN Special Representative for Afghanistan and head of UNAMA, Lakhdar Brahimi, promised a "light footprint" in terms of international presence, based on lessons learned from East Timor and elsewhere, in practice there has been an extremely heavy international footprint in Kabul and an extremely light—in fact, barely visible—footprint outside the capital. This has generated negative views toward the international community among the Afghan population and is likely to have significant political repercussions, particularly in the Pashtun south, which feels excluded by the political settlement and has received little in the way of international reconstruction and development aid. Policies to eradicate drugs also play into this dynamic, since the predominantly Pashtun south and east are the main opium-growing areas. The UK government, which has taken a lead on this issue, has set a target of a 70 percent reduction in opium poppy crops by 2008 and 100 percent by 2013. However, unless there are serious efforts to invest significant development resources in poppy-growing regions, eradication measures, as already demonstrated in 2002, will exacerbate underlying political tensions and conflicts.

Attracting Western-educated Afghans is also likely to be a central challenge, one that, again, depends largely on the provision of basic security and the state's ability to mobilize and redistribute resources. A decentralized and criminalized economy is no basis for genuine social and political legitimacy, let alone poverty reduction and social progress. However, as already emphasized, attempting to curtail the shadow economy through law enforcement alone will be counterproductive. Rather than negative sanctions, policy should seek to create positive inducements to encourage profiteers to invest in legitimate business. For example, many businessmen involved in the *hawalla* system could potentially make the transition into the formal banking sector with the right kind of support and institutional framework.

The shadow economy has thrived because of the relative weakness of the official economy and because of Afghanistan's geographic position and transnational social networks. However, these comparative advantages could be mobilized in support of efforts to reconstruct the licit Afghan economy. Afghanistan has the potential to become a hub for a thriving and productive regional trade, although the preconditions for this are regional stability, safe roads, and reliable communication networks—all of which presuppose the creation of a strong central government. A massive investment in infrastructure concentrated in high export potential sectors will be required. At one time, for example, Afghanistan provided 40 percent of the world's raisin market. There is clearly great potential for developing regional cooperation in areas such as water, power, and trade. Forms of intraregional collaboration are already being developed or explored. For instance, Iran and Pakistan both made aid commitments at Tokyo and have provided assistance in areas such as humanitarian aid and infrastructure programs. Pipeline construction talks between Pakistan, Turkmenistan, and Afghanistan have also recommenced.

As emphasized earlier, development assistance also must be directed beyond Afghanistan's borders. The problems of failing states, chronic poverty, and social exclusion are regional phenomena and need to be addressed as such. More thought needs to be given to how development policies can complement efforts to build human security. While a number of the smaller bilateral donors such as Switzerland and the UK have explored policy approaches that seek to do this, the IFIs have, to a large extent, been "conflict blind." Privatization policies in particular have accentuated tensions and played into greed and grievance dynamics by providing opportunities for elite enrichment, while stripping away forms of social protection.[115] An attempt by the European Bank for Reconstruction and Development to link loans to improvements in human rights in

Uzbekistan may be evidence of the emergence of a more politically informed approach.

Recommendations and Conclusion

Afghanistan lies at the heart of a regional conflict complex. The *systemic* nature of this regionalized complex has been highlighted, as has its capacity to mutate and change over time. If, as Duffield argues, such conflict systems are analogous to organisms, then understanding them requires an analysis that emphasizes their interconnections, their mutability, and their processes of renewal and self-transformation.[116] To a considerable degree, exploring these defining features of the combat, shadow, and coping economies in Afghanistan also takes us away from the view that Afghanistan can somehow be separated out and dealt with in isolation from the core regional conflict system and wider networks of which it is part.

The idea that in "postconflict" settings donors need to think and act regionally is neither new nor original. The Marshall Plan was essentially about regional transformation in Europe, as are similar policy approaches discussed in relation to postwar reconstruction in Southeast Europe (see discussion in Chapter 5 of this book). Before the fall of the Taliban, Rubin and his colleagues argued that institution building and reconstruction needed to precede and act as a catalyst for political agreements and that both sets of policy needed to be tackled within a regional framework.[117] However, although there is now an international tailwind behind peace-building and reconstruction, there is limited evidence that donors are thinking in coherent terms beyond the national level. Donors find it difficult to think outside of their "country boxes" and a regional perspective is frequently missing from policy design and implementation.[118] For instance, donors have not matched their funding pledges for Afghanistan with substantial increases in support for poverty eradication or social protection programs in neighboring countries, including Pakistan, Tajikistan, and Kyrgyzstan. Although Afghanistan may be a "strategic node" in the conflict system, this does not mean that policy should be limited only to this "node." Following an acupuncture analogy, there are multiple pressure points in the conflict system that need to be tackled simultaneously in order to have a systemwide effect. Tackling drug production within Pakistan in the 1980s, for instance, merely contributed to the displacement of the problem across the border to Afghanistan. Therefore, "winning the peace" must entail a sustained and coherent engagement by international actors at the regional as well as the national level.

One factor that constrains emerging policy is a lack of data, which leads to poor empirical modeling and analysis. There is a dearth of empirically based research on Afghanistan in general, and on livelihoods, smuggling, and the opium economy in particular.[119] Likewise, very little research has been devoted to understanding the perspectives of those living in borderlands, yet such perspectives are crucial if we are to better understand the dynamics of the Afghan political economy. Research in live conflict zones presents a number of practical, ethical, and methodological challenges,[120] but without it, policy and practice are likely to be based upon questionable assumptions. Only further research can make the "invisible flows" discussed in this chapter more "visible."

A political economy framework goes beyond the "breakdown model," which posits that conflict is irrational and chaotic, and beyond the "greed"-based model, where actors are assumed to be self-interested profiteers. As this chapter has shown, characterizations of the war economy as wholly negative and predatory are neither analytically helpful nor useful in terms of informing effective policymaking. By desegregating and analyzing the different types of economic behavior that emerge in conflict-affected zones—here conceptualized as the combat, shadow, and coping economies—it is possible to get a more nuanced understanding of the different types of actors, networks, and motivation systems involved. The combat and shadow economies provide many livelihoods and incomes in the context of an enduring conflict. A large number of people now have an important stake in these economies, from the poor farmer, to the opium trader and shopkeeper, to the commander who controls and taxes the trade. Their involvement is perfectly rational given both the lack of alternatives and the lucrative nature of the activities involved. In important respects, too, the "bazaar economy" has brought a modicum of development to previously peripheral areas.

The existence of these various interrelated and overlapping economies suggests that a successful transition from war to peace is unlikely to be achieved by simply attempting to fence in and marginalize the combat and shadow economies and those who benefit from them. This strategy is based upon a poor conceptualization of the processes at work. These are not, in fact, separate, closed, and bounded categories—the networks involved in survival, profiteering, and war-making overlap with and reinforce one another. However, drug policies in Afghanistan have tended to focus on border controls and checking the flow of illicit drugs. But other than declaring a ban on poppy cultivation and production, there has been a reluctance to tackle head-on the cultivation of opium poppy *within* Afghanistan.[121] Thought will need to be given to how to engage with conflict entrepreneurs and to create the right incentives for accumulated profits to be invested in the licit economy. Development and drug-related policy in Afghanistan needs to be based upon a better understanding of the roles and motivations of the various actors involved at different locations and levels within the opium economy in order to support the multiple transitions there.

The effectiveness of such processes will also depend, crucially, on the ability of the transitional administration to develop power-sharing institutions and processes that are able to take the lead, albeit progressively, in building peace. While the precise balance between a donor-directed versus an internally led peacebuilding process, or a "heavy footprint" versus a "light footprint," can be debated, it is clear that sufficient state power needs to be generated to break the fragmented de facto power structure that has emerged in the wake of the Taliban's fall. Only time will tell whether the failure to extend the ISAF's mandate beyond Kabul was a costly mistake. A minimalist approach by the international community, which equates peace with getting rid of Al-Qaida and the Taliban, will not be effective. Furthermore, a "bargain basement" model of reconstruction that combines ambitious state-building objectives with limited commitment and resources is doomed to fail.

Without a strong, legitimate state with a monopoly of force, the criminalized war economy will simply become a criminalized peace economy.[122] The donor fantasy of a minimal, liberal, and decentralized state, strips the state of its developmental role in historical context.[123] The combat and shadow economies thrive in the absence of a state that can provide security and welfare for its citizens. Understanding incentives is crucial: What kinds of incentives can be created to turn the warlord into a statesman or the black-marketeer into a legitimate businessman? If warlords can continue to generate revenue, either locally or through external backers, they will have few incentives to engage with a central state. Similarly, profiteers will continue to invest in short-term, low-risk activities until there is a state that can provide a secure and predictable environment for legitimate commerce. The first-order question remains one of security— and this can only be achieved through sustained international engagement in the region.

Notes

1. This chapter is based on two fieldwork studies. The first, in 1997–1999, on NGOs and complex political emergencies, was funded by the DFID; the second, in 2001, on the Afghan war economy, was for the Overseas Development Institute. This chapter draws primarily on two subsequent papers: Jonathan Goodhand, "Frontiers and Wars: A Study of the Opium Economy in Afghanistan," paper pre-

sented at the Canadian Social Science Research Council conference "Beyond Borders," Vancouver, July 2002, final draft 2003; and M. Bhatia, J. Goodhand, H. Atmar, A. Pain, and M. Suleman, "Profits and Poverty: Aid Livelihoods and Conflict in Afghanistan," in Sarah Collinson et al., *Power, Livelihoods, and Conflict: Case Studies in Political Economy Analysis for Humanitarian Action*, Humanitarian Practice Group (HPG) Report no. 13 (London: HPG, February 2003).

2. Peter Wallensteen, *Understanding Conflict Resolution: War, Peace, and the Global System* (London: Sage, 2002), p. 205.

3. An important limitation that affects all researchers working on Afghanistan is the lack of reliable data. Even before the war, Louis Dupree wrote that statistics on Afghanistan were "wild guesses based on inadequate data," in *Afghanistan* (Princeton: Princeton University Press, 1980). This reflected the centralized but weak nature of the Afghan state. Mapping and conducting a census, the state's technologies of control that make society more legible and therefore more governable, were weakly developed. The problem of statistics was accentuated by what Dupree terms the "mud curtain," which was erected by villagers to keep an interfering state at bay—state officials visiting the countryside were met with evasion on questions related to land (because of taxation) and family members (because of conscription). Over two decades of conflict has compounded this problem and there has been virtually no long-term anthropological research inside Afghanistan during the war years, so that knowledge is partly stuck at prewar levels. Finally, there are inherent problems in obtaining any kind of meaningful data on the invisible and extremely sensitive nature of the opium economy, and statistics cited from secondary sources in this chapter should be treated as illustrative rather than authoritative.

4. Adam Pain and Jonathan Goodhand, "Afghanistan: Current Employment and Socio-Economic Situation and Prospects," Infocus program on crisis response and reconstruction, Working Paper no. 8 (London: International Labour Organization, March 2002), p. 2.

5. W. Byrd, "Afghanistan's Reconstruction. Regional and Country Context," World Bank discussion paper, revised draft, October 31, 2002, p. 2.

6. From 1956 to 1978 the Soviet Union provided Afghanistan with U.S.$1.265 billion in economic aid and roughly U.S.$1.250 billion in military aid. See Barnett J. Rubin, *The Fragmentation of Afghanistan: State Formation and Collapse in the International System* (Lahore, Pakistan: Vanguard Books, 1996).

7. In 1972 the two greatest single sources of national wealth—agriculture and livestock—yielded a mere 1 percent of state revenues. A. Hyman, *Afghanistan Under Soviet Domination, 1964–1991*, 3rd ed. (Basingstoke: Macmillan, 1992), p. 32. State-generated finances during the 1960s depended almost entirely on heavy duties on imported goods, which the merchant class was too politically weak to resist.

8. N. Cullather, "Damming Afghanistan: Modernization in a Buffer State," *Journal of American History*, September 2002, p. 529.

9. The Ghilzai are one of the more power Pashtun tribes who are scattered all over Afghanistan. There is thus no proper Ghilzai land. See B. Glatzer "Afghanistan: Ethnic and Tribal Disintegration?" in W. Maley, ed., *Fundamentalism Reborn? Afghanistan and the Taliban* (Lahore, Pakistan: Vanguard Books, 1998).

10. UNDCP, "Afghanistan Annual Poppy Survey 2000," Islamabad, 2000.

11. C. Schetter, "The Bazaar Economy of Afghanistan," in C. Nölle-Karimi, C. Schetter, and R. Schlagintweit, eds., *Afghanistan: A Country Without a State?* (Frankfurt: IKO-Verlag für Interkulturelle Kommunikation, 2002), p. 111.

12. "Because the Pushtun ethno-territory . . . straddles the border with Afghanistan, Pushtun control the most lucrative smuggling route into Balochistan [and] also operate most of the shops where the smuggled goods are sold, as well as half the buses taking the goods to Pakistan's major urban centers. Baloch transporters find themselves in a relatively weak position relative to Pushtun in this regard." Paul Titus, "Routes to Ethnicity: Roads, Buses, and Differential Ethnic Relations in Pakistani Baluchistan," in Paul Titus, ed., *Marginality and Modernity: Ethnicity and Change in Post-Colonial Baluchistan* (Oxford: Oxford University Press, 1996), pp. 291–294.

13. Hyman, *Afghanistan Under Soviet Domination*, p. 36.

14. Barnett R. Rubin, "The Political Economy of War and Peace in Afghanistan," *World Development* 28, no. 10 (2000): 1789–1803.

15. A. Giustozzi, "Respectable Warlords? The Transition from War of All Against All to Peaceful Competition in Afghanistan," London School of Economics Research Seminar, January 29, 2003, p. 7.

16. John K. Cooley, *Unholy Wars: Afghanistan, America, and International Terrorism* (London: Pluto Press, 1999), p. 131.

17. Ibid.

18. A. Rashid, *Taliban: Islam, Oil, and the New Great Game in Central Asia* (London: I. B. Tauris, 2000), p. 121.

19. M. von der Schulenburg, "Illicit Opium Production in Afghanistan," in Nölle-Karimi, Schetter, and Schlagintweit, *Afghanistan*, pp. 129–138.

20. Human Rights Watch, "Afghanistan: Crisis of Impunity—The Role of Pakistan, Russia, and Iran in Fueling the Civil War," Working Paper 13, no. 3 (July 2001): 23.

21. Cited in Rubin, "The Political Economy of War and Peace," p. 1794.

22. See S. Lautz, N. Nojumi, and F. Najimi *"Qaht-e Pool:* 'A Cash Famine'— Food Security, Malnutrition, and the Political Economy of Survival: A Report from Kabul, Heart, and Qandahar, Afghanistan," Feinstein International Famine Centre, February 2002, www.odihpn.org/pdfbin/afghanistan.pdf.

23. Virtually all the Taliban leaders studied in religious schools (madrasas) in Pakistan with strong links to the Deobanid political party, Jamiat ul-Ulema-i Islam.

24. Ahmed Rashid, "The Taliban: Exporting Extremism," *Foreign Affairs* 78, no. 6 (November–December 1999): 27.

25. O. Roy, "The Transnational Dimension of Radical Islamic Movements," in *Talibanisation: Extremism and Regional Instability in South and Central Asia* (Brussels: Conflict Prevention Network and Stiftung Wissenschaaft und Politik, 2001).

26. The United National Islamic Front for the Salvation of Afghanistan (Jabha-yi Muttahid-i Islami-yi Milli barayi Nijat-i Afghanistan) was formed in 1996 as an alliance opposed to the Taliban. The president of the ousted government, Burhanuddin Rabbani, remained the president of Afghanistan and the titu-

lar head of the UF, although real power lay with Commander Ahmad Shah Massoud, the minister of defense. Human Rights Watch, "Afghanistan," p. 12.

27. Human Rights Watch, "Afghanistan," p. 40.

28. Rashid, *Taliban*.

29. Ibid., p. 167.

30. W. Maley, ed., *Fundamentalism Reborn? Afghanistan and the Taliban* (London: Hurst, 1998); M. Fielden and J. Goodhand, "Beyond the Taliban? The Afghan Conflict and United Nations Peacemaking," *Conflict, Security, and Development* 1, no. 3 (2001): 5–32.

31. Mark Duffield, *Global Governance and the New Wars. The Merging of Development and Security* (London: Zed Books, 2001), p. 39.

32. Jonathan Goodhand, "Aiding Violence or Building Peace? The Role of International Aid in Afghanistan," *Third World Quarterly* 23, no. 5 (2002): 847.

33. Zareen Naqvi, *Afghanistan-Pakistan Trade Relations* (Islamabad: World Bank, 1999).

34. Rashid, *Taliban*.

35. Ibid., p. 189.

36. Rubin, "The Political Economy of War and Peace," p. 1798.

37. Cooley, *Unholy Wars*, p. 47.

38. At the international level there has been a geographical shift in the production of opium. In the 1980s illicit opium was produced and illegally exported in more than nine countries; however, by 2000 its cultivation was concentrated in two countries—95 percent of all illicit opium originated from Afghanistan and Burma.

39. United Nations Office on Drugs and Crime (UNODC), "The Opium Economy in Afghanistan: An International Problem," Vienna, 2003, p. 93.

40. Ibid.

41. UNDCP, "The Impact of the Taliban Prohibition on Opium Poppy Cultivation in Afghanistan," Islamabad, May 28, 2002.

42. Von der Schulenburg, "Illicit Opium Production in Afghanistan."

43. Institute of War and Peace Reporting (IWPR), "The Killing Fields of Afghanistan," Afghan Recovery Report no. 16, June 26, 2002.

44. Von der Schulenburg, "Illicit Opium Production in Afghanistan."

45. *Agreement on Provisional Arrangements in Afghanistan Pending the Reestablishment of Permanent Government Institutions* (Bonn Agreement), S/2001/1154, signed in Bonn on December 5, 2001.

46. C. Johnson, W. Maley, A. Their, and A. Wardak, "Afghanistan's Political and Constitutional Development," Humanitarian Practice Group, Overseas Development Institute Report, January 2003, p. 3.

47. B. Woodward, *Bush at War* (New York: Simon and Schuster, 2002).

48. Mark Duffield, "Globalization, Transborder Trade, and War Economies," in Mats Berdal and David M. Malone, eds., *Greed and Grievance: Economic Agendas in Civil Wars* (Boulder, CO: Lynne Rienner, 2000), pp. 69–89.

49. UNODC, "Afghanistan, Strategic Study no. 9: Opium Poppy Cultivation in a Changing Policy Environment. Farmers' Intentions for 2002/3" (Kabul, Afghanistan: UNODC, May 2003).

50. UNDCP, "Impact of the Taliban Prohibition," p. 8.

51. High-level officials within the government are allegedly tied to the drug trade.

52. IWPR, "Killing Fields of Afghanistan," p. 1.

53. A *qawm* is a group united by a norm of solidarity within the group and by competition with parallel groups. Rubin, *Fragmentation of Afghanistan*, p. 346.

54. "Iran and U.S. Vie for Influence on the Front Line," *Daily Telegraph* (London), June 2, 2002, p. 8.

55. D. Sagramoso, "The Illegal Proliferation of Small Arms and Light Weapons in Central Asia," in K. Pinnick and J. Green, eds., *Central Asia and the Post-Conflict Stabilization of Afghanistan* (London: International Institute for Strategic Studies, 2002), p. 82.

56. W. Maley, "Talibanization and Pakistan," in Denise Groves, ed., *Talibanization: Extremism and Regional Instability in South and Central Asia* (Brussels: CPN and Stiftung Wissenschaaft und Politik, 2001).

57. Duffield, "Globalisation."

58. M. Sedra, "Challenging the Warlord Culture: Security Sector Reform in Post-Taliban Afghanistan," paper no. 25, Bonn International Centre for Conversion, 2002, p. 15.

59. Giustozzi, "Respectable Warlords?" p. 7.

60. Rashid, *Taliban*, p. 118.

61. M. von der Schulenburg, "Peace in a Glasshouse," unpublished report, July 2002.

62. Cited in UK, House of Commons, International Development Committee, "Afghanistan: The Transition from Humanitarian Relief to Reconstruction and Development Assistance—First Report of Session 2002–3," report together with the proceedings of the committee, minutes of evidence, and appendices, January 14, 2003, p. 31.

63. Johnson et al., "Afghanistan's Political and Constitutional Development," p. 11.

64. Ibid.

65. J. Hirshleifer, *The Dark Side of the Force: Economic Foundations of Conflict Theory* (Cambridge: Cambridge University Press, 2001).

66. A. Davis, "How the Taliban Became a Military Force," in W. Maley, ed., *Fundamentalism Reborn? Afghanistan and the Taliban* (Lahore, Pakistan: Vanguard Books, 1998), p. 59.

67. UNODC, *The Opium Economy in Afghanistan: An International Problem* (New York: United Nations, 2003).

68. David Mansfield, "The Economic Superiority of Illicit Drug Production: Myth and Reality," paper presented at the international conference "Alternative Development in Drug Control and Cooperation," Feldafing, Germany, August 2001.

69. UNODC, "Afghanistan."

70. Ahmed Rashid, "How the Taliban Became a Political Force," in Maley, *Fundamentalism Reborn?* pp. 72–89.

71. M. Chingono, *The State, Violence, and Development: The Political Economy of War in Mozambique, 1975–1992* (Aldershot: Avebury, 1996).

72. Jonathan Goodhand, "From Holy War to Opium War? A Case Study of the Opium Economy in North Eastern Afghanistan," *Central Asian Survey* 19, no. 2 (2000): 265–280.

73. D. Turton and P. Marsden, "Taking Refugees for a Ride? The Politics of Refugee Return to Afghanistan," Afghan Research and Evaluation Unit, Issues Paper Series, December 2002.

74. One hectare of opium requires as much as 350 person-days compared to 41 for wheat. Women play a central role in minimizing labor costs. They are involved in planting, weeding, thinning, lacing the capsules, collecting gum, clearing fields, breaking the capsules and removing seed, cleaning the seed, and processing by-products such as oil and soap. David Mansfield, "Alternative Development in Afghanistan: The Failure of the Quid Pro Quo," paper for the International Conference on Alternative Development in Drug Control and Cooperation, Feldefing, Germany, p. 10. Children also play a vital role. Attendance of boys at madrasas drops considerably during the weeding and harvesting season. Finally, reciprocal labor (known as *ashar*) by families and friends plays an important role.

75. Von der Schulenberg, "Peace in a Glasshouse."

76. One farmer interviewed said that the dried poppy stalks from his fields provided fuel for up to six months of the year, an important consideration since fuel takes up a quarter of the family income.

77. This section draws heavily on the excellent work of UNODC, "Afghanistan," and Mansfield, "Economic Superiority of Illicit Drug Production," the only studies to have been based upon extensive field research in Afghanistan.

78. Mansfield, "Economic Superiority of Illicit Drug Production."

79. "Armies" of itinerant laborers travel around the country following the poppy harvest.

80. Mansfield, "Economic Superiority of Illicit Drug Production."

81. In 2001 a World Food Program survey estimated that in Kandahar province only 20 percent of the livestock remained.

82. UNODC, "Afghanistan."

83. Turton and Marsden, "Taking Refugees for a Ride?"

84. Duffield, *Global Governance and the New Wars.*

85. A disturbing example of the latter is the young children who act as porters, crossing the border at Torkham between Pakistan and Afghanistan and carrying a range of commodities from scrap metal to drugs.

86. Schetter, "Bazaar Economy of Afghanistan," p. 114.

87. Rashid, *Taliban*, p. 118.

88. C. Nordstrom, "Shadows and Sovereigns," *Theory, Culture, and Society* 17, no. 4 (2000): 37.

89. Ibid.

90. Von der Schulenberg, "Illicit Opium Production in Afghanistan."

91. Paul Collier, "Doing Well Out of War: An Economic Perspective," in Berdal and Malone, *Greed and Grievance,* pp. 91–112.

92. This point draws on Mark Bradbury's analysis in relation to Somalia. Mark Bradbury, "Living with Statelessness: The Somali Road to Development," *Journal of Conflict, Security, and Development* 3, no. 1 (April 2003): 7–25.

93. Cited in UK, House of Commons, International Development Committee, "Afghanistan."

94. Tony Vaux and Jonathan Goodhand, *Disturbing Connections: Aid and Conflict in Kyrgyzstan,* Conflict Assessments no. 3 (London: Centre for Defence Studies, King's College, July 2001).

95. C. Cramer and Jonathan Goodhand, "Try Again, Fail Again, Fail Better? War, the State, and the Post-Conflict Challenge in Afghanistan," *Development and Change* 33, no. 5 (2002): 904.

96. Johnson et al., "Afghanistan's Political and Constitutional Development," p. 19.

97. Simon Chesterman, "Walking Softly in Afghanistan: The Future of UN State-Building," *Survival* 44, no. 3 (Autumn 2002): 37–46.

98. A. Suhrke, J. Leslie, and A. Strand, "A Review of Peace Operations: A Case for Change. Afghanistan (A Snapshot Study)," Conflict, Security, and Development Group, King's College, London, March 10, 2003.

99. ICG Afghanistan Briefing, "The Afghan Transitional Administration: Prospects and Perils," Kabul/Brussels, July 30, 2002.

100. Chesterman, "Walking Softly in Afghanistan," p. 38.

101. Cited in ibid., p. 4.

102. UNODC, "Afghanistan: Strategic Study no. 9—Opium Cultivation in a Changing Policy Environment, Farmers Intentions for 2002/3," Kabul, Afghanistan, May 2003.

103. For instance, the Kabul Declaration on Good Neighborly Relations involves group pledges on action against "terrorism, extremism and drug trafficking." In the months immediately following the signing of the declaration, however, there was limited progress on these issues. M. Berniker, "Back to Bad Habits," *Asia Times* (Hong Kong), December 25, 2002.

104. Cited in UK, House of Commons, International Development Committee, "Afghanistan," p. 6.

105. The UNAMA mandate is outlined in UN General Assembly/Security Council, *Report of the Secretary-General on the Situation in Afghanistan and Its Implications for International Peace and Security,* A/56/875-S/2002/278, March 18, 2002.

106. Suhrke, Leslie, and Strand, "Review of Peace Operations."

107. Ibid.; UK, House of Commons, International Development Committee, "Afghanistan."

108. World Bank, UN Development Programme, and Asian Development Bank, "Afghanistan: Preliminary Needs Assessment for Recovery and Reconstruction," January 2002.

109. CARE International in Afghanistan, "Rebuilding Afghanistan: A Little Less Talk, a Lot More Action," policy brief, September 2002.

110. Paul Collier and Anke Hoeffler, "Aid, Policy, and Growth in Post-Conflict Societies," June 11, 2002, econ.worldbank.org/files/15710_collierhoeffleraidpostconflict.pdf.

111. UK, House of Commons, International Development Committee, "Afghanistan," p. 13.

112. Ibid., p. 16.

113. UK, House of Commons, International Development Committee, "Afghanistan."

114. Turton and Marsden, "Taking Refugees for a Ride?"

115. Vaux and Goodhand, *Disturbing Connections*.

116. Duffield, *Global Governance and the New Wars*.

117. B. Rubin, A. Ghani, W. Maley, A. Rashid, and O. Roy, "Afghanistan: Reconstruction and Peacemaking in a Regional Framework," Peacebuilding Reports 2001, Swiss Center for Peacebuilding (KOFF), Bern, June 2001, p. 4.

118. An exception is the World Bank study "Afghanistan's Reconstruction."

119. Exceptions are the UNDCP strategic studies and works by Mansfield.

120. For an exploration of these challenges, see Jonathan Goodhand, "Research in Conflict Zones: Ethics and Accountability," *Forced Migration Review* 8 (August 2000): 12–15.

121. Von der Schulenberg, "Illicit Opium Production in Afghanistan."

122. Rubin, "Political Economy of War and Peace."

123. Cramer and Goodhand, "Try Again, Fail Again, Fail Better?"

4

Sierra Leone in West Africa

This chapter examines the domestic and regional political economies that fueled Sierra Leone's descent into armed conflict and its perpetuation, and that have affected past and current attempts at peacebuilding. Sierra Leone is an interesting case study for several reasons. First, the latest phase of peacebuilding, which began with the signing of a new peace agreement in May 2001, has had the opportunity to be informed by recent and current debates about the role of economic agendas in conflict. Second, Sierra Leone has experienced a series of failed peace agreements, as well as more generally flawed intervention throughout the 1980s and 1990s. It is useful to evaluate the extent to which past failures and flaws have been acknowledged and, ideally, remedied by current peacebuilding approaches. Third, understanding the regional political economy of war and peace in Sierra Leone has implications for our understanding of the dynamics driving and sustaining conflicts that have erupted elsewhere in the region—notably, Liberia and Côte d'Ivoire.

The chapter examines a number of themes that are dealt with in the following order:

- Narratives of the Sierra Leone conflict have emphasized the role of economic agendas. In theory, this should have enhanced understanding of the dynamics of the conflict. However, the dominant view of this conflict as one driven by rebel greed has obscured proper understanding of the broader dynamics underpinning the war economy in Sierra Leone.
- Sierra Leone's descent into conflict and its ensuing war economy were not only a function of top-down corruption mediated through local

and regional patronage networks and shifting alliances of conflict and collaboration between key actors. The combat economy was rooted in long-standing regional networks and traditions of shadow trade that exploited differences in the economic and regulatory environments of the countries in the region. These conditions created bottom-up, structural incentives for participation in shadow trade. Actors in the combat economy adapted these networks and more thoroughly integrated them into the global shadow economy.

• Neoliberal development policies of the international financial institutions (IFIs) in the 1980s and 1990s critically weakened the state and fueled discontent. Successive leaders used IFI demands for reductions in state expenditure, privatization, and the use of foreign firms to weaken rivals and reward their own patrons, as IFI demands for cuts in state spending, in state employment, and in basic subsidies exacerbated social tensions, thus inhibiting the prospects for peace. Worryingly, many of the same neoliberal precepts are being advocated yet again, with some predictable results.

• Although the diamond economy is now widely recognized as a mainstay of the war, international action on this issue was slow to materialize. Moreover, while a variety of domestic, regional, and global regulatory initiatives have now been put in place, their effectiveness remains questionable. Indeed, the speedy adaptation of regional shadow networks to the new geography of regulation highlights the challenge of transforming war economies.

• Successful peacebuilding and sustainable development in Sierra Leone will require sustained and adequately funded peacekeeping; greater policy attention to the regional dynamics of conflict in West Africa, particularly the regional market in arms, mercenaries, and conflict goods; less donor insistence on the fundamentals of macroeconomic stability and greater priority for creating alternative livelihoods and strengthening state capacities; and more holistic and flexible agencies of intervention to respond to the challenges of adaptive "illicit" networks that survive into peace.

Historical Background: Evolution of the
Political Economy of Conflict in Sierra Leone

The conflict in Sierra Leone began in March 1991 when Revolutionary United Front (RUF) fighters, aided by Charles Taylor's National Patriotic Front of Liberia (NPFL) crossed from Liberia to Sierra Leone. It formally concluded on January 18, 2002, with the joint declaration ending the war.

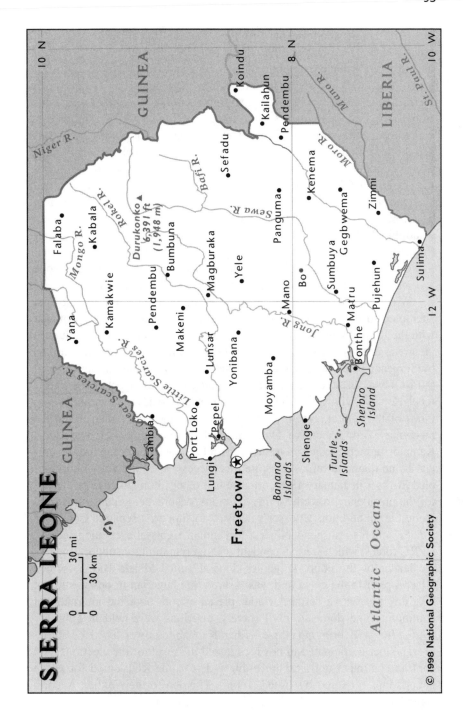

SIERRA LEONE

The period in between was marked by vicious conflict and a succession of failed peace agreements in 1996, 1997, and 1999. Both the composition of the initial force that crossed into Sierra Leone and Taylor's motivations for supporting the RUF highlight the regional dynamics that underpinned Sierra Leone's conflict. The 300 or so fighters not only included dissidents from Sierra Leone but also "special forces" of Taylor's NPFL and mercenaries from Burkina Faso.[1] Taylor's motivation for supporting the rebels had three elements. The first was to force the withdrawal of Sierra Leone from Economic Community of West African States Cease-Fire Monitoring Group (ECOMOG) peacekeeping forces in Liberia. Sierra Leone had been the staging post for ECOMOG intervention in 1990 and was the rear base for Nigerian soldiers in Liberia. The second motivation was to help install his RUF allies in power, and the third goal was to capture revenues from Sierra Leone's diamond industry.[2] As will be noted below, the diamond trade became a mainstay of the combat economy in Sierra Leone and was crucial to the financing of the RUF's military campaign.

With support from ECOMOG, the Sierra Leonean army at first attempted to defend the country. However, against the backdrop of war with the RUF, dissatisfaction with high-level corruption, and the failure of the government to properly meet its needs, the military staged a coup led by Sergeant Valentine Strasser. The National Provisional Ruling Council (NPRC) was established and initially attempted to negotiate with the rebels. By 1995, however, the RUF had managed to advance within twenty miles of the capital, Freetown. In desperation, the government hired the mercenary firm Executive Outcomes, which in conjunction with local Kamajor fighters[3] managed to drive the rebels back and recapture the crucial Kono diamond mines. Despite this success, a second army coup toppled Strasser in January 1996, after he had reneged on a pledge not to run for the presidency in forthcoming elections, despite being constitutionally ineligible. In addition, Strasser's decision to support a separate Commonwealth action to suspend Nigeria for human rights abuses alienated the NPRC forces, which were dependent on Nigerian military support. Indeed, the leader of the coup, Brigadier-General Julius Maada Bio, informed Nigeria prior to the event and was assured that Nigerian troops would not take any preventive action.[4] Under pressure from both the international community and domestic civil society, elections were held in February 1996, ultimately bringing Ahmed Tejan Kabbah to power. The RUF, however, neither participated in nor recognized the result of the elections, and conflict continued until, facing military defeat, the RUF opted for peace negotiations brokered by Côte d'Ivoire. This led to the Abidjan Accord, signed in November 1996. The implementation of the accord was supposed to be accompanied by a UN peacekeeping force. However, as UN member states were unwilling to meet the U.S.$47 million bill for 700 soldiers, that force never materialized.[5]

The Abidjan Accord was derailed by yet another military coup in May 1997. This time however, the Sierra Leonean army and the rebels whom they were supposedly fighting joined forces and formed the Armed Forces Revolutionary Council (AFRC) under the leadership of Major Johnny Paul Koromoh. In response to these events, the Security Council, largely at the behest of Britain, the former colonial power, imposed an oil and arms embargo on the country.[6] In addition, ECOMOG forces blockaded Freetown and launched bombing raids on junta positions. The junta entered into negotiations that resulted in the Conakry Agreement of October 1997, but the junta quickly began to criticize key provisions and the agreement was never implemented.

In February 1998, ECOMOG troops launched an attack that returned Kabbah to power. Shortly thereafter, in July 1998, the Security Council established the UN Observer Mission in Sierra Leone (UNOMSIL), consisting of seventy military observers deployed for an initial period of six months.[7] Kabbah's return had generated hopes that the RUF had finally been defeated. Within months, however, the RUF, with external assistance from Liberia and Burkina Faso, regained the military initiative.[8] Moreover, the new civilian regime in Nigeria, the principal troop contributor to ECO-MOG, became unwilling to continue shouldering the human and financial cost of its operations, which had grown to as much as U.S.$1 million a day, and signaled its wish for a phased withdrawal. Faced with the prospect of losing military protection and under pressure from external donors to sue for peace, the government signed a cease-fire agreement in May 1999 and a new peace agreement, the Lomé Accord, in July. This was underwritten by the creation of the UN Mission in Sierra Leone (UNAMSIL), a 13,000-strong peacekeeping force.[9]

The Lomé Accord was controversial from the outset. It provided an amnesty for RUF rebels who had committed vicious human rights abuses. In addition, Foday Sankoh, the leader of the RUF, was rewarded with the status of vice president and chairmanship of the Strategic Mineral Resources Commission, giving him control over the country's diamond resources. Furthermore, the implementation of the agreement was flawed in several respects. Fighting continued in the countryside. The RUF was reluctant to allow UNAMSIL into its key diamond-producing areas. And in May 2000 the RUF took 500 peacekeepers hostage.[10] However, following the deployment of British troops and more assertive action by UNAMSIL, the military balance changed, and in November 2000 a cease-fire agreement was signed in Abuja between the RUF and the government. This was followed in May 2001 by a second—and more far-reaching—agreement (Abuja II), a formal declaration of peace in 2002, and the holding of elections in May of the same year.

Representation of the Conflict

Unlike the conflict in Southeast Europe and, to a degree, in Afghanistan, the narrative of conflict developed by commentators on Sierra Leone has given particular prominence to the role of economic agendas in both inciting and prolonging war. Sierra Leone does not, therefore, stand as a war in which narratives of "ancient ethnic hatreds" obscured other agendas, as was certainly the case in Bosnia. Nevertheless, the particular representations of the conflict have been problematic in ways that bear closer examination.

Sierra Leone and the broader region have suffered from its location—in geographic, economic, and political terms—on the global periphery. A number of consequences have arisen from this fact, not least of which has been an unwillingness to provide the sustained financial and political commitment that has underpinned peacebuilding in Bosnia and Herzegovina. A further consequence, however, was the relative lack of attention paid to the conflict in the media. As Hans-Henrik Holm's study of Danish media coverage shows, Sierra Leone receives very little coverage in general and less on specific political developments.[11] International news agencies, such as Reuters, provide more extensive coverage but, by their very nature, tend to focus on events rather than the causes of war and state failure.[12] Similarly, as the newspaper *The Guardian* noted at the time that UK forces had been dispatched to the country, for most of the British public: "Sierra Leone is more likely to be mistaken for a car model off a Ford assembly line, and as to the competing virtues of Foday Sankoh or President Kabbah, fewer than one in 100,000 could even pretend to have an opinion."[13]

Ironically, the preceding arms-to-Africa scandal involving British government officials and the mercenary company Sandline had made the country of slightly more interest to the media in the UK. This was not so much because of Sierra Leone's intrinsic problems, but because of the domestic political ramifications of a case that represented one of the first scandals of the New Labour administration and an apparent breach of its much-vaunted ethical foreign policy.[14] Arguably, the media interest this case created presented an ongoing domestic political imperative for New Labour to ensure the success of the Kabbah regime. What it did not do, however, was to offer an informed understanding of the dynamics driving conflict.

The effect of such limited and sporadic coverage on Sierra Leone was to provide a *tabula rasa* on to which commentators have been able to imprint broader stereotypes of civil conflict in Africa. Thus the violence in the country could be neatly pigeonholed by Kaplan as typical of "what is occurring in West Africa and much of the underdeveloped world: the withering away of central governments, the rise of tribal and regional domains, the unchecked spread of disease, and the growing pervasiveness of war."[15] The country could be passed off by Robert Cooper, one of Tony Blair's key foreign policy advisers, as one of those premodern states in which "chaos is the norm."[16] Indeed, the dominant tropes in accounts of Sierra Leone's conflict are the collapse of an effective state, the inhuman and nihilistic nature of the conflict, its absence of ideology, and emphatic reports of cannibalism and of the use of drugs and magic potions to fortify fighters.[17]

Typical of this representation is John MacKinlay's classification of the RUF—together with the NPFL in Liberia—as a "lumpen insurgent force."[18] This characterization of the RUF consciously echoes those accounts of Sierra Leone's conflict that emphasize the low level of education among RUF fighters and the preponderance of unemployed and crime-prone elements.[19] However, MacKinlay's stereotyping of the RUF takes such accounts further, suggesting a pseudo-scientific classification that has unnerving echoes of the eugenics debates of the early twentieth century. For MacKinlay, such forces arise from the "volatile lumpen culture itself and not from an intellectually developed ideology." The lumpen lieutenant dominates by his formidable presence, the unit commander may suffer "personality distortions," and his utterances take on a "messianic quality." Drugs and alcohol are used as controlling devices. These lumpen insurgents are the "antithesis" of a true soldier, conditioned by training and unmotivated by personal gain. Moreover, while MacKinlay concedes, in passing, that such forces may trade globally, their international structures are nevertheless considered to be undeveloped.[20] Other commentators have similarly declared that conflict in Sierra Leone had nothing to do with globalization.[21] Not only can this representation of RUF fighters be questioned—Thomas Dempsey, for instance, argues it was precisely the high level of discipline and political indoctrination of RUF fighters that hindered disarmament and demobilization in the country[22]—but it also frames the conflict as essentially driven by internal factors and explained by reference to its irrational and essentially inexplicably primordial qualities.

As already noted, this perspective is not untypical of the way in which contemporary conflicts, particularly those in Africa, have been represented. One effect has been to tar much of Africa, and particularly West Africa, as an arena of "new barbarism" and "coming anarchy,"[23] while silencing narratives of progress toward constitutional democracy in states such as

Benin, Ghana, Mali, and Senegal.[24] Such representations have also been used to justify arguments either for nonintervention or for a new "voluntary imperialism." The former contends that the practitioners of nihilistic anarchy neither deserve to be saved from themselves—especially at the cost to western lives—nor are they receptive to being saved. The latter contends that postmodern states have both an interest and an obligation to "bring order and organisation"[25] to the premodern world—a sort of twenty-first-century "white man's burden." This is, of course, precisely the discourse that animates and underpins the architects of Duffield's "liberal peace."[26]

The events of September 11, 2001, and the consequent "war on terror" have created a new representation of failed states as lawless areas, ripe for both cultivating and hiding terrorists. Duffield has already highlighted the way in which the new aid discourse has securitized underdevelopment as threatening the developed world through the transmission of drugs, crime, and refugees. Since September 11, however, underdevelopment, and particularly state failure, has also been framed as a *military security issue* for a Western world concerned about the threat of terrorism.[27] Thus, U.S. enthusiasm for the development of a certification regime for conflict diamonds notably increased following reports of Al-Qaida involvement in the trade in conflict diamonds from Sierra Leone and Liberia. Similarly, not only has U.S. military expenditure been substantially increased for the "war on terror" and the invasion of Iraq, but so too has U.S. development aid. In some respects, the consequent increase in foreign aid clearly represents a boon. For instance, Guinea's presence on the Security Council at the same time that the United States was pressing for war on Iraq meant it was the beneficiary of U.S.$2.1 million in aid for the care of Liberian refugees hosted by the country.[28] At the same time, however, it may also presage a return to a Cold War style of aid and intervention, where donor munificence is correlated with subscription not only to the economic fundamentals of neoliberalism, but also to the political fundamentals of the war on terror. This may leave the priorities of local peacebuilding even lower on the agenda of donors than they are now.

Of course, explanations of the conflict in Sierra Leone have also highlighted the role of economic agendas in driving the conflict, in particular the role of the diamond trade in providing both motivation and funding for conflict. Potentially, this represents an advance on the "new barbarism" explanation of the conflict. However, the process by which war economies, including that of Sierra Leone, have been problematized has served to mark them out as exceptional and distinct rather than reflective of broader responses to both globalization and the structural violence inherent in North-South relations. Indeed, as Duffield has noted, "conflict trade," such as that in diamonds from Sierra Leone, tends to be represented as a form of criminalized deviancy perpetuated by violent leaders or warlords whose interests exist outside of, and in opposition to, those of the broader society they inhabit.[29] Such trade is thereby demarcated as an aberration grafted onto decent society by the conditions of war, leading to the concomitant assumption that the conclusion of war and the defeat or reincorporation of the deviant will create conditions for cessation of the trade—especially with a little dose of good governance and neoliberalism. However, war economies not only reflect social transformations that create alternative systems of profit, power, and protection,[30] but they also have roots in pre-conflict economic structures, which either persist in, or adapt to, the conditions of postconflict peace. As will be shown below, Sierra Leone is no exception.

Moreover, as Joanna Spear has noted, the dominant representation of conflict in Sierra Leone as motivated by rebel greed presents a one-dimensional snapshot that ignores the interactions between greed and grievance factors and fails to inject a temporal dimension into analyses of these interactions.[31] Thus, particularly in its onset, the conflict can be better understood as a result of accumulated grievances with economic mismanagement, corrupt officials, the stresses associated with International Monetary Fund (IMF) structural adjustment, and the disaffection of junior officers excluded from the patronage system.[32] Similarly, while the role of economic agendas may have become more pronounced as the conflict developed, it is also the case that the prosecution of the war has left a legacy of *new* grievances that further complicate the challenge of peacebuilding.[33] Even in an analysis concerned with the economic dimensions of the conflict and their legacy for peace, it is important not to lose sight either of the *politics* in the political economy of conflict or of the way in which the pursuit of economic agendas can reflect or reinforce grievance.

From Shadow Economy to War Economy

This section charts the evolution of Sierra Leone's war economy. It will be argued that both those explanations that emphasize rebel greed and those that, instead, focus on the role of corruption and patrimonialism neglect the influence of bottom-up structural incentives to engage in shadow trade. Rather, Sierra Leone's war economy exploited the shadow networks and practices that had their roots in long-standing traditions of shadow trade that took advantage of different economic and regulatory environments in the region.

Some narratives of Sierra Leone's gradual descent into a kleptocratic state and then into armed conflict place an emphasis on processes of top-down elite corruption and the impact of a neopatrimonial system that distributed control of, or participation in, the diamond sector to key supporters. The effect, it has been argued, was to undermine the country's economy, to starve the government of a resource base that could fund effective governance, and ultimately to discredit both its corrupt leaders and the institutions of state. As William Reno notes of Sierra Leone's leaders: "Like the predatory organisations that arose in the 1990s, their political networks and strategies were deeply rooted in exploiting diamonds . . . the war did not mark a change in the logic of Sierra Leonean politics so much as the rise of competition among groups that had already mastered the tasks of violent manipulation of markets."[34] Thus the consequent conflict can be understood, in part, as an acute manifestation of a constantly shifting pattern of conflict and collaboration between local actors to control the benefits of both the "licit" and "illicit" diamond economy. This is epitomized by the "sobel" (soldiers by day, rebels by night)[35] phenomenon under which the Sierra Leonean army either engaged in its own independent mining operations or actively collaborated with the RUF.

An example of the former occurred in mid-1990, just prior to the RUF invasion, when then-president Joseph Momoh ordered the army to evict gangs of "illicit" diamond miners (IDMs) from Kono's mining areas. His motivation was to simultaneously pave the way for investment by a foreign company and to assert his own control over Sierra Leone's diamond economy, which was still largely under the influence of his predecessor, Siaka Stevens. The ensuing operations forced as many as 30,000 miners out of the area and further fueled popular alienation from the government. The effectiveness of the army's operation, however, was both a function of ordinary soldiers' interest in setting up their own IDM operations and the concern of senior officers to expand their own power base by gaining access to the informal diamond market controlled by Stevens.[36] The apotheosis of the latter occurred after the military coup of 1997, when the AFRC invited the RUF to share power, thus formalizing the economic cooperation that had been occurring in the midst of a supposed war between the two entities.[37] In this context, capturing the institution of the state was only important insofar as it provided the sovereign legitimacy that facilitated the provision of external aid and trade that could be further exploited for personal enrichment, and to the extent that it offered opportunities for the distribution of rewards to supporters.

This combination of top-down corruption and shifting patrimonial networks of competition and collaboration is certainly important in understanding the nature of the shadow diamond economy that undermined the state and then fueled war. However, the regionalized war economy that developed during the 1990s also had its roots in long-standing networks and traditions of shadow trade that combined with regional economic dynamics to create bottom-up structural incentives to participate in the "illicit" diamond trade. To understand Sierra Leone's combat economy, then, it is necessary to understand the prewar shadow and coping economies from which it emerged.

The regionalized war economy that developed in Sierra Leone has its roots in a much longer tradition of shadow trade that, as Kate Meagher demonstrates, can be traced back to the precolonial long-distance trading networks that operated across large areas of Africa, particularly in East and West Africa.[38] With the advent of colonialism, this interregional trade continued, although the type of goods changed. In West Africa, the Sahel, and savanna, forest, and coastal regions, trade was originally in primary products such as salt, dried fish, livestock, and gold. Colonialism meant that traditional West African circuits became dwarfed by more profitable opportunities. Crucially, the opportunities for shadow trade were created by differences in the fiscal, legal, and import regulations adopted in French and British colonies. In other words, regional actors were able to exploit the shadow spaces created not only by physical borders, but also by the differential economic and regulatory practices of the colonial powers. In short, currency zones replaced ecological zones in structuring the direction of traditional trade, while the goods traded also changed in response to new markets.[39] The opportunity to exploit differences in regulatory regimes continued into independence. For instance, a major motive for shadow trade was provided by differences between economies with internationally convertible currencies, notably the franc-zone countries, and those with foreign-exchange controls. Traders from the latter could obtain convertible currency through export trade in agricultural and other primary commodities to the former and use the funds to purchase goods such as cigarettes, textiles, and electronics for onward export.

Diamond traders and "illicit" diamond miners in Sierra Leone have exploited differential economic and regulatory practices of this sort since the discovery of diamonds in the 1930s. The colonial authorities had, in fact, concluded an agreement with De Beers's Sierra Leone Selection Trust (SLST) that gave the company a monopoly in mining and prospective rights over the entire country for ninety-nine years. However, IDM activity rapidly grew and by 1956 there were an estimated 75,000 "illicit" miners in the Kono District, with armed bands of 400–500 men raiding SLST areas.[40] The scale of IDM had an impact on other sectors of the economy—rice production fell markedly as young men abandoned the rice fields for the diamond fields. By the end of the 1950s, Sierra Leone, initially a net exporter of rice, had become an importer.[41] However, IDM activity was given widespread legitimacy due to a general perception that the SLST monopoly was a racket aimed at robbing locals of their resources and enriching foreigners. According to one report, "anyone engaged in illicit mining and smuggling was seen as a hero not a crook."[42] This attitude continued to provide legitimacy for IDM activity even after independence. Indeed, Siaka Stevens fanned such feelings, partly as a political strategy to gain power, partly to encourage SLST to give up its rich holdings, and partly to legitimize his own involvement in the shadow diamond trade.[43]

The buyers and smugglers of shadow diamonds were mainly Mandingo traders from neighboring West African states and, increasingly, Lebanese traders who had first arrived in the country in the nineteenth century.[44] The latter's role in Sierra Leone's economy had been encouraged by the British, through the use of loans and other incentives, largely because they were seen as an alternative to Krio traders who were deemed too disloyal and independent for a colonial people.[45] Later, the Lebanese diamond trade from Sierra Leone would become an important tax base for the various militias involved in Lebanon's civil war.[46]

At first, smuggling was conducted via Freetown, from which diamonds would be routed to Beirut and into European markets. However, smuggling via Liberia became increasingly common for several reasons. First, the tightening of security between Kono and Freetown in the early 1950s meant that diamonds were more easily transported via Liberia, which established fictitious diamond mines as cover for its role in the laundering of diamonds. Diamond merchants from Antwerp and Israel rapidly established offices in Liberia. De Beers followed suit in an attempt to keep as much of the trade under its control as possible.[47] Second, the price differentials that existed between Sierra Leone and Liberia were an incentive for the smuggling trade via Liberia—dealers could get better prices for their diamonds in Liberia. This had already been the case in the 1950s when Liberian dealers could offer higher untaxed prices. The effect of price differentials became even more pronounced in the late 1970s, as world price increases were not passed on to local dealers and diggers in Sierra Leone.[48] Conversely, reforms that had been initiated in 1959 produced a rise in local prices, and an upsurge in diamonds passing through official channels.[49]

Third, differences in currency regimes and/or the relative strength of the leone influenced the attraction of shadow trade. For instance, in the mid-1970s, the leone was tied to the pound sterling. The leone was thus more acceptable as a hard currency and the attraction of smuggling diamonds to Liberia to acquire U.S. dollars was correspondingly less. However, in 1978 the leone was detached from the pound and has since been perennially weak, suffering a series of devaluations. For most of this period, diamond buying in Sierra Leone should have been conducted in leones, thereby increasing the incentive for shadow trade, either as a strategy to obtain higher leone returns from illicit domestic transactions or as a strategy to obtain stronger foreign currencies by smuggling diamonds abroad.[50] For instance, in the early 1990s, goods such as rice and petroleum were imported by dealers who were paid in leones, but at an advantageous (nonmarket) rate. The leones were then used to purchase diamonds at above-market rates when compared to prices calculated using the official exchange rate. Most of the diamonds purchased in this manner would then be smuggled out of the country, where payments were more likely to be in an alternative stronger currency.[51] This latter phenomenon was also related to a fourth factor, which was the periodic imposition of a requirement to deposit a proportion of hard currency earnings from diamond exports with the Bank of Sierra Leone.

All these factors came together in 1987, when crisis in the economy resulted in the imposition of an economic emergency program. To forestall the precipitous collapse of the leone, the government required all foreign exchange earnings to be deposited with the Bank of Sierra Leone and all economic activity to be conducted in leones. It also included the monopolization of diamond export pricing by the Government Gold and Diamond Office, which had the effect of pushing prices down. While the emergency program temporarily reduced inflation and halted the fall in the leone, the impact on official diamond exports was both immediate and catastrophic. Almost overnight, official exports collapsed, and by the second half of 1988 a country that had recorded official exports of over 2 million carats in 1970 was recording none.[52]

Thus, both formal and informal regional economic structures provided an incentive for and facilitated IDM trading. Such structural and bottom-up drivers to informal mining were reinforced in Sierra Leone by a process of top-down elite corruption and a neopatrimonial system that frequently expressed itself in the allocation of diamond resources to key supporters. This meant not only that the Sierra Leonean "shadow state"[53] had neither the resources nor the legitimacy to repel what was initially a rather limited incursion by the RUF, but also that the networks established to support the peacetime shadow and coping economies could be easily developed and adapted to support the combat economy.

The Genesis of the Regional Combat Economy

As already noted, the final spark that led to the outbreak of armed conflict in Sierra Leone came in 1991 with the incursion of RUF soldiers supported by Charles Taylor of Liberia. In many respects, the war that followed mirrored the neighboring conflict in Liberia, where all the warring factions were exploiting the country's natural resources to fund war and profit making. In 1995 alone, U.S.$300–500 million worth of diamonds and gold, U.S.$53 million of timber, and U.S.$27 million of rubber were exported to Europe and Southeast Asia by Liberia's warlords.[54] Charles Taylor was no exception. Indeed, he was adept at exploiting contacts originally made with foreign companies as a senior official in the Doe regime to establish lucrative export trades in iron ore, timber, and agricultural products in territory he seized.[55] By 1991, for instance, he had become France's third largest supplier of tropical hardwoods and also received U.S.$10 million a month from a consortium of North American, Japanese, and European mining companies.[56] Estimates of Taylor's total earnings from such trade vary from U.S.$75 million to as much as U.S.$400 million per year.[57] Taylor received backing from Libya and, within the region, Burkina Faso and Côte d'Ivoire.[58] Arms were airlifted from Libya to Burkina Faso to Côte d'Ivoire and then on to Liberia. This same network was also an outward route for Taylor's export trade. In particular, goods were transported via Gbarnga in Liberia through the Ivorian town of Danane and on to the ports of San Pedro and Abidjan, from where they would be shipped to Europe and the United States. Thus, as Abdel-Fatah Musah has noted, the road from Gbarnga to Danane became a strategic "minerals for guns" route.[59]

By late 1990, Taylor's forces had moved to the border with Sierra Leone, and NPFL fighters organized in special commando units had established control over the cross-border trade in diamonds, gold, and agricultural products conducted by Mandingo traders. Initially, Taylor and his associates dealt directly with individual officials in Sierra Leone, and also Guinea, who engaged in clandestine cross-border trade. However, this arrangement broke down amid disputes over the spoils of trade. Indeed, it was just such a dispute—over a deal to smuggle cars into Sierra Leone—that was the immediate cause of the RUF incursion into the country.[60]

Once the Kono diamond fields were secured by the RUF, it created a mining unit under the leadership of "Lt. Col. Kennedy," which was subsequently transformed into an entity the RUF referred to as RUFP Mining Ltd.[61] The group also moved to establish an office in Brussels, claiming it wanted to work in the capital of Europe—rather conveniently, it was also close to Antwerp's diamond markets.[62]

RUF fighters initially mined diamonds themselves or used forced labor. Later, modified forms of forced labor were developed that allowed local diggers to retain a proportion of the diamonds they found. One system required diggers to work four days in a week for the RUF and two for themselves, with a day off for rest. A more common system was the "two pile" system in which diggers created one pile of diamondiferous gravel for the RUF and one for themselves. What they found in their own pile they could retain for themselves, except for sizable diamonds, which were retained by the rebels.[63] The conditions in which the miners worked, however, were exceedingly harsh.

RUF diamonds left the country in a variety of ways, all of which relied on the exploitation of flexible and mutable regional networks. Some were traded by the RUF within Sierra Leone. For instance, RUF traders from the Tongo diamond fields would bring their merchandise to Kenema, where there were more than forty diamond dealers, many of them Lebanese, despite the fact that their official and proper source of diamonds was supposedly out of reach in RUF territory. These dealers were also major importers of food and consumer goods, which they would exchange for diamonds. The diamonds would then either be laundered through the official export system or, more commonly, smuggled out of the country. The UN Expert Panel on Sierra Leone noted, for instance, that many prominent exporters from Sierra Leone were also exporters from the Gambia. This was particularly the case after the 1997 coup in Sierra Leone, when a large number of Lebanese traders fled to the Gambia as well as other countries such as Guinea, Liberia, and Côte d'Ivoire, but retained their business contacts in Sierra Leone. In the case of the Gambia, the UN Expert Panel reported that, despite producing no diamonds of its own, the country had become a "mini-Antwerp," exporting over $100 million per annum between 1996 and 1999. An estimated 90 percent of these exports were said to consist of diamonds originally sourced from Sierra Leone.[64] Other routes for RUF diamonds included Guinea, where there were reports, for instance, of RUF commanders trading diamonds for supplies and sometimes weapons with mid-level Guinean military officers.[65] As with the Gambia, imports into Belgium from Guinea were substantially greater than production or recorded exports (see Table 4.1).

However, the main transit point for RUF diamonds was Liberia, with diamonds being carried by RUF commanders and trusted Liberian couriers to Foya-Kama or Voinjama, and then on to Monrovia, from which they were often transferred to Côte d'Ivoire. The RUF's main diamond agent was a Burkinabé "general," Ibrahim Bah, who would shuttle regularly between Monrovia and Ouagadougou trading the diamonds and making substantial profits in the process. Another actor in the trade from Sierra Leone to Liberia was Talal El-Ndine, a key figure in the inner circle of Charles Taylor, who acted as paymaster to the RUF, bringing diamonds out of Sierra Leone and to arms brokers transporting weapons into Liberia. Other major purchasers of RUF diamonds in Liberia were Lebanese mer-

Table 4.1 West African Diamond Production and Antwerp Imports, 1990–1998, in thousands of carats

	Sierra Leone		Liberia		Guinea		Ghana		Côte d'Ivoire	
	Prod.[a]	Import[b]	Prod.	Import	Prod.	Import	Prod.	Import	Prod.	Import
1990	78	331	100	5,523	127	287	650	597	12	825
1991	243	534	100	658	97	374	700	675	15	946
1992	347	831	150	1,909	153	526	656	689	15	868
1993	158	344	150	5,006	167	1,021	591	526	15	683
1994	255	526	100	3,268	381	875	740	498	84	605
1995	213	455	150	10,677	365	780	632	643	75	1,614
1996	270	566	150	12,320	205	439	715	608	302	2,214
1997	104	803	150	5,803	205	533	830	531	307	885
1998	8.5	770	150	2,558	205	596	800	n/a	307	n/a

Source: Ian Smillie, Lansana Gberie, and Ralph Hazleton, *The Heart of the Matter: Sierra Leone, Diamonds, and Human Security* (Ottawa: Partnership Africa Canada, 2000), p. 33.

Notes: a. Diamond production in West African countries.

b. Antwerp imports of West African diamonds.

n/a = not available.

chants such as Aziz Nassour and Samih Ossaily, both of whom had extensive business interests in West Africa and who supplied the RUF with weapons, medical supplies, and mining equipment.[66] Indeed, between December 2000 and September 2001, Aziz is reported to have employed couriers who took weekly flights from Antwerp to Abidjan and then on to Liberia, from whence they would travel to meet with RUF commanders. On each trip, the couriers are reported to have carried U.S.$300,000, which would be exchanged for RUF diamonds.[67]

Subsequently, Bah, Nassour, and Ossaily have been linked with Al-Qaida purchases of RUF diamonds amounting to as much as U.S.$20 million, possibly in an attempt at money laundering. For example, Bah is reputed to have arranged visits by Al-Qaida representatives to RUF-held areas of Sierra Leone in late 1998, where they obtained diamonds for cash.[68] The significance of such Al-Qaida links in the political economy of Sierra Leone's conflict should not be overestimated, however. The RUF has long been held up as an example of a profoundly nonideological movement motivated primarily by economic aims, particularly as the conflict evolved. Moreover, while both Nassour and Ossaily admit their involvement in the diamond trade from Sierra Leone, both deny any links with Al-Qaida. At most, it seems likely that any Al-Qaida connections that did exist were probably incidental to the pursuit of profit through the trade in diamonds.

Whatever the case, Liberia represented the main transit point for RUF diamonds, from which they would either be moved on to other countries in West Africa or out to Europe and the United States. Indeed, like the Gambia, the disparity between Liberia's domestic production of diamonds and imports into Antwerp was substantial (see Table 4.1).

Many of the firms supposedly exporting diamonds from Liberia to Antwerp, however, existed in name only. Mail for these companies was in fact routed to the International Trust Company, which subsequently became the International Bank of Liberia Ltd. Later still, mail was also forwarded to the Liberian International Ship and Corporate Registry, based in Virginia with offices in New York. The latter is an important revenue generator in its own right for Liberia. Despite Charles Taylor's inability to keep Monrovia's single set of traffic lights in operation, Liberia's status as a flag-of-convenience state means it has the second largest maritime fleet in the world. Consequently, the maritime register generates significant funds, estimated at U.S.$18 million in 2000, some of which have been diverted to fund arms purchases, particularly after the imposition of UN sanctions on Liberia's diamond trade.[69]

In sum, therefore, the scale of the RUF's export operations was substantial. De Beers estimated that RUF exports amounted to some

U.S.$70 million in 1999, while a World Bank study of the same year estimated that U.S.$137 million worth of diamonds were "illicitly" exported from the country. Other estimates of the RUF's average annual earnings range from U.S.$25 to U.S.$125 million.[70] In comparison, annual government revenue amounted to just U.S.$60 million in 1994–1995 and exports of minerals (diamonds, gold, bauxite, rutile) had collapsed from U.S.$134 million in 1991 to just U.S.$0.9 million.[71]

These earnings funded not only personal enrichment but also the acquisitions of arms and other supplies with which to prosecute war. As with the export of diamonds, these provisions principally came through Liberia, with the RUF able to take advantage of Charles Taylor's network of allies, arms dealers, mercenaries, and transport companies. For instance, mercenaries from Eastern Europe conducted bombing raids from bases in Liberia; training was provided by South African, Ukrainian, and Nigerian nationals, among others; and mercenaries from a range of countries, particularly Burkina Faso, took part in RUF operations.[72]

A network of air firms was drawn upon to fly arms to Liberia and sometimes on to the RUF in Sierra Leone. Some of the firms were registered in Liberia, though not necessarily based there, taking advantage of its lax license and tax laws. Others were both registered in and operated from other countries. Whatever the case, such companies would fly in arms (often via Burkina Faso) for onward transfer to the RUF. One example, recorded by the UN, occurred in March 1999, when a cargo of sixty-eight tons of weapons was flown from the Ukraine to Burkina Faso under a contract with a Gibraltar-based company. The weapons, which were ostensibly destined for the Burkina Faso Defense Ministry, were then shipped to Liberia aboard an aircraft operated by a company registered in Monaco that was owned by the well-known Ukrainian arms dealer Leonid Minin.[73]

According to Abdel-Fatah Musah, a secret airstrip in eastern Kenema, manned by the RUF, became the main entry point for "illegal" arms, including surface-to-air missiles from Eastern Europe.[74] However, the UN has reported that the destruction of landing strips in RUF areas gradually forced it to use helicopters to transport arms and equipment.[75] In addition, the infrastructure of the timber industry in Liberia has been drawn upon, not only to pay for[76] and supply arms, but also to transport troops and weapons within Liberia (see Table 4.2). For instance, there have been occasions where the Oriental Timber Company (OTC), the principal timber firm operating in Liberia, has managed the whole process of weapons transfer, starting with disembarkation at Buchanan port and continuing with the use of its own trucks to transport arms along logging roads it has constructed.[77]

Table 4.2 Purchasers and Suppliers of Liberian Timber: A Selective List

Buyer	Supplier	Log Supplier Arms Links?
Global Star (Asia) Trading Ltd. c/o Natura Holdings, Singapore	Oriental Timber Company (OTC)	Yes
DLH Nordisk A/S, Denmark	OTC	Yes
	Maryland Wood-Processing Industries (MWPI)	Yes
Timber Trade Service, Italy	OTC	Yes
Messrs. Bonomi Prefabbricati ILL Sri, Italy	OTC	Yes
HBT Holzhandel GMBH, Germany	OTC	Yes
TREEMEX, Germany	OTC	Yes
SIBA, Senegal	OTC	Yes
TECNOALP, Italy	OTC	Yes
General Wood Ltd., London	OTC	Yes
Simla Trade, India	OTC	Yes
Sumas Trading PTE Ltd.	Royal Timber Company (RTC)	Yes
World Best Trading, Dubai	OTC	Yes

Source: Global Witness, *Taylor-Made: The Pivotal Role of Liberia's Forests in Regional Conflict* (London: Global Witness, September 2001), p. 16.

Such arms and timber deals were financed through a network of bank accounts controlled by Talal El-Ndine, Charles Taylor's financial adviser and paymaster to the RUF. According to Global Witness, two accounts were established in Burkina Faso, one at the Central Bank of West African States and the other at the Banque International du Burkina (BIB). These were held in the name of Jean Paul Some. A third was set up in Switzerland in 1993. Funds from the Liberian timber industry would be deposited into the Swiss account and then transferred to the Burkinabé accounts, which were then used to pay for shipments of arms, ammunition, and fuel both for Taylor's own purposes and for those of the RUF. The BIB account also received funds from Libya.[78]

Thus the political economy of Sierra Leone's conflict should not be understood only as a function of a greed-based search for diamonds in the midst of war, nor simply as a function of top-down corruption and patrimonialism within the country. It also needs to be understood as the product of preconflict regional economic dynamics that both created structural incentives for shadow trade and facilitated the development of regionwide networks to engage in this trade. The wartime trade networks developed by the RUF and its ally Charles Taylor simply built upon existing practices, adapting and refining the regional networks of the shadow economy, as well as more thoroughly integrating them into global shadow markets.

The very nature of this regionalized combat economy also partly explains the viciousness of the violence perpetrated by the RUF. As Musah has noted, the RUF's access to such an extended economic space meant that it did not have to rely on the local population for supplies and other material support. Thus the insurgents did not need to cultivate legitimacy among the local population in the way that would have been imperative if they had been operating within a more enclosed political economy.[79]

Contemporary Efforts to Transform the War Economy in Sierra Leone

At first glance, the most recent attempt at peacekeeping and peacebuilding in Sierra Leone since early 2002 can be counted as a relative success for the UN.[80] After eleven years of fighting, the war was officially declared at an end on January 18, 2002. Since then, government authority has been successfully reasserted across the country. Parliamentary elections, in which 81 percent of the population voted, were held in May 2002 and President Kabbah was returned to power with 70 percent of the vote. The RUF's political wing, the RUF-P, received just 1.7 percent of the vote. In addition, 72,000 combatants from the RUF, the Sierra Leonean army, and the Civil Defense Force (CDF) have been demobilized. The combination of UN sanctions on Liberia and a domestic diamond certification regime has increased the flow of diamonds through the official system. Gross domestic product (GDP), which had fallen by 25 percent between 1997 and 1999, grew by 3.8 percent in 2000 and by 5.4 percent in 2001.[81] In March 2002, the country reached the point where it became formally eligible for interim debt relief under an enhanced highly indebted poor country (HIPC) initiative.[82] As long as the economy continues to perform according to the benchmarks of the IMF poverty reduction program, debt relief will continue. Enhanced HIPC assistance could see the country's ratio of debt service to export drop from 74 percent in 2002 to 5 percent in 2005.[83] Moreover, despite continued conflict elsewhere in the region, the presence of UNAMSIL, one of the largest UN peacekeeping operations ever mounted—17,000 strong at its peak and costing some U.S.$2 billion—has ensured relative stability in the country.

However, the record of earlier peacebuilding efforts in the region has been less impressive, marked by a lack of commitment, underfunding, and a failure to fully appreciate the underlying dynamics of the conflict. More troubling, however, many of the economic prescriptions that contributed to the conflict in the 1990s are again being advocated by external donors. In addition, current programs on crucial issues such as the trade in dia-

monds, disarmament and demobilization, and corruption suffer from significant flaws. Thus the extent to which external intervention has managed
to embed a stable peace able to survive the departure of UNAMSIL is
questionable.

On the issue of the limited political and economic commitment to
peacebuilding in the region, it is worth noting that, at the same time that the
international community was pledging U.S.$5.1 billion for the reconstruc-
tion of Bosnia, implementation of the Abidjan Accord in 1996 was undermined by the unwillingness of donors to stump up the U.S.$47 million bill
for a peacekeeping force.[84] In 2000 a donor conference for Southeast Europe
managed to find pledges of U.S.$1.8 billion, while, at much the same time,
a mere U.S.$150 million was found for Sierra Leone.[85] Perhaps more
telling, however, was the discrepancy between the sum of donor pledges and
the RUF's estimated annual earnings of U.S.$25–125 million from its trade
in conflict diamonds; international assistance was insufficient to offset the
economic incentives for continued war, as subsequent events proved.

Moreover, while the UK now celebrates the success of its intervention
in Sierra Leone, an earlier request by Momoh for military advisers and
support for improved communication and intelligence capabilities was
turned down.[86] In 1999, Peter Penfold, then British ambassador to Sierra
Leone, was told not to request more British funding, due to more urgent
needs in Kosovo.[87] UNAMSIL peacekeeping forces sent to oversee the
Lomé peace agreement were ill equipped and underfunded. Indeed, the
commander of UNAMSIL complained in a leaked memorandum that most
units had arrived with little or no equipment, that a shortage of transport
meant that staff officers had been forced to travel in minibuses, and that
shortages of equipment prevented him from communicating directly with
his battalion commander.[88]

There is an obvious and oft-repeated lesson here. Early and well-
funded commitments to conflict prevention, peacekeeping, and peacebuilding are a prerequisite for durable peace. Even the U.S.$2 billion now com-
mitted to peace in Sierra Leone (roughly the cost of one B-2 stealth bomber)
is a relatively small amount, compared to more conventional expenditures
on national security. Indeed, at U.S.$19.9 billion, total UN expenditures for
peacekeeping in the 1990s amounted to just 0.3 percent of the U.S.$6.9 tril-
lion in global military expenditure over the same period. In 1994, the most
expensive year in peacekeeping history, the United States spent $290 on
national defense for every dollar spent on UN peacekeeping.[89]

The next section seeks to examine the way in which the policies of
external agencies, in particular the IFIs, actually exacerbated Sierra
Leone's descent into conflict, and the way in which current approaches to
peacebuilding in the country are in danger of repeating the same mistakes.

The International Financial Institutions

As William Reno has noted, the economic crisis that accompanied Sierra Leone's collapse was not merely a function of pervasive state corruption, but also of the way in which local elites were able to take advantage of creditor demands for reductions in state services and the introduction of foreign firms, to reinforce their patronage and political power.[90] In particular, IFI requirements to streamline the state were used by ruling elites to justify eliminating or weakening alternative institutions and actors that presented potential challenges. In addition, the process of privatization was used both as a mechanism to reward allies and as a vehicle under which state functions could be farmed out to politically nonthreatening outside companies.

This kind of adaptation to the agenda of neoliberalism was already in evidence in the mid-1970s, when under the guise of increasing market competition the Government Diamond Office, responsible for exporting the country's diamonds, was relieved of its monopoly. The effect, however, was to increase control over diamond marketing among associates of then-president Siaka Stevens. Indeed, one of the firms that received an export license belonged to Jamil Said Mohammed, a key business partner of the president.[91] Stevens also engaged in bogus privatization exercises that were applied to state agencies for agricultural marketing, road transport, and oil refining.[92] Stevens's rule was marked by the wasting away of state services and growing corruption mediated through a patronage network that increasingly dominated both the formal and informal economies. Stevens manipulated state regulation of the economy to sabotage rival economic ventures and undermine political challengers. Budget cuts eroded the capacity of the armed forces, while state spending on health and education fell by 60 percent between 1980 and 1987.[93] Real per capita GDP peaked in 1970 and then proceeded to drop by over a third between 1971 and 1989.[94] The combined collapse of state services reinforced the centrality of Stevens's "official" clandestine market, which was used for basic survival.

Stevens retired in 1985, but the rule of his successor, Joseph Momoh, was no better. Momoh was chosen partly for his loyalty to Stevens and partly because he lacked his own political network with which to challenge the de facto control of key sections of the economy held by Stevens and his business partners. However, in the absence of his own patronage network, Momoh began selling off state assets and granting concessions to private firms. In this way he could use external firms to wrest control over the economy from Stevens's business partners and the IDM gangs.[95] These external firms were deemed reliable partners precisely because they were not connected to other centers of political power in Sierra Leone.

They could be co-opted by Momoh as allies in his attempt to cut off his own political rivals from independent sources of wealth and authority. Thus, while Momoh launched various operations to shut down informal mining, a succession of foreign firms were given concessions to mine diamonds. This move not only prompted a coup attempt against Momoh by Stevens's supporters in 1987, but also fueled alienation from the state among "illicit" miners. As noted above, Momoh ultimately replaced the civilians engaged in IDM activity with soldiers who then engaged in their own IDM trade.

Likewise, the privatization of port management, customs, and fishery royalties offered Momoh a further opportunity to "shut potential rival strongmen off from autonomous accumulation."[96] The firms themselves were not generally successful. However, Momoh's strategy of cutting back the state and cultivating partnerships with external companies corresponded with the agenda of external creditors, who argued that the country's problems lay in corruption and the loss of control to IDM operators. In their view, the solution was to use foreign firms to restore control, particularly over the diamond industry. As Reno notes:

> Both the IMF and the president envisioned foreign firms as contributing to a centralization of control over coercion and resources. IMF advisers viewed this as occurring in a formal institutional framework; the president most likely imagined a reconstituted patronage network. Instead external intrusion shifted control of resources to armed IDM gangs even further divorced from central control.[97]

IMF and World Bank conditionalities also exacerbated the social stresses created by underdevelopment. In the mid-1980s, for instance, the government agreed to execute a structural adjustment program that included cuts in the numbers of civil servants, removal of subsidies on food and petroleum, limits on public expenditures, and a reduction of the budget deficit. Among the measures implemented were increases in the tariffs on electricity, cuts in education and health, and limits on civil service pay—the latter contributing to a "brain drain" of experienced civil service staff, further weakening the institutions of the state.[98] In addition, subsidies on rice and petrol were significantly reduced: prices for a fifty-kilogram bag of rice (imports of which had been privatized) were raised from 85 to 680 leones by 1988. The price of petrol rose from 8 leones per gallon to 55.[99] Ironically, however, the government's continued accumulation of arrears led to a temporary break with the IMF and World Bank, which meant that most of the funding for a public investment program that was supposed to accompany structural adjustment did not arrive.[100]

Similarly, a structural adjustment package agreed in 1991, the same year as the RUF incursion, came with the usual IFI stipulations for debt repayment, deregulation, privatization, and reform of the public sector. By 1994, and in the midst of a civil war, 40 percent of state employees had been dismissed.[101] For the World Bank, this was a sign of progress. Indeed, despite the ongoing conflict, a 1992 coup by the AFRC, rampant corruption, and the withering away of state institutions, the World Bank considered the early 1990s to be marked by "considerable progress in stabilizing and restructuring the economy."[102] Notably, for the Bank, during the three year period between 1992 to 1994 inflation declined from 100 to 20 percent and real GDP growth improved.[103] In reality, as David Francis has noted, structural adjustment in the late 1980s and early 1990s

> marginalised those already below the poverty line and also excluded and impoverished the middle class and petty bourgeoisie. . . . [It] led to the expansion of the informal economy, whilst the state's economic policies further impoverished the peasant producers. The consequence of SAPs [structural adjustment policies] intensified political unrest and generated a wave of popular political actions by trade union workers, students and teachers.[104]

Despite such protests, however, the government, as David Keen has noted, was "remarkably successful in promoting itself as a model student of financial orthodoxy . . . while tolerating and participating in increasingly violent forms of extortion."[105] Indeed, at the international level, the conflict in Sierra Leone was concealed by "a veil of silence," behind which humanitarian operations and the provision of loans substituted for a more effective intervention.[106] Despite a coup in 1996, further IFI loans followed in return for strict adherence to reform. Indeed, an IMF press release announcing a U.S.$34 million loan to the government in December 1995 had an eerily familiar ring to it:

> The bulk of . . . fiscal adjustment will have to be borne by expenditures, particularly in the area of defense, through economies in the purchase of military hardware and downsizing the army. Other fiscal measures include an increase in the rate of duty on premium gasoline which was effected in November . . . implementation of a civil service retrenchment program [and] removing from the public enterprise sector a number of enterprises whose functions can be managed more efficiently by the private sector.[107]

Despite war, coups, and flawed peace attempts, budget cuts continued. At the same time, rising GDP, inflation of only 6 percent in 1996, and further privatizations earned the country more plaudits from the World Bank.[108] Successive leaders, however, were able to use precisely these processes to jettison the state as an alternative to their own personal patronage and to eliminate the need for reliance on internal strongmen by forging alliances with foreign companies. Indeed, Sierra Leone engaged in what Reno refers to as a process of imperialism by invitation,[109] a process that reached its apotheosis with the provision of diamond concessions to a branch of the mercenary firm Executive Outcomes.

IFI conditionalities in Sierra Leone reflected both the deep level of intervention of the IFIs and the unrealistic ambition of the reforms that were instituted in the context of state collapse. As Marina Ottaway has documented, an extensive list of tasks was required of the government by the IMF following the Lomé peace agreement. In theory, the memorandum only set out the most urgent problems to be addressed. A brief sample from the more exhaustive list includes demobilization, disarmament, and reintegration of former combatants, initiation of a program of national reconstruction, reduction of inflation, liberalization of the petroleum market, revision of the tax system, and elections by January 2001. As Ottaway has also observed, this was "a set of prescriptions for state reconstruction . . . so exhaustive that it cannot possibly be followed in practice."[110]

The IFI intervention that accompanied both the war and the flawed peace initiatives of the 1990s not only failed to alleviate the conflict, but also actively contributed to the decline of state capacity and legitimacy. Not only did IMF policies give ruling elites increased opportunities for self-enrichment, but they also helped them to deny economic space for political rivals. Requirements to end subsidies for basic commodities, deregulate the economy, devalue the national currency, and reduce public expenditure did not so much reinvigorate the economy as fuel alienation and legitimize the agenda of top-down corruption pursued by the country's elite. Indeed, IFI-imposed cuts in the rice ration to the military, coupled with pressure to evict Executive Outcomes, contributed to the 1997 coup that ousted the democratically elected Kabbah government.[111]

Strikingly, the IFI reforms currently being pursued echo the failed agendas of the 1990s. In a context where an estimated 90 percent of people between ages eighteen and thirty-five are unemployed, and where the rank-and-file civil service earn an average of a dollar a day (equivalent to the UN's definition of absolute poverty), lower taxes and lower inflation still remain central goals. Despite the fact that previous reforms reduced the number of state-owned firms to twenty-nine and despite the manner in which leaders were able to capture the process of privatization, the World Bank continues to promote this policy.[112] Indeed, in 2001 the Sierra Leone government approved a strategic plan for the divestiture of state enterprises and established a national commission for privatization to support the processes.[113] As in the past, creditors view privatization, coupled with formal anticorruption initiatives, as the way to eliminate corruption and promote efficiency, especially in the mining sector.[114]

However, there are strong indications that local elites are adapting to these demands in the same old ways. The government is widely accused of corruption. A survey on the perception of corruption in the country conducted in May–August 2000 found that 95 percent of respondents considered corruption to be rampant in most government departments.[115] The cabinet is formed largely along lines of patronage,[116] and at least four senior members of the government have reportedly engaged in "illicit" diamond mining.[117] Closed-door decisions to grant large and long-term diamond and oil concessions to foreign companies reflect a continued lack of transparency and accountability.[118] Old firms linked to the conflict are now returning to claim their concessions. Most notably, the Canadian mining firm DiamondWorks, which is linked to the mercenary companies Sandline and (the now defunct) Executive Outcomes, announced in 2002 that it would resume mining operations in Koidu.[119] The current head of DiamondWorks, Antonio "Tony" Teixeira, was among a number of people named in 2000 by British foreign minister Peter Hain as sanctions busters in Angola.[120] Thus the nexus of privatized security purchased on the back of the country's natural resources has extended its legacy into the peace.

In line with the precepts of liberal peace, the government agreed in 2000 to implement a national anticorruption strategy. At the same time, an anticorruption commission was established with funding from the UK's Department for International Development (DFID).[121] The latter's role is to investigate those found guilty of breaking anticorruption laws. It can arrest suspects, but lacks the mandate to prosecute. Instead, suspects are handed over to the attorney general, who then determines which cases will proceed. However, the operation of both the anticorruption strategy and the commission have suffered from a number of problems. First, to date, the government has largely failed to implement the anticorruption strategy. Second, the attorney general is also the minister of justice, leading to concerns that the demarcation between the decision to prosecute and the political interests of the government is not sufficiently clear.[122] Third, as the International Crisis Group (ICG) noted in 2002, at least thirty-five cases brought before the attorney general by the anticorruption commission have been essentially ignored. In effect, the commission has become a tool to deter and punish political opponents, "a key instrument of Presidential authority rather than an impartial body."[123] Again, this echoes previous practice in Sierra Leone, in which, for example, Strasser used corruption investigations focused on low-level officials as a means of reinforcing his authority.[124] More broadly, this illustrates the ways in which, despite the best intentions of the IFIs, local actors are able to adapt the complex web of externally imposed reforms to suit their own political and profit-making agendas. It also underlines the way in which externally imposed reforms can be simultaneously hobbled by the competing priorities of external actors. Thus, donors have been reluctant to comment on the flaws of a Kabbah government, which they publicly describe as "a dream team,"[125] for fear of jeopardizing the move to elections that could presage a reduction in the UN's peacekeeping force.

The Diamond Economy: Sanctions and Certification

Given Sierra Leone's abundant diamond endowments, addressing the domestic, regional, and global dynamics of the diamond sector is critical to the country's recovery from conflict. In some respects, this is an area where international action has markedly improved. While the role of diamonds in Sierra Leone's conflict is now widely recognized, action on this issue was initially slow. In part, this was because of the international community's reluctance to properly engage in a crisis that was, at best, of sporadic interest to domestic electorates; in part, it was because the narratives of "new barbarism" outlined above had the effect of obscuring both the extensive economic networks and the regional dynamics that underpinned the conflict.

Moreover, to the extent that external intervention was undertaken, it sometimes had ambivalent effects on the political economy of the conflict. For example, both ECOMOG and UN peacekeeping troops reputedly engaged in trading arms and drugs for RUF diamonds.[126] This issue came to a head with the leaking of a memorandum of May 2000 by the Indian commander of UNAMSIL, Major-General Vijay Kumar Jetley, in which he accused the Nigerian contingent of obtaining "massive benefits" from informal diamond mining and alleged that a "tacit understanding" of mutual noninterference had been reached between the RUF and ECOMOG. Indeed, he claimed that a former ECOMOG commander, Brigadier-General Maxwell Khobe, was known as the "ten million man," after receiving U.S.$10 million to permit the mining activities of the RUF to continue unobstructed. Jetley also suggested that ECOMOG force commander Major-General Gabriel Kpambe was involved in "illegal diamond mining in connivance with RUF leader Foday Sankoh."[127]

When international action to address the role of diamonds in Sierra Leone began to coalesce, it reflected a broader focus on the issue of conflict diamonds that developed in the late 1990s, particularly following a Global Witness report on the role of diamonds in the Angolan conflict.[128]

The publication in 2000 of reports on Sierra Leone by Partnership Africa Canada and a UN Expert Panel both reflected and reinforced a growing focus on the link between war and diamonds in the country. Indeed, in July of the same year (some nine years after the conflict began), the UN finally imposed sanctions on the direct and indirect import of rough diamonds from Sierra Leone, with an exemption for those sold by the government once a certificate-of-origin scheme was brought into operation[129]—which duly occurred in October 2000. This scheme includes the use of a specially designed, "tamperproof" certificate of origin and a set of rules on import and export procedures. Under the scheme, only diamonds "legally" mined in areas under the control of the government can be officially exported.

Reputedly, diamond brokers from the Lebanese community, who play a pivotal role in Sierra Leone's diamond economy, have voluntarily resolved to work within the official system as a contribution to the country's national recovery effort.[130] The government has also introduced a mining community development fund to be distributed among chiefdoms in the mining areas. The aim of the fund is to demonstrate to Sierra Leone's citizens that they have a material interest in supporting the official export system, as funds for the program are derived from the government's 3 percent export tax on diamonds. The amount allocated to the fund represents 0.75 percent of the total export value of Sierra Leone's diamonds. By the end of 2001, approximately U.S.$195,000 had been distributed.[131]

At the regional level, the UN has also imposed a ban on the export of diamonds from Liberia, Guinea has introduced a certificate-of-origin system for its diamonds (in June 2001), Liberia has produced a draft scheme of its own, and Côte d'Ivoire has expressed interest in a regional certification scheme.[132] Since January 2003, these initiatives have also been reinforced by the introduction of a global certification scheme for rough diamonds that aims to prevent the trade in conflict diamonds globally.

 These initiatives have yielded some positive results. Action against RUF diamond exports, coupled with the introduction of the diamond certification scheme, has seen official diamond sales in Sierra Leone rise from just U.S.$1.2 million in 1999 to U.S.$26 million in 2001, providing a larger tax base from which the central administration can—at least in theory—distribute the rewards of peace. A DFID-funded study of the diamond industry in Sierra Leone has suggested that the value of diamond exports could rise to U.S.$180 million by 2006, which government officials in Sierra Leone view as a conservative estimate.[133] Similarly, since the imposition of diamond sanctions on Liberia in May 2001, no official exports from Liberia have been recorded by the Liberian Central Bank or the Ministry of Finance. Nor have imports of Liberian stones been recorded in Antwerp.[134]

Diamond certification, however, has not been without flaws. The rise in official diamond exports from Sierra Leone may reflect the gradual extension of government authority across the country, as much as the efficiency of the domestic certification system in Sierra Leone. More troubling, a substantial proportion of "illicit" diamonds continued to be smuggled out of the country directly or laundered into the system. For instance, in October 2001 a UN Expert Panel reported that the RUF, which then retained a firm grip on key diamond areas, was channeling diamonds through Freetown. In particular, Freetown traders were bringing diesel, petrol, soap, rice, secondhand clothes, and other consumer goods to Koidu—the capital of the Kono diamond fields—and exchanging them for diamonds, cassava, and mangoes. The traders then either sold the stones to licensed dealers in Sierra Leone or smuggled them to other states in West Africa. In July 2001 the RUF and the state-backed civil militia, the Civil Defense Force, agreed to a moratorium on diamond mining in Kono under UNAMSIL supervision. However, this sparked protests from locals, who demanded to know how else they were to make their living, and ultimately proved unenforceable.[135]

Effective implementation of the diamond certification scheme in Sierra Leone is hampered by the very nature of the problem it seeks to address. Sierra Leone's diamond endowments are overwhelmingly in the form of alluvial diamonds deposits. Alluvial diamond fields are created by the disintegration of volcanic rock (kimberlite) and can be carried by river systems over a wide area. In contrast with kimberlite diamond deposits located deep underground, the extraction of which requires expensive and capital-intensive operations, alluvial mining can be done by anyone equipped with a sieve and shovel. Thus, as one ICG report notes, "mining" in Sierra Leone is often "more like farming in that it involves tens of thousands of persons and is virtually impossible to control."[136]

A significant proportion of diamonds are still being smuggled out of the country—some in diplomatic bags. One report has suggested that as much as 60 percent of Sierra Leone's diamond exports are smuggled, mainly to Guinea and the Gambia.[137] The latter, it should be noted, is a significant exporter of diamonds, despite producing none itself. There are also reports that Charles Taylor continued to purchase significant quantities of diamonds from Sierra Leone—both from agents acting for him in Kono and from traders who had already smuggled the diamonds into Liberia.[138] It is also notable that the quality of diamonds exported through the official system is lower than average for Sierra Leone, suggesting that better-quality diamonds are not being routed through the official system.[139]

In part, incentives for continued smuggling stem from the regulations imposed on exporters. In a move redolent of previous counterproductive initiatives, the governor of the Bank of Sierra Leone added a clause to the export system requiring traders to bring the dollar value of diamonds they officially export back into the banking system. Given that many traders use the hard currency from diamond sales to pay for imported commodities, the only way to retain hard currency is through unofficial exports. Notably, the governor is reportedly involved with a diamond-exporting firm, NAMINCO, and may thus have a commercial motive for discouraging other exporters and withholding his signature on the export certificates of competitors.[140] Corruption in the system is also facilitated by a dearth of trained mine monitors (down to 78 from a prewar total of 108), who in addition are poorly paid or not paid at all.[141] Moreover, many monitors and police choose not to report the illegal dealings they discover because of their reluctance to challenge powerful illicit diamond miners, particularly in the absence of backing from Freetown.[142]

The implementation of the community development fund has also been problematic. Initially, government officials wanted traditional community authorities to design specific projects before funding was disbursed, but nongovernmental organizations (NGOs) and external advisers, concerned about state corruption, insisted the money be disbursed straightaway. In the event, few of the chiefs actually used the money for the benefit of their communities. Instead, opportunities for corruption were simply channeled further down the pipeline. As Lansana Gberie has also noted, this episode underlines how the antigovernment bias of NGOs and donors and their perception of officials as uniformly corrupt often leads to conflict, obstruction, and failure.[143]

The postconflict period has also witnessed the emergence of numerous "youth councils" that claim to be community policing groups but that also operate as protection rackets. These groups do in fact perform local good works (neatly illustrating the often symbiotic relationship between mafia and coping economies). However, they are also involved in intimidation of local communities, illegal mining, and obstruction of licensed miners. For example, the LBYC is reported to have made a deal with former RUF combatants to incorporate them into its structures,[144] while the Movement of Concerned Kono Youth, based in Kono, has a fleet of twenty-five to fifty motorcycles that are allegedly used to smuggle diamonds across the border into Guinea.[145] This group argues that all foreigners, particularly the Lebanese, should leave the district, and in early 2002 they took a Lebanese trader hostage, allegedly ransoming him for U.S.$1,700.[146]

Adaptation of Regional Networks

The Diamond Trade

Regional shadow networks have also adapted to the new economic incentives created by the differential regulatory environments shaped by the ban on Liberian exports and the certificate-of-origin scheme in Sierra Leone. According to a 2001 UN Expert Panel report, the problem of RUF diamonds being smuggled out via Liberia has been reversed, with Liberian diamonds now being laundered through Sierra Leone and Côte d'Ivoire via dealers specializing in purchasing Liberian rough-diamond stocks. Indeed, one dealer in Sierra Leone claimed the official certification system made it *easier* to launder diamonds, as it was no longer necessary to go through the complicated process of smuggling through other West African countries[147]—although, more recently, the escalating civil war in Liberia appears to have disrupted supplies into Sierra Leone. The global certification scheme, which aims to prevent the trade in conflict diamonds, has several flaws of its own, raising serious questions about its likely effectiveness in counteracting the trade.

The Market for Mercenaries

Both the Liberians United for Reconciliation and Democracy (LURD) insurgency in Liberia and the more recent civil war in Côte d'Ivoire reflect and influence the shifting conflict dynamics that are an integral part of the political economy of the region. The LURD insurgency in Liberia, which began in 1999 when rebels crossed into Liberia from Guinea, has developed familiar patterns of economic behavior. Both LURD and government forces engage in looting captured villages—in the latter case, to substitute for the lack of pay from the state. LURD itself consists of members drawn from factions in Liberia's previous civil war, but has also recruited mercenaries from Guinea, Côte d'Ivoire, and Sierra Leone, who have been offered a retention fee of U.S.$200 and a share of the spoils of conflict.[148] Mercenaries from Sierra Leone include former RUF fighters and former members of the Kamajor CDF, factions who were on opposite sides during Sierra Leone's civil war. To confuse matters more, former RUF soldiers also account for 90 percent of Liberia's Antiterrorism Unit (ATU), Charles Taylor's most trusted security force.[149]

Similarly, rebel forces in Côte d'Ivoire are supported by mercenaries from Liberia and Sierra Leone. Indeed, in the case of two of the rebel groups, the Movement for Justice and Peace (MJP) and the Ivorian Popular Front Movement of the Great West (MPIGO), mercenaries are reputed to account for 90 percent of their forces.[150] Liberian fighters, in particular, are reported to have engaged in the looting of drugs, weapons, and cars in the Ivorian city of Man, after its capture by rebels in December 2002.[151] For its part, in September 2002 the government recruited former employees of the mercenary company Executive Outcomes through the assistance of a Saudi Arabian diamond speculator. The mercenaries were reportedly paid £4,000 a month. By early 2003, however, their numbers seemed to have been cut to just a handful as a result of pressure from France.[152]

In part, the regional market for mercenaries reflects the general attractions of mercenary work and the prospect of sharing the booty in the context of severe underdevelopment (unemployment in Liberia is estimated at 75–80 percent).[153] In the case of Sierra Leone, however, the steady supply of mercenaries also reflects problems with a disarmament, demobilization, and reintegration (DDR) process that the ICG has called "more cosmetic than substantive."[154] In particular, the UN reintegration program experienced a substantial shortfall in funding from donors. As another report noted: "as the CNN effect wore off and high visibility activities such as symbolic weapons burnings gave way to the more mundane tasks of providing training and housing, funding dried up."[155] The DDR process was further undermined by the fact that the RUF moved their better weapons into Liberia, keeping them available for later use or sale. This diversion of arms was aided by UNAMSIL's apparent willingness to accept substandard disarmament—for example, by declaring an area as "disarmed" when only one third of combatants had given up a third of their weapons.[156] By December 2002, there were still some 18,000 former combatants awaiting reintegration.[157] This lack of movement has bred discontent among former combatants, sometimes leading to street protests as well as to the emergence of aggressive youth groups who continue to usurp government authority in mining areas.[158] The lack of alternative economic opportunities has also enhanced the attractiveness of mercenary employment for former combatants who have few, if any, other marketable skills.

The market for mercenaries, like the wider political economy of conflict in the region, is fed by widespread poverty, unresolved land disputes, and other aspects of underdevelopment, all of which are exacerbated by IFI demands and the operations of the global market. In Côte d'Ivoire, for instance, growing ethnoreligious tensions have been compounded by mass unemployment, layoffs, privatization, and stagnant salaries since the imposition of structural adjustment in the mid-1980s.[159] Cocoa and coffee, which together make up 60 percent of the area under cultivation, are the mainstay of the economy. Indeed, Côte d'Ivoire is the world's largest producer of cocoa, accounting for over 40 percent of world production. Yet the end in 1999 of the country's thirty-seven-year stabilization system, under which the state marketing board guaranteed prices to exporters, has coincided with a 30 percent slump in world cocoa prices.[160] The slump was, in fact, partly a function of trade liberalization in Côte d'Ivoire, as the marketing board had previously employed a financing system that enabled sales to be phased throughout the year. When the old system was abandoned, producers sold their harvest at the same time, flooding the market and leading to predictable consequences for international prices. The collapse in cocoa prices, in turn, exacerbated social unrest in Côte d'Ivoire, as cocoa growers protested at the way in which the government had liberalized their industry.[161] World prices for coffee have also fallen precipitously—by as much as 70 percent.[162] Moreover, the share that farmers are paid accounts for a dwindling proportion of the retail price of coffee, which is currently just 7 percent per penny,[163] as value is increasingly added elsewhere in the supply chain. The collapse in coffee prices is also a function of oversupply; an increasing number of countries, advised by the IFIs to pursue export-led growth policies in areas of comparative advantage, have entered the market or expanded production.

At the same time, the conduct of the conflict itself has centered on key areas of cocoa and coffee production, as government and rebel forces have attempted to seize control of these economic assets. Both the strategic cocoa town of Daloa as well as Man, the center of Ivorian coffee production, have become key areas of contention. Similarly, San Pedro, Côte d'Ivoire's second largest port, has become a prime rebel target.[164] Not only does it represent a strategic outlet for exports to the international market, but traditionally it also has served as a key nodal point in the regionwide networks established for "illicit" arms imports.

Shifting Alliances

The West African conflict complex is characterized by a continually shifting array of military, political, and economic alliances. Taylor's backing of the RUF insurgency has been replicated throughout the region. Thus, in Liberia, LURD insurgents have been supported by the government of Guinea in response to Taylor's backing for rebel incursions into the country. In part, Guinea's support for LURD has been motivated by a desire to keep Charles Taylor tied up militarily, similar to the way in which Taylor used RUF forces in response to Sierra Leone's support for ECOMOG in Liberia. Like the RUF, LURD also appears notably bereft of an alternative political program for Liberia, other than the removal of Charles Taylor. LURD forces have also attacked and occupied mining districts in Liberia. LURD diamonds, as well as coffee and cocoa, have been sold to Guinean brokers in Conakry, to Guinean commanders in return for arms, and to dealers in Sierra Leone.[165] There are also reports of Liberian government forces conducting raids in Sierra Leone to obtain food and other goods.

In this context, it is worth noting that Liberia has accused both Britain and the United States of supplying and training LURD forces, allegations that have been denied. Nevertheless, as an ICG report has noted, the insurgency has certainly benefited from the "calculated indifference"[166] of the United States and the UK, given their perception of Taylor as the Milošević of West Africa. However, the removal of Taylor by a group with no clear political program, composed of former Liberian warlords and former RUF mercenaries, will not solve the region's problems. Essentially, the political economy that supports LURD is much the same as the economy that drove the RUF, and before them, Taylor himself. Changing the actors in the theater of conflict may change the composition, and even direction, of the regional networks that underpin conflict, but will do little to address the fundamentals of the regional political economy that promotes conflict.

Just as Guinea has supported LURD operations in Liberia, it has also been alleged that Charles Taylor has directly sponsored the MJP and MPIGO rebel groups in Côte d'Ivoire and that their attacks were planned and launched from Liberia. In particular, the River Gbeh camp of the Liberian logging company Maryland Wood-Processing Industries (MWPI), has been used as an operational center and a transit point for troops and arms. The camp has also served as a storage facility for cars and motorcycles looted from Côte d'Ivoire.[167] Global Witness has further alleged that Taylor was planning renewed insurgency in Sierra Leone, claiming that he had already established four cells in the country predominantly manned by idle young former combatants. Arms were also reportedly being smuggled into the country with weapons often offloaded at sea onto small boats that then ferry them into a Sierra Leone port.[168]

The Arms Trade

Although Liberia has been under a UN arms embargo since 1992, and while members of the Economic Community of West African States (ECOWAS) have committed themselves to a moratorium on the import, export, and manufacture of light weapons,[169] the region nevertheless remains awash with small arms and light weapons.[170] The embargo on Liberia certainly does not appear to have had a significant impact on Charles Taylor's ability to acquire arms—either for use in his own civil war, or in wars he has successively sponsored throughout the region. As a UN Expert Panel report on Liberia noted in 2001: "Despite nine years of an embargo on arms and military equipment to Liberia, a steady supply of weapons has reached the country. Indeed, in their conversations with the Panel, the Liberian authorities appeared not bothered about the embargo and never complained about it."[171] The same report details numerous examples of sanctions busting in Liberia. For instance, in August 1999 the Singapore-based parent company of the Oriental Timber Company, a firm with significant timber operations in Liberia, arranged a U.S.$500,000 payment for an arms shipment. The infrastructure of the timber industry also supported the transfer of arms and troops, with industry-owned ships bringing in arms two to three times every month. In addition, the OTC's militia was periodically incorporated into the government's ATU forces and may even have been absorbed into the Liberian-backed rebel groups in Côte d'Ivoire.[172]

The arms trade in the region also continues to be maintained through the complex regional and global networks that are the mainstay of the shadow arms economy. An example of one arms shipment to Liberia neatly illustrates this point. A consignment of rifles was purchased from the Slovak Republic for the Ugandan military through an Egyptian arms broker with Culworth Investments Corporation, a company that has offices in Liberia. On receipt of the consignment, the Ugandans discovered that it did not conform to their specifications. An Illyushin-18, registered in Moldova but chartered by Centrafrica Airlines, a company in the Central African Republic, arrived in November 2000, supposedly to fly the weapons back to the Slovak Republic. In fact, a new purchaser, Pecos Company of Guinea, had been found. Pecos had an end-user certificate from Guinea's Ministry of Defense, but the Illyushin actually flew to Monrovia with seven tons of sealed boxes on board, which included 1,000 submachine guns. The Liberian representative on the flight was Carlos Alberto La Plaine, a Portuguese diamond dealer. Three days later the plane flew back to Uganda to pick up a second consignment of 1,250 machine guns but was impounded by the Ugandan authorities, which suspected that the plane was engaged in sanctions busting.[173]

Prospects and Recommendations

Peacebuilding efforts in Sierra Leone since the early 2000s have been a marked improvement over their predecessors in the 1990s. Distinguishing the latest peace process is the newfound willingness of the international community to make a sustained commitment, at least over the medium term, in the form of a robust UN peacekeeping force, increased funding, and broader international action on conflict diamonds. Potential peace spoilers have not—at least not yet—been able to regroup. However, the current generation of peacebuilding initiatives also exhibits some familiar flaws, particularly in the area of DDR, that render uncertain Sierra Leone's potential to develop a political economy of peace that can be sustained beyond the planned drawdown of UNAMSIL (currently projected to be cut from its peak of 18,000 troops to roughly 5,000 by the end of 2004).[174]

This uncertainty is magnified by the conflicts in Liberia and Côte d'Ivoire, both of which are at risk of spilling back into the country. In addition, IFI development policies echo the failed solutions of the 1990s. Then as now, local politicians have been adept at exploiting neoliberal reforms for their own political and economic benefit. Indeed, external initiatives to deal with corruption appear to have been simply incorporated as another mechanism of punishment and patronage available to Sierra Leone's leaders. Again, there is a risk of resurgent corruption, state decay, and widespread popular alienation.

While the international community has committed substantial funds to Sierra Leone, such resources have not always been applied appropriately. The reintegration of demobilized combatants, for instance, has been undermined by delays in funding. Furthermore, although the introduction of a domestic certification scheme has increased the value of diamonds exported through the official system, local and international initiatives have not succeeded in curtailing the trade in illicit diamonds. In fact, current developments in the shadow diamond and arms economies of the region underscore the way in which flexible shadow networks are able to adapt to, and exploit, a new regulatory geography. In the case of both the shadow diamond and arms economies, ineffective regional controls are exacerbated by global control initiatives that are notable for the lack of rigor applied to their implementation and enforcement. Thus there are a number of key lessons for future policy that can be derived from Sierra Leone's experience, some of them depressingly familiar.

Resourcing the Peace

At a general level, the importance of early and consistent engagement backed up with sufficient funds and manpower is perhaps a cliché, but is no less relevant for peacebuilding in Sierra Leone than elsewhere. One of the challenges for academics and policymakers is to make the case that the U.S.$2 billion spent on peacebuilding in Sierra Leone is not only worthwhile, but actually a relatively cheap investment when compared with the funds spent, for instance, on more conventional national security projects such as the B-2 stealth bomber or the war on Afghanistan. Of course it might be argued that these examples represent core national security issues whereas Sierra Leone does not. However, building peace in Sierra Leone has implications not only for stability in the whole of West Africa, but also for the global stability of various commercial sectors (e.g., diamonds, coffee, cocoa). Preventing a recurrence of state collapse in Sierra Leone also helps address the broader actual and perceived threats to security in the "zones of peace." For instance, underdevelopment and state failure can produce permissive conditions for the spread of AIDS, the movement of refugees, and the growth of terrorism, or as in Sierra Leone's case, the exploitation (albeit incidental) of shadow networks to facilitate terrorist financing.

Adopting a Consistent Regional Approach to Regulating Conflict Trade

The experience of Sierra Leone also demonstrates the need to understand the regional dynamics of conflict. International inattention to the conflict there, which was compounded by its representation as an arena of anarchy, inhibited both a proper appreciation of the regional factors underpinning the conflict, and perhaps more important, appropriate action to address them. Since the turn of the twenty-first century, peacebuilders have taken some steps in this direction. The UN, for instance, has imposed diamond and arms embargoes on the RUF and Liberia. It has also created a West Africa office in Dakar and appointed a Special Representative of the Secretary-General to head the office. Furthermore, in 1998 ECOWAS states signed a moratorium on the export and import of light weapons and in 1999 adopted an ECOWAS security mechanism. This latter includes a call for improved cooperation in early warning, conflict prevention, peacekeeping operations, cross-border crime, and trafficking in small arms. As part of this process four zonal observation bureaus for gathering political, economic, and social information have been proposed for the Gambia, Benin, Liberia, and Burkina Faso.[175] In addition, Guinea, Liberia, and Sierra Leone have agreed to restart the Mano River Union to facilitate cooperation on economic affairs and security, including the deployment of security units along common borders.[176]

There are, however, several loopholes in the UN diamond and arms embargoes and the ECOWAS moratorium. First, both suffer from lax implementation, both within the region and beyond it. Partly this is a function of the acute security dilemmas that actors in the region face and that condition the effectiveness of intraregional initiatives. But it is also a function of weak regional capacity for monitoring arms and diamond embargoes. Support for the development of civil radars to better track the regional airspace and better funding for the ECOWAS secretariat to oversee the moratorium would help address such issues. To be effective, UN embargoes on arms or diamonds need funding for monitors on the ground and a greater willingness among all member states to punish sanctions busters. Otherwise, sanctions will remain acts of symbolism. Better enforcement of UN arms and commodity embargoes also requires more stringent global regulatory frameworks that set standards for all firms to follow, and that result in real punishment when caught. As noted in Chapter 6, severe financial punishments are levied against states and firms that offend the precepts of neoliberalism, yet the enforcement mechanisms on arms and conflict goods such as diamonds are largely tokenistic.

Second, in May 2003 the UN belatedly extended sanctions to incorporate the Liberian timber industry (initially for a ten-month period effective starting July 7, 2003),[177] thus attempting to address the role of the industry in the provision of funds and the infrastructure for the movement of arms and troops. However, as with the current embargoes on arms and diamonds, this is unlikely to be effective unless measures are also taken to address the potential for the current networks to adapt and mutate in response. This would certainly require enforcement at the regional level and, in the longer term, the development of a global system to prevent the trade in conflict timber—albeit one with more teeth than the current certification system for rough diamonds.

Making Development Aid Conflict Sensitive

It is now fashionable to argue for donor and IFI initiatives to take into account their role in and impact on peacebuilding. The efforts to incorporate a conflict lens in development initiatives are both conceptually and operationally nascent, and their effectiveness remains untested. As the trajectory of Sierra Leone's descent into conflict illustrates, the economic prescriptions of the IFIs have been counterproductive at best. Their emphasis on macroeconomic stability, privatization, and withdrawal of the state from economic management contributed to new forms of corruption and patrimonialism, an upsurge of popular discontent, and a corrosion of state legitimacy and capacity that left the country vulnerable to armed insurgency. This is not to suggest that alternative development policies are not problematic. Indeed, as elsewhere, peacebuilding in Sierra Leone essentially presents policymakers with a paradox.[178] Bypassing or reducing the state undermines its effectiveness and legitimacy, while creating opportunities for the capture of economic life by local strongmen allied to networks of patronage. Conversely, however, expanding the capacity and reinforcing the authority of the state runs the risk that it will be captured by dominant elites and used as an instrument of private gain rather than a vehicle for the maximization of public wealth. Nevertheless, while securing peace often requires the determined engagement of outside actors, sustaining it requires local ownership of the processes of peacebuilding. While donors often pay lip service to this principle, it is rarely reflected in practice. A more successful strategy of external engagement, then, is almost the reverse of current practice; it is one in which external actors make a credible and long-term commitment in funds and troops that ensures an effective security guarantee to the state and to domestic society groups, but where the minutiae of economic governance are owned by domestic actors. Indeed, if anything, the emphasis on controlling inflation and establishing macroeconomic stability needs to give way to a greater emphasis on the importance of job creation and institution building, in Sierra Leone as in other postconflict countries.[179] A good model in this respect might be the initiatives in Sierra Leone aimed at improving the effectiveness of budget-setting and parliamentary oversight.[180] In sum, there is a need to go "back to the future" and to bring both the state and Keynesian policies into peacebuilding.

Promoting Regional Cooperation

There are several opportunities for external actors to promote regional cooperation that may more effectively address the challenges of peacebuilding in Sierra Leone and neighboring countries. Rather than gradually drawing down UNAMSIL's troop strength as peace in Sierra Leone slowly takes hold, it may be more appropriate to transform it into a regional peace operation. Perhaps more important, however, the experience of Sierra Leone points to the need for donors and IFIs to plan policy responses in relation to *regional* conflict dynamics. Initiatives that seek to promote economic recovery and build peace in Sierra Leone, but inadvertently facilitate dynamics that promote conflict elsewhere in the region, merely enhance the risk of conflict being reimported into Sierra Leone. The most obvious example is the studied neglect by the United States and the UK of the threat posed by the LURD insurgency in neighboring Liberia.

IFIs in particular need to adopt a more explicitly regional approach to policies that affect regional trade and commerce. For instance, in the diamond trade, part of the problem of smuggling relates to the different tax and regulatory practices employed in different countries. Efforts to harmonize policies across the region would not only avoid the dangers of a race to the regulatory bottom through "beggar thy neighbor" competition, but would also reduce at least some of the incentives for participation in the shadow diamond economy. Over the longer term, the establishment of regional diamond cutting and polishing centers might address the current inability of these countries to add value to their diamond exports, and may help develop a more skilled and better-paid work force, while offering a cooperative mechanism for states in the region to overcome their present security dilemmas—rather as the European Coal and Steel Community did in Europe after World War II.

A further challenge in need of a regional response is the proliferation of mercenaries. While mercenaries are a global problem, as reflected in the 1989 UN Convention on Mercenaries, West Africa has suffered particularly from the prevalence of mercenaries. Much has been made of the positive role played by the mercenary company Executive Outcomes in Sierra Leone's conflict.[181] However, Executive Outcomes' role was at best ambivalent. Moreover, West Africa's primary mercenary problem does not come from external corporate mercenary groups, but rather from indigenous mercenaries from across the region that have fueled a succession of conflicts. Mercenarism is an intrinsic part of the West African security dilemma, and initiatives to address this issue could represent a further element in the building block of strategies necessary to move to a regional political economy of peace. An effective solution, however, will require more than the empty rhetoric of a regional agreement. One option worth exploring is the creation of regionwide targeted programs—that is, initiatives not necessarily connected to standard DDR programs for combatants of specific conflicts—for the demobilization and alternative employment of former mercenaries, with effective monitoring mechanisms to ensure implementation. Of course, the necessary corollary of any regionwide approach is a clearer commitment on the part of the international community to ensure the security of both the people and the governments of legitimate regimes. Without such guaranteed protection, the incentive for weak governments to resort to privatized security forces in the face of threats to regime survival will remain.

Another innovative approach to addressing the West African regional conflict complex might be to move away from a diplomatic approach that emphasizes the negotiation of separate peace agreements for each state. Although more difficult to effect, a diplomacy that acknowledges the way in which the various conflicts and threats across the region are interconnected and pursues concurrent negotiations as part of a regionwide peace process is worth attempting. This could include interlocking domestic and regional agreements on the cessation of specific conflicts, on arms control, and on the regulation of conflict goods such as timber and diamonds. Such an approach would require the support and sponsorship of the international community. Indeed, an essential element of shifting the regional political economy from war to peace would be a renegotiation of the global system of trade that perpetuates inequalities related to resources such as diamonds, cocoa, coffee, and timber and that reinforces underdevelopment and social tensions in the region. In some sense, this sort of arrangement would combine elements of the regional approach to peacemaking that has been undertaken in the Democratic Republic of Congo with aspects of the trade reforms forwarded under the New Partnership for African Development (NEPAD). What it would of necessity have to avoid, though, is becoming yet another vehicle for the reflexive extension of the kind of neoliberal prescriptions that contributed to conflict in Sierra Leone in the first place.

Promoting Holistic and Flexible Peacebuilding Strategies

While the above recommendations relate mainly to strategies that might best be adopted in support of regional cooperation, the capacities of the actors responsible for supporting such peacebuilding initiatives are also important. There is a need for holistic and flexible forms of intervention, and a willingness to conceive of altering programs and targets, not as an embarrassing admission of failure but as an integral element of a strategy of adaptation to, and engagement with, changing conditions on the ground. One of the key lessons of the prolonged conflict in Sierra Leone and elsewhere in the wider region is the way in which local and regional combatants and war entrepreneurs have constantly adapted to shifting opportunities in the security and regulatory environments. Indeed, the networks that sustain war and survive into peace display a robust ability to ignore borders and rapidly mutate in response to changing circumstances. In comparison, peacebuilding interventions are conducted primarily by international agencies that are hampered by cumbersome bureaucracies, political infighting, and often functional or geographic restrictions of their mandates. As Bruce Jones has noted, in Sierra Leone a year of collective efforts to produce a strategic framework to coordinate the peacebuilding efforts of outside actors produced little more than a general statement of existing coordination problems and an exhortation for better links between political, development, and humanitarian actors. Indeed, at one point Sierra Leone was graced with four distinct UN coordination structures, "none of which bore any formal or substantive relationship to the others."[182] External agencies also tend to operate with fixed targets that are difficult to shift once set. The question of who generally wins in such an environment—the external agencies or the local criminal and warlord networks—is, in American slang, a "no-brainer."

Given the realities of international bureaucracy, the prospect of greater flexibility and coherence within and among the organizations' efforts are probably slim. An alternative may be to support the development of nongovernmental regional monitoring groups with a mandate to track arms and shadow diamond shipments to and from the region. The success of existing NGOs such as Global Witness in uncovering such flows suggests that properly funded regional monitoring groups may at least be able to introduce greater transparency on such issues. There is of course a risk that such groups would simply duplicate the work of organizations like Global Witness. There is also a risk that local governments would suborn local groups. However, formally linking them to a wider global network of NGO monitoring groups could both ensure a complementarity of objectives and provide them with external support and protection for their work.

Finally, the contention that failed states such as Sierra Leone present either breeding grounds for terrorism or anarchic spaces in which terrorists can hide, operate, and raise funds needs to be interrogated. In Sierra Leone's case, this thesis has taken the form of apparent Al-Qaida links to the trade in conflict diamonds. In the paradigm of the liberal peace, terrorism is being cast as another element of "the virus of disorder" in the developing world, which threatens the developed world. For this reason, it bears reminding that transnational terrorists groups such as Al-Qaida operate in strong states in the developed world too, and seem equally adept at exploiting the freedoms that come with development and democracy as they are at exploiting the chaos of war-torn states. It would be unfortunate, therefore, if in the light of September 11, 2001, underdevelopment were to be not only securitized as it has been in the liberal peace paradigm, but also subordinated to the priorities of national military security for Western donors. Doing so would risk engendering a "September 11" version of common Cold War practice, in which the nature and recipients of donor support are determined by supplicants' willingness not only to sign up to neoliberalism but also to endorse the geostrategic priorities of powerful donors. In effect, this would push the requirements of effective peacebuilding even further down the agenda of donors than they are now. The need is not for more aid in the name of the donor's national security but for more aid targeted at effective local peacebuilding.

Conclusion

Sierra Leone's descent into conflict cannot be adequately understood as a manifestation of a nihilistic "new barbarism." Nor should it be seen solely as a function of a greed-based warlordism that stands outside the "normal" political economy of the state, the region, or indeed the globalized world. Sierra Leone's conflict was certainly spurred and exacerbated by a process of top-down corruption mediated through patronage networks in which the country's resources were used as levers to buy loyalty amid shifting points of conflict and collaboration between local and regional actors. However, it is also the case that the shadow economy that preceded the conflict, and that was subsequently adapted to service conflict, was a function of bottom-up structural incentives to engage in shadow trade. In part, these incentives were shaped by chronic poverty and underdevelopment, but they were also a function of the way in which differential regulatory practices across the region created shadow spaces for power and profit that a combination of regional kinship and other networks were able to exploit. In the course of the conflict, regional shadow trading networks became thoroughly integrated into the "illicit" global economy.

In addition, explanations of conflict in Sierra Leone that construe it as some variant of elite or social pathology, explicable only by reference to its inexplicability, neatly serve to obscure the destabilizing impact of the neoliberal prescriptions demanded by external creditors, both in the onset of conflict and in the struggle to emerge from it. As described in this chapter, the effect was not the introduction of an efficient and prosperous market economy, as envisaged by creditors, but the further erosion of state capacity and legitimacy under IFI sanction. At worst, the IFIs became agents to the conflict. At best, they were accidental anarchists.

The early years of Sierra Leone's conflict were marked by a reluctance on the part of the international community to properly engage with the crisis. In this context, aid and humanitarian intervention represented a substitute for more effective and sustained engagement. The lack of robust policy action was also reflected in the unwillingness to fund peace efforts adequately and in the delay in meaningful action on the issue of conflict diamonds. The lack of international concern reached its apotheosis in the Faustian bargain that was the Lomé peace agreement, when donors pressured the Sierra Leone government to sue for peace with a patently unpacific RUF in an effort to secure peace on the cheap.

To the extent that peacebuilding efforts in the early 2000s have been marked by a more sustained and more substantial commitment, some of the errors of past policy have been rectified. However, the continued application of the neoliberal model, and the failure to recognize the ways in which local actors are able to adapt the mechanisms of liberal peace to suit their own agendas, raise serious questions about the sustainability of both peace and development in Sierra Leone. Moreover, while there has now been some belated acknowledgment of the regional dimensions of the conflict in Sierra Leone, they have still not been sufficiently understood and, crucially, the mechanisms to address them remain underdeveloped.

Notes

1. John L. Hirsch, *Sierra Leone: Diamonds and the Struggle for Democracy,* International Peace Academy Occasional Paper Series (Boulder, CO: Lynne Rienner, 2001), p. 31.

2. Adekeye Adebajo, *Building Peace in West Africa: Liberia, Sierra Leone, and Guinea-Bissau,* International Peace Academy Occasional Paper Series (Boulder, CO: Lynne Rienner, 2002), p. 82.

3. Originally a guild of hunters among the Mende people in the southeast of the country, these were mobilized and expanded to defend villages during the civil war. They became the main element in the country's civil defense force.

4. Adebajo, *Building Peace in West Africa,* p. 85.

5. International Crisis Group (ICG), *Sierra Leone: Time for a New Military and Political Strategy,* ICG Africa Report no. 28 (Freetown: ICG, April 11, 2001), p. 11.

6. UNSC Resolution 1132 of October 8, 1997.

7. By UNSC Resolution 1181 of July 13, 1998.

8. Hirsch, *Sierra Leone.*

9. UNSC Resolution 1270 of October 22, 1999.

10. Adekeye Adebajo and Chris Landsberg, "Back to the Future: UN Peacekeeping in Africa," *International Peacekeeping* 7, no. 4 (Winter 2000): 177.

11. Hans-Henrik Holm, "Failing Failed States: Who Forgets the Forgotten?" *Security Dialogue* 33, no. 4 (December 2002): 457–471.

12. Ibid.

13. "In the Line of Fire," *The Guardian* (London), May 15, 2000, cited in Paul Williams, "Fighting for Freetown: British Military Intervention in Sierra Leone," *Contemporary Security Policy* (Special Issue: "Dimensions of Western Military Intervention") 22, no. 3 (December 2001): 157.

14. Rhiannon Vickers, "Labour's Search for a Third Way in Foreign Policy," in Richard Little and Mark Wickham Jones, eds., *New Labour's Foreign Policy: A New Moral Crusade?* (Manchester: Manchester University Press, 2000), p. 40.

15. Robert Kaplan, "The Coming Anarchy," *Atlantic Monthly,* February 1994, p. 48.

16. Robert Cooper, "Why We Still Need Empires," *The Observer,* April 7, 2002.

17. William Shawcross, *Deliver Us from Evil: Warlords and Peacekeepers in a World of Endless Conflict* (London: Bloomsbury, 2000), pp. 169–178; Kofi Annan, "Africa: The Horror," *Washington Post,* August 1, 1999; Jon Swain, "The Making of a Monster," *Sunday Times,* May 21, 2000.

18. John MacKinlay, *Globalisation and Insurgency,* Adelphi Paper no. 352 (Oxford: Oxford University Press for the International Institute of Strategic Studies, 2002).

19. For instance, see Ibrahim Abdullah and Patrick Muana, "The Revolutionary United Front of Sierra Leone: A Revolt of the Lumpenproletariat," in Christopher Clapham, ed., *African Guerrilla* (Oxford: James Currey, 1998), pp. 172–193.

20. Ibid.

21. Lord William Wallace, comments at an Economic and Social Research Council seminar, Sheffield, 2002.

22. Thomas Dempsey, "Warlords and Diamonds: Disarming Rebel Groups in Liberia and Sierra Leone," paper presented at the International Studies Association (ISA) conference, New Orleans, March 24–27, 2002.

23. Kaplan, "The Coming Anarchy."

24. Comfort Ero, Waheguru Pal Singh Sidhu, and Augustine Toure, *Towards a Pax West Africana: Building Peace in a Troubled Sub-Region*, report on IPA-ECOWAS, September 27–29, 2001, Abuja Seminar (New York: International Peace Academy, 2001), p. 6.

25. Cooper, "Why We Still Need Empires."

26. Mark Duffield, *Global Governance and the New Wars: The Merging of Development and Security* (London: Zed Books, 2001).

27. Mark Pythian, "Intelligence and the Illicit Arms Trade: Problem or Solution?" paper presented at the British International Studies Association conference, LSE, London, December 16–18, 2002, p. 9; "Hewitt Links World Poverty with Terror," *The Guardian* (London), February 1, 2003.

28. "Poor and Corrupt but World Players for a Day," *The Guardian* (London), February 1, 2003.

29. Duffield, *Global Governance and the New Wars,* pp. 130–140.

30. David Keen, *The Economic Functions of Violence in Civil Wars,* Adelphi Paper no. 320 (Oxford: Oxford University Press for the International Institute of Strategic Studies, 1998), p. 11.

31. Joanna Spear, "The Security Sector: The Political Economy of Private Military Security—The Case of Sierra Leone," paper presented at the British International Studies Association (BISA) conference, LSE, London, December 16–18, 2002, p. 13.

32. Paul Richards, *Fighting for the Rain Forest: War, Youth, and Resources in Sierra Leone* (London: James Currey, 1996); Alfred B. Zack-William, "Sierra Leone: The Political Economy of Civil War, 1991–1998," *Third World Quarterly* 20, no. 1 (1999): 143–162; Woodrow Wilson International Center for Scholars and the International Peace Academy, *The Economics of War: The Intersection of Need, Creed, and Greed,* conference report (New York: Woodrow Wilson International Center for Scholars, 2002), pp. 13–17.

33. Spear, "The Security Sector," p. 14.

34. William Reno, "Resources and the Future of Violent Conflict in Sierra Leone," paper presented at the British International Studies Association (BISA) conference, LSE, London, December 16–18, 2002, pp. 2–3.

35. Abiodun Alao, "Diamonds Are Forever . . . But So Also Are Controversies: Diamonds and the Actors in Sierra Leone's Civil War," *Civil Wars* 2, no. 3 (Autumn 1999): 43–64.

36. Comfort Ero, *Sierra Leone's Security Complex,* Security and Development Group Working Paper no. 3 (London: Centre for Defence Studies, June 2000), p. 19.

37. Dena Montague, "The Business of War and the Prospects for Peace in Sierra Leone," *Brown Journal of World Affairs* 9, no. 1 (Spring 2002): 229–238.

38. Kate Meagher, "Informal Integration or Economic Subversion? Parallel Trade in West Africa," in Réal Lavergne, ed., *Regional Integration and Cooperation in West Africa* (Trenton, NJ: Africa World Press with the International Development Research Center, Ottawa, 1997), pp. 165–187.

39. Ibid., p. 175.

40. Ian Smillie, Lansana Gberie, and Ralph Hazleton, *The Heart of the Matter: Sierra Leone, Diamonds, and Human Security* (Ottawa: Partnership Africa Canada, 2000), p. 40.

41. Ibid.

42. Lansana Gberie, *War and Peace in Sierra Leone: Diamonds, Corruption, and the Lebanese Connection*, Occasional Paper no. 6 (Ottawa: Partnership Africa Canada, November 2002), p. 7.

43. Smillie, Gberie, and Hazleton, *Heart of the Matter*, p. 43.

44. Ibid., p. 39.

45. Gberie, *War and Peace in Sierra Leone*, p. 10.

46. Smillie, Gberie, and Hazleton, *Heart of the Matter*, p. 5.

47. Ibid., p. 40.

48. John Williams, Donald Sutherland, Kimberley Cartwright, and Martin Byrnes, *Sierra Leone: Diamond Policy Study*, January 2002, p. 120, www.dfid.gov.uk.

49. Ibid., p. 44.

50. Ibid., p. 49.

51. Ibid., p. 50.

52. Smillie, Gberie, and Hazleton, *Heart of the Matter*, p. 5; Williams et al., *Sierra Leone*, p. 121.

53. William Reno, "Clandestine Economies, Violence, and States in Africa," *Journal of International Affairs* 53, no. 2 (Spring 2000): 433–460.

54. Adebajo, *Building Peace in West Africa*, pp. 47–48.

55. Keen, *Economic Functions of Violence in Civil Wars*, p. 30.

56. Adekeye Adebajo, "Liberia: A Warlord's Peace," in Stephen John Stedman, Donald Rothchild, and Elizabeth M. Cousens, eds., *Ending Civil Wars: The Implementation of Peace Agreements* (Boulder, CO: Lynne Rienner, 2002); Adebajo, *Building Peace in West Africa*, p. 46.

57. ICG, *Sierra Leone*, p. 14; Abiodun Alao and Funmi Olonisakin, "Economic Fragility and Political Fluidity: Explaining Natural Resources and Conflicts," *International Peacekeeping* 7, no. 4 (Winter 2000): 29.

58. Herbert Howe, "Lessons of Liberia: ECOMOG and Regional Peacekeeping," *International Security* 21, no. 3 (1996): 149.

59. Abdel-Fatah Musah, "Privatization of Security, Arms Proliferation, and the Process of State Collapse in Africa," *Development and Change* (Special Issue: "State Failure, Collapse, and Reconstruction") 33, no. 5 (November 2002): 926.

60. Mats Berdal and David Keen, "Violence and Economic Agendas in Civil Wars: Some Policy Implications for Outside Intervention," *Millennium: Journal of International Studies* 26, no. 3 (1997): 801.

61. United Nations, *Report of the Panel of Experts Appointed Pursuant to UN Security Council Resolution 1306 (2000), Paragraph 19, in Relation to Sierra Leone*, S/2000/1195, December 20, 2000, p. 13, par. 71.

62. William Reno, *Warlord Politics and African States* (Boulder, CO: Lynne Rienner, 1999), p. 124.

63. United Nations, *Report of the Panel of Experts Appointed Pursuant to UN Security Council Resolution 1306 (2000), Paragraph 19, in Relation to Sierra Leone,* p. 12, par. 70.

64. Ibid., p. 14, par. 80.

65. Ibid., p. 15, par. 38.

66. Gberie, *War and Peace in Sierra Leone,* p. 14.

67. "Bin Laden's $20m African 'Blood Diamond' Deals," *The Observer,* October 20, 2002.

68. Gberie, *War and Peace in Sierra Leone,* p. 14.

69. United Nations, *Report of the Panel of Experts Appointed Pursuant to Security Council Resolution 1343 (2001), Paragraph 19, Concerning Liberia,* S/2001/1015, October 26, 2001, pp. 84–91.

70. United Nations, *Report of the Panel of Experts Appointed Pursuant to UN Security Council Resolution 1306 (2000), Paragraph 19, in Relation to Sierra Leone,* p. 14, par. 79; Small Arms Survey, *Small Arms Survey 2002: Counting the Human Cost* (Oxford: Oxford University Press, 2002), tab. 3.10, p. 142.

71. Reno, *Warlord Politics and African States,* p. 127.

72. United Nations, *Report of the Panel of Experts Appointed Pursuant to UN Security Council Resolution 1306 (2000), Paragraph 19, in Relation to Sierra Leone,* p. 36, pars. 184–186.

73. Ibid., pp. 39–41, pars. 204–212.

74. Musah, "Privatization of Security," p. 927.

75. United Nations, *Report of the Panel of Experts Appointed Pursuant to UN Security Council Resolution 1306 (2000), Paragraph 19, in Relation to Sierra Leone,* p. 39, pars. 200–202.

76. For instance, in August 1999 the Liberian government signed an agreement exempting the Liberian-based Exotic Tropical Timber Enterprise from all due taxes related to its timber operations as a way of repaying a U.S.$2 million debt to the company. Although the agreement did not state how the debt had been incurred, it is notable that the chairman of the company was Leonid Minin, the purported head of the Ukrainian mafia and a notorious arms trafficker. See Global Witness, *Taylor-Made: The Pivotal Role of Liberia's Forests in Regional Conflict,* September 2001, pp. 9–10, www.globalwitness.org.

77. Global Witness, *The Role of Liberia's Logging Industry on National and Regional Insecurity: Briefing to the UN Security Council by Global Witness,* January 2001, www.globalwitness.org.

78. Global Witness, *The Usual Suspects: Liberia's Weapons and Mercenaries in Côte d'Ivoire and Sierra Leone—Why It's Still Possible, How It Works, and How to Break the Trend,* March 2003, pp. 16–18, www.globalwitness.org.

79. Abdel-Fatau Musah, "A Country Under Siege: State Decay and Corporate Military Intervention in Sierra Leone," in Abdel-Fatau Musah and J. 'Kayode Fayemi, eds., *Mercenaries: An African Security Dilemma* (London: Pluto Press, 2000), p. 86.

80. Lotta Hagman (rapporteur), *Security and Development in Sierra Leone,* International Peace Academy Workshop Report (New York: International Peace Academy, undated), p. 4.

81. World Bank, *Transitional Support Strategy for the Republic of Sierra Leone*, March 3, 2002, p. 13, www-wds.worldbank.org/servlet.

82. This was initiated in 1996 by the World Bank and the IMF and is designed to bring the debt of the poorest countries down to sustainable levels as a reward for implementation of appropriate macroeconomic reforms.

83. United Nations, *United Nations Interagency Appeal for Relief and Recovery: Sierra Leone 2003* (New York: United Nations, 2003), p. 10.

84. ICG, *Sierra Leone*, p. 11.

85. Adebajo, *Building Peace in West Africa*, p. 102.

86. Shawcross, *Deliver Us from Evil*, p. 172.

87. Adebajo, *Building Peace in West Africa*, p. 94.

88. Major-General Vijay Kumar Jetley, "Report on the Crisis in Sierra Leone," www.sierra-leone.org.

89. Harriet Hentges and Jean-Marc Coicaud, "The Dividends of Peace: The Economics of Peacekeeping," *Journal of International Affairs* 55, no. 2 (Spring 2002): 355–356.

90. Rita Abrahamsen, "Development Policy and the Democratic Peace in Sub-Saharan Africa," *Journal of Conflict, Security, and Development* 1, no. 3 (2001): 89.

91. Williams et al., *Sierra Leone*, p. 47.

92. Reno, "Resources and the Future of Violent Conflict," p. 11.

93. Adebajo, *Building Peace in West Africa*, p. 81.

94. World Bank, *Transitional Support Strategy*, p. 1.

95. Reno, "Resources and the Future of Violent Conflict," p. 12.

96. Rita Abrahamsen, "Development Policy and the Democratic Peace in Sub-Saharan Africa," *Journal of Conflict, Security and Development* 1, no. 3 (2001): 89–90.

97. Reno, "Resources and the Future of Violent Conflict," p. 13.

98. United Nations, *United Nations Conference on the Least Developed Countries: Country Presentation by the Government of Sierra Leone* (Geneva: United Nations, 1990), p. 3.

99. Ibid., p. 2.

100. Ibid., p. 4.

101. Abrahamson, "Development Policy and the Democratic Peace," p. 89.

102. IMF, "IMF Approves Augmented ESAF Loan for Sierra Leone," Press Release no. 95/68, December 18, 1995.

103. World Bank Country Brief, www.worldbank.org/afr/sl2.htm.

104. David J. Francis, *The Politics of Economic Regionalism: Sierra Leone in ECOWAS* (Aldershot: Ashgate, 2001), p. 80.

105. David Keen, "Incentives and Disincentives for Violence," in Mats Berdal and David M. Malone, *Greed and Grievance: Economic Agendas in Civil Wars*, International Peace Academy Occasional Paper Series (Boulder, CO: Lynne Rienner, 2000), p. 74.

106. Ibid.

107. IMF, "IMF Approves Augmented ESAF Loan."

108. World Bank Country Brief, www.worldbank.org/afr/sl2.htm.

109. Reno, *Warlord Politics and African States*, p. 133.

110. Marina Ottaway, "Rebuilding State Institutions in Collapsed States," *Development and Change* (Special Issue: "State Failure, Collapse, and Reconstruction") 33, no. 5 (November 2002): 1008.

111. Neil Cooper and Michael Pugh, *Security-Sector Transformation in Post-Conflict Societies,* Conflict, Security, and Development Group Working Paper no. 5 (London: Centre for Defence Studies, 2002), p. 39.

112. IMF, "IMF Completes Review Under Sierra Leone's PRGF Arrangement and Approves $25 Million Disbursement," Newsbrief no. 02/97, September 19, 2002.

113. World Bank, *Transitional Support Strategy,* p. 8.

114. Ibid., p. 9.

115. Anti-Corruption Commission 1991, www.sierra-leone.org/accreport.html.

116. ICG, *Sierra Leone After Elections: Politics as Usual,* ICG Africa Report no. 49 (Freetown: ICG, July 12, 2002), p. 3.

117. ICG, *Sierra Leone: Managing Uncertainty,* ICG Africa Report no. 35 (Freetown: ICG, October 24, 2001), p. 11.

118. Ibid.

119. Greg Campbell, *Blood Diamonds: Tracing the Deadly Path of the World's Most Precious Stones* (Boulder, CO: Westview Press, 2002), p. 207.

120. Gberie, *War and Peace in Sierra Leone,* p. 19.

121. "Corruption and Governance," speech by Clare Short, UK secretary of state for international development, at the British Council Auditorium, Freetown, February 27, 2002.

122. ICG, *Sierra Leone After Elections,* p. 16.

123. Testimony by John Prendergast before House International Relations Committee, Africa Subcommittee, www.intl-crisis-group.org/projects.

124. Reno, *Warlord Politics and African States,* p. 126.

125. ICG, *Sierra Leone After Elections,* p. 17.

126. Eric G. Berman, *Re-Armament in Sierra Leone: One Year After the Lomé Peace Agreement,* Small Arms Survey Occasional Paper no. 1 (Geneva: Small Arms Survey, 2000).

127. Major-General Vijay Jetley, "Report on the Crisis in Sierra Leone," May 2000, www.sierra-leone.org/jetley0500.html; William Reno, "War and the Failure of Peacekeeping in Sierra Leone," in Stockholm International Peace Research Institute, *SIPRI Yearbook 2001: Armaments, Disarmament, and International Security* (Oxford: Oxford University Press, 2001), p. 158.

128. Global Witness, *A Rough Trade: The Role of Companies and Governments in the Angolan Conflict,* December 1998, www.globalwitness.org/campaigns/diamonds/reports.php.

129. Foreign and Commonwealth Office (FCO), "Cook Welcomes UN Diamond Embargo on Sierra Leone," press release, July 6, 2000, www.fco.gov.uk/news.

130. Williams et al., *Sierra Leone,* p. 64.

131. Ibid., p. 91; Gberie, *War and Peace in Sierra Leone,* p. 7.

132. United Nations, *Report of the Panel of Experts Pursuant to Security Council Resolution 1343 (2001), Paragraph 19, Concerning Liberia,* p. 83.

133. Gberie, *War and Peace in Sierra Leone,* p. 6.

134. United Nations, *Report of the Panel of Experts Appointed Pursuant to Security Council Resolution 1395 (2002), Paragraph 4, in Relation to Liberia,* S/2002/470, April 19, 2002, p. 23, pars. 102–104.

135. United Nations, *Report of the Panel of Experts Appointed Pursuant to Security Council Resolution 1343 (2001), Paragraph 19, Concerning Liberia,* p. 80, pars. 370–371.

136. ICG, *Sierra Leone: Managing Uncertainty,* p. 4.

137. Gberie, *War and Peace in Sierra Leone,* p. 9.

138. Global Witness, *The Usual Suspects,* p. 17.

139. Ibid., p. 8.

140. Ibid., p. 9.

141. United Nations, *Report of the Panel of Experts Appointed Pursuant to Security Council Resolution 1395 (2002), Paragraph 4, in Relation to Liberia,* p. 27, par. 123.

142. Global Witness, *The Usual Suspects,* p. 37.

143. Gberie, *War and Peace in Sierra Leone,* p. 8.

144. Global Witness, *The Usual Suspects,* p. 38.

145. Ibid.

146. Gberie, *War and Peace in Sierra Leone,* p. 8.

147. United Nations, *Report of the Panel of Experts Appointed Pursuant to Security Council Resolution 1343 (2001), Paragraph 19, Concerning Liberia,* p. 78, par. 361.

148. United Nations, *Report of the Panel of Experts Appointed Pursuant to Security Council Resolution 1395 (2002), Paragraph 4, in Relation to Liberia,* p. 12, par. 39.

149. Global Witness, *The Usual Suspects,* p. 15.

150. Ibid., p. 7.

151. "Liberian Fighters Enter Ivory Coast War," Associated Press, February 20, 2002.

152. "British Mercenaries Find a New Ferocity in Ivory Coast," *The Guardian* (London), February 22, 2003.

153. ICG, *Liberia: Unravelling,* ICG Africa Briefing (Freetown: ICG, August 19, 2002), p. 6.

154. ICG, *Sierra Leone: Managing Uncertainty,* p. 4.

155. Hagman, *Security and Development in Sierra Leone,* p. 5.

156. ICG, *Sierra Leone: Managing Uncertainty,* p. 5.

157. United Nations, *Sixteenth Report of the Secretary General on the United Nations Mission in Sierra Leone,* S/2002/1417, December 24, 2002, par. 19.

158. Ibid.

159. West Africa Network for Peace-Building, *Crisis in Côte d'Ivoire,* WARN Policy Brief, November 6, 2002, p. 2, www.wanep.org/aboutwanep.htm.

160. See website of the Institute for Security Studies, www.iss.co.za.

161. Oxfam, *Rigged Rules and Double Standards: Trade, Globalisation, and the Fight Against Poverty* (Oxford: Oxfam, 2002), p. 165.

162. Ibid., p. 13.

163. Oxfam, *Bitter Coffee: How the Poor Are Paying for the Slump in Coffee Prices,* Oxfam International Background Briefing, May 2001 (Oxford: Oxfam, 2001), www.oxfam.org.uk/policy/papers/coffee.htm.

164. West Africa Network for Peace-Building, *Côte d'Ivoire Crisis,* WANEP Policy Briefs Update, December 3, 2002, www.wanep.org/wanep_policy_briefs_ update.htm.

165. United Nations, *Report of the Panel of Experts Appointed Pursuant to Security Council Resolution 1343 (2001), Paragraph 19, Concerning Liberia,* p. 30, par. 127, and p. 79, par. 363.

166. Testimony by John Prendergast, p. 5.

167. Global Witness, *The Usual Suspects,* p. 31.

168. Ibid., p. 33.

169. Joseph P. Smalldone, "Mali and the West African Light Weapons Moratorium," in Jeffrey Boutwell and Michael T. Klare, eds., *Light Weapons and Civil Conflict: Controlling the Tools of Violence* (Lanham, MD: Rowman & Littlefield, 1999), pp. 129–145.

170. Ero, Sidhu, and Toure, *Towards Pax West Africana,* pp. 23–24.

171. United Nations, *Report of the Panel of Experts Appointed Pursuant to Security Council Resolution 1343 (2001), Paragraph 19, Concerning Liberia,* p. 36, par. 159.

172. Global Witness, *The Usual Suspects.*

173. Ibid., pp. 39–42.

174. United Nations, *Seventeenth Report of the Secretary General on the United Nations Mission in Sierra Leone,* S/2003/321, March 17, 2003, pp. 2–3, pars. 10–14.

175. Ero, Sidhu, and Toure, *Towards a Pax West Africana,* p. 16.

176. United Nations, *Report of the Panel of Experts Appointed Pursuant to Security Council Resolution 1343 (2001), Paragraph 19, Concerning Liberia,* p. 32, pars. 135–140.

177. House of Commons, *Official Report,* May 21, 2003, col. 794W, www. parliament.uk/about_commons/about_commons.cfm.

178. Reno, "Resources and the Future of Violent Conflict," p. 18.

179. Susan L. Woodward, *Economic Priorities for Peace Implementation,* IPA Policy Paper Series on Peace Implementation (New York: International Peace Academy, October 2002).

180. ICG, *Sierra Leone After Elections,* p. 16.

181. See, for instance, David Shearer, *Private Armies and Military Intervention,* Adelphi Paper no. 316 (Oxford: Oxford University Press for the International Institute of Strategic Studies), pp. 49–55.

182. Bruce D. Jones, "The Challenges of Strategic Coordination," in Stedman, Rothchild, and Cousens, *Ending Civil Wars,* p. 107.

5

Bosnia and Herzegovina in Southeast Europe

Mobilization of grass roots support for change [is] still lacking.
World Bank report, October 2002

There is no evidence that liberalization in BiH has been to the detriment of the poor.
Poverty Reduction Strategy Paper, draft,
Sarajevo, December 2002

As one of the first major peacebuilding experiments of the post–Cold War period, the experience of Bosnia and Herzegovina (BiH) has been notable mainly for its difficulties, especially regarding efforts to address the political economy and regional and transnational dimensions of the conflicts and their legacies. At the end of the war in 1995, little thought was being given in international policymaking circles to the political economy of armed conflict, and perhaps even less to the opportunities and challenges posed by the tendencies of conflicts to spill over state boundaries. Moreover, unlike in Afghanistan and Sierra Leone, BiH had no lootable natural resource endowments, but rather fixed assets (such as industrial and hydroelectric power plants) as well as low-value extractive resources (such as softwood and coal). Thus the economy of this conflict complex depended less on shipping out domestic assets than on exploiting cross-territory military support and consumer shortages, and on trafficking throughout the region. War entrepreneurs with vested interests in controlling routes and flows counted upon territorial fragmentation, besieged towns, and externally imposed sanctions to increase their economic leverage. Subsequently,

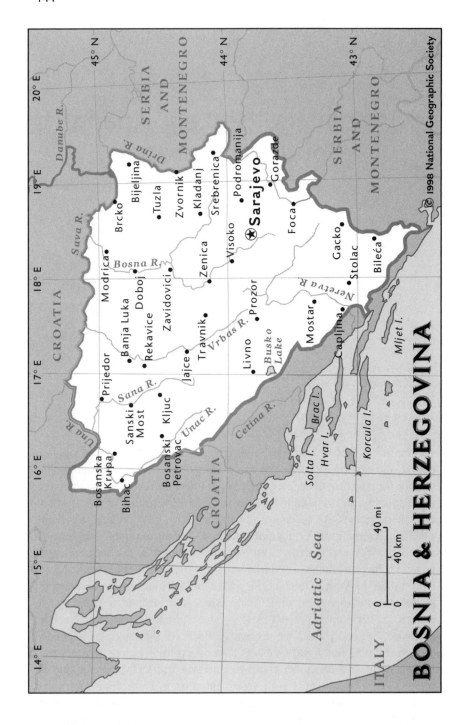

BOSNIA & HERZEGOVINA

the policies of postconflict transformation failed to counter the economic interests of these entrepreneurs in maintaining a weak, fragmented state. Further, the neoliberal economic policies that accompanied the peacebuilding efforts there offered entrepreneurs further opportunities to capitalize on state weakness.

The importance of regional dynamics in the European context is also significant. In the words of Wolfgang Petritsch, then High Representative of the Peace Implementation Council, "Bosnia and Herzegovina is a European project."[1] Unlike the other cases, the former Yugoslavia had known economic integration, experiments in industrial democracy and nascent sectors of postindustrial activity and wealth. Its geographical position has also meant that it has greater strategic priority for NATO and Western Europe. The region (defined as the former Yugoslavia and Albania) may be on the periphery of the European capitalist core, but by global standards it participates in post-Fordist, nonsubsistence economic activity and is significantly more networked into global exchange and information than West Africa or Central Asia.

While the challenges of transformation from a war to a peace economy in and around BiH may seem overstated when compared to other war-torn states, significant problems remain. On the one hand, widespread violence has faded, elections and other democratic processes are well under way, displaced persons are moving back to their homes, reconstruction has made significant headway, the worst of shortages have been surmounted, and a degree of normality in everyday life is evident to the casual observer. Although the area shares some of the impoverishment of underdeveloped countries, the average life expectancy at birth between 1995 and 2001 was officially claimed to be seventy-three years,[2] school attendance is high, and basic nutritional standards are being met. The 2001 Human Development Index placed BiH between Iran and Jordan, at about the world average.

On the other hand, however, the transformation has been attenuated and wartime regional shadow economies have become institutionalized. As a consequence of war, destruction, and dislocation, and also the diminution of the formal economy, a great many people remain impoverished and vulnerable, especially the elderly, the unemployed, the low and infrequently paid employed, farmers, and those in social and educational services. After seven years of peacebuilding by outsiders, the BiH economy in 2002 produced only half its prewar per capita gross domestic product (GDP). By comparison, after World War II, and in conditions of international isolation, it took less than five years to reach prewar levels of GDP. The World Bank calculates that a return to prewar levels, originally predicted for 2002, is now likely to be achieved in 2010 *only if economic reform is rapidly implemented,*[3] an injunction, it will be argued, that is likely to aggravate the situation. Poverty is said to be deeper here than in any other country in the region, despite the infusion of considerable external financial assistance.[4] Social dislocation, political corruption, and economic stagnation pervade the country's political economy. How and why has transformation failed in these respects? The chapter is structured around the following broad arguments:

• Narratives of the war in BiH, as constructed by the media and politicians, focused largely on ethnic hatreds and failed to factor in the struggles for economic control. This had profound implications for the manner in which external actors attempted to resolve the crisis. In the peace process and the implementation of the Dayton Accord, cartographies of ethnic space eclipsed a considered analysis of the economic challenges that needed to be addressed, other than assuming the superiority of free market rigor.

• Economic warfare began before, and continued during, the outbreak of active hostilities. The economic crisis that struck Yugoslavia in the 1980s unleashed the conditions for unregulated self-help, predation, and the untrammeled exploitation of resources and markets that helped to keep the war going.

• The economic structures, processes, and attitudes of wartime survived into the "liberal peace." War entrepreneurs adapted well to the post-Dayton period and have fostered networks to expand shadow spaces in conditions of peace—by trafficking in goods and people, for example. Not only did the actions of international agencies legitimize the nationalists' capture of political power through "democratic" elections, but their economic policies and activities also presented opportunities for further wealth creation among the winners.

• Elements of economic transformation have been dysfunctional. In particular, in the absence of sustainable growth, aid dependency has persisted. The imposition of macroeconomic stability through monetarism has denied local ownership over the formal economy as well as depressed growth and purchasing power. A reliance on privatization, deregulation of the market, and foreign direct investment to stimulate growth has not produced the anticipated sustainable development.

• The shadow economy flourishes in part because it is a coping mechanism, one made all the more attractive by the impact of neoliberal restructuring, that increases employment opportunities and reduces social inequalities. It is underpinned by opportunities and collaboration offered by the dominant model of global economic policy. Mafias take advantage of Dayton's political boundaries to manipulate financial premiums, but also trade unofficially across spatial boundaries regardless of political or ethnic affiliations.

• Regional economic transformation has been neglected. The direction that integration and harmonization with the European Union (EU) should take remains an unresolved issue. The Stability Pact for Southeast Europe remains weak and is largely a mechanism for coordinating donor support and fund distribution. The region is expected to develop its own pattern of integration, but domestic institutions will first need to be strengthened nationally as a precondition of regional integration.

• Alternatives to the current orthodoxy, both for BiH and Southeast Europe, are available and could include strengthening public institutions and transferring ownership over macroeconomic policy; the generation of production through import controls and government intervention to boost employment and public services; increasing purchasing power through a less restrictive fiscal regime; and developing a regional customs union that allows for mutual protection.

State Creation, Collapse, and Conflict

The role of violent conflict in the emergence of strong states in Europe has been a significant theme in historical research, particularly in the work of Charles Tilly.[5] Since the demise of Byzantine supremacy in the eleventh century, the history of the Adriatic rim of Southeast Europe (from Albania to Slovenia) has been characterized by its subjugation to imperial control, the mass movement and settlement of migrants, and in spite of prolonged periods of military activity, a resistance to building a robust state system in conformity with the Western model elucidated by Tilly. Indeed, as the Ottoman Empire declined, Albania was nursed into independence under international administration in 1913–1914. Contrary to dominant Western narratives, however, weak statism has been a permissive rather than causal factor in unrest. There were long periods when different groups in the region lived side by side and worked together within their differences.[6] The collapse of the Austro-Hungarian Empire after World War I led to the creation of a kingdom of many nationalities, the South Slav Union (Yugoslavia). This dynastic dictatorship disintegrated during World War II and Yugoslavia was subdivided during the occupation by Nazi Germany. After the liberation, led by the communist partisans under Enver Hoxa in Albania and Josip Broz (Tito) in Yugoslavia, the two countries experienced parallel fates as political systems bound mainly by national militaries, command economies, and political dictatorship.

Although Tito's Yugoslavia enjoyed a degree of economic prosperity and a nonalignment policy that facilitated Western trade, investment, and tourism, by the time of Tito's death in 1980 the country's political cohesion had begun to fragment, though not solely along nationalist lines.[7] A new constitution in 1974 created an eight-member federal presidency with a rotating chair. It decentralized almost every state function except defense and foreign policy. However, the 1974 constitution also fostered the creation of alternative power bases that challenged federal control. Confronted with a dual transition after the Cold War—to political pluralism and to capitalism—"the Yugoslav state community did not have sufficient social, political and institutional capacities at its disposal to democratically resolve the crisis."[8]

The rapid consolidation of leaders such as Milan Kučan in Slovenia, Franjo Tudjman in Croatia, and Slobodan Milošević (as defender of Serbs at a rally in Kosovo in 1987) signaled the end of federalism in Yugoslavia. In March 1989 the autonomy of Vojvodina (with its large Hungarian minority) and Kosovo (with its overwhelming Albanian majority) was revoked, causing widespread unrest in the latter province. By the beginning of 1990, Milošević had become president of Serbia; Slovenia, the most ethnically homogenous republic, had taken steps toward independence; and extremists in the Croat Democratic Union (HDZ) had gained ground in Croatia. Multiparty elections later in 1990 confirmed nationalist elements in power. In the Yugoslav federal system, BiH had been designated a republic with no nation of its own but comprising three constituent nations (Serb, Croat, and Muslim). As Yugoslavia disintegrated, they elected three nationalist leaders to a power-sharing government, with Alija Izetbegović of the (mainly Muslim) Party of Democratic Action (SDA) as president. In 1991, Macedonia declared its independence without resistance. Slovenia and Croatia (both gaining external recognition) followed suit, the former winning minor skirmishes against the Yugoslav National Army, but the latter meeting resistance and full-scale assaults. Serbs in the Krajina area of Croatia, led by the Serb Democratic Party (SDS), declared an autonomous region in response to denial of citizenship rights by the Zagreb government and began an armed struggle. In early 1992, with the BiH government threatening to pull out of the Federation too, the SDS in BiH, led by Radovan Karadžić, declared independence, as did the HDZ for the Croat statelet of Herceg-Bosna. Just as peacekeepers of the UN Protection Force (UNPROFOR) began arriving in Croatia in March 1992 to monitor (temporary) cease-fires there, violence was spreading to BiH.[9] In April of that year, the European Community recognized the independence of BiH, even as it was ceasing to exist as such.

For three and a half years, regulars, militias, and guerrilla forces fought localized but interconnected wars, frequently committing atrocities against civilians.[10] To begin with, Bosnian Serbs supported by Belgrade fought Muslims and Croats. But in 1993 the Croats, supported from Zagreb, turned on Muslim civilians in Mostar, Dalmatia, and central BiH. However, initiatives to stop fighting between Croats and Muslims came from the United States, which wanted to turn the military balance against the Serbs, from Croats in Central Bosnia who were often cut off and vulnerable to Muslim attacks, and from the Bosnian government, which wanted a unified state and replaced "Muslim" with the appellation "Bosniak." In 1994 the Washington Agreement created the Croat-Bosniak Federation, which underpinned Croat nationalist aspirations by guaranteeing a confederation between the Federation and Croatia proper. Bosnian Serbs founded their own union, the Republika Srpska (RS). Peacekeepers from UNPROFOR and the UN High Commissioner for Refugees (UNHCR) struggled to maintain a humanitarian relief supply system and to cope with the whole-sale displacement of people. The creation of UN-protected safe areas for Sarajevo and other besieged urban areas proved to be a contradiction in terms, since defending them would have cost the UN its neutrality and the member states provided only half the number of troops requested by the UN Secretary-General.[11] However, the humiliating fall of Šrebrenica and the massacre of Bosniaks by Serb forces in July 1993 as well as the attack on a marketplace in Sarajevo in February 1994 were important turning points.[12] NATO eventually became increasingly systematic in its air attacks against RS positions, and by the summer of 1995 Britain, France, and the Netherlands had sent a combat-capable rapid reaction force. The RS parliament vetoed the Vance-Owen Plan to allow for autonomous entities within a state, incurring Milošević's displeasure. In response, he announced a blockade of the Bosnian Serbs in August 1994. However, it was not until a U.S.-backed Croatian offensive against the Krajina Serbs in August 1995 produced a "hurting stalemate" that the parties agreed to the Dayton Accord of December of that year. A NATO-led Implementation Force (IFOR) was established to secure the accord and stabilize the fragmented state of BiH.

Representation of the Conflict and Its Consequences

The conflicts in the former Yugoslavia, and especially in Bosnia and Herzegovina, were predominantly portrayed as resulting from historic, centuries-old ethnic hatred. Perhaps this was unsurprising, given that "ethnic cleansing" was the dramatic and horrific manifestation of the conflict, its ghastly immediacy readily transferred into print and to screen by the media. In dominant popular and political interpretations, the bewildering descent into "savagery" was structured around what Paul Shoup called "a witch's brew of ethnic Slav nationalities."[13] Similar accounts by Robert Kaplan and Misha Glenny reportedly had a profound influence on President Bill Clinton and key personnel in his administration.[14] Observers concluded that Southeast Europe was reverting to type: intractable violence nursed by ancient ethnic cleavages. In more sophisticated accounts, the conflict was archived as a narrative of dysfunctional constitutions in which the nationalities question had remained stubbornly unresolved.[15] Other commentators admitted that Yugoslavia's ethnic and national groups had lived harmoniously for years and indeed intermarried, but contended that the shaping and manipulation of identity through the political discourse of extreme nationalism was able to mobilize groups for conflict. The fact that Tudjman and Milošević together plotted to dismember BiH illustrates the realpolitik that lay behind this manipulation.[16]

The ethnic problematization of the conflict profoundly affected the construction of external policy responses. Initially, this representation of "the Balkans," a term already synonymous with endemic instability, induced caution among external actors about getting involved and sending peacekeepers.[17] Second, it allowed extremists to determine the nature of the problem in terms of ethnicity and territory through, among others means, "hate speech" (that is, political discourse of inflammatory denigration directed at other, in this case ethnic, groups).[18] As a result, diplomatic efforts to end the war focused on constitutional arrangements and territorial subdivision that "embodied the very nexus between identity and territory on which the protagonists relied."[19] Drawing and redrawing maps became a preoccupation that squeezed nonethnic solutions out of contention. The Vance-Owen Plan of spring 1993 was a prime example, with only one of its ten proposed provinces designated as "mixed" and another (Sarajevo) admitting a degree of interethnic power-sharing. Peacemakers could not overcome the contradiction in preserving multiethnicity by dividing the country into ethnic territories and institutionalizing a weak central state (see below).[20] Moreover, the fixation with ethnic cartography provided the antagonists with an incentive to continue fighting to win more ethnic space.

Third, both the orthodox narrative of ethnic hatred and its variants—constitutional dysfunction and political manipulation—masked other factors and external responsibilities that had contributed to the trajectory of the conflicts and their regional dimensions. The political manipulation variant of the ethnicity narrative pinned responsibility almost exclusively on indigenous agency, particularly that of the Serb nationalists. In doing so, it fostered silences around the economic sources of conflict. Economic issues did not fit neatly into an analytical framework that corralled the Yugoslavs into a zone of nationalist unrest governed by political opportunists. Moreover, a political economy analysis could hardly be undertaken without some recognition of the prewar roles of the international financial institutions (IFIs), structural adjustment programs, and economic integration with the rest of Europe. So little on the economic dimensions of the conflicts entered mainstream writing about the Yugoslav wars that the deficit can be interpreted as the "systematic exclusion of economic causes that could point to the West as being part of the problem."[21] It was not that the potential for debate was absent. Several analysts, particularly within Yugoslavia or from the Yugoslav diaspora, had long been addressing political economy issues and the external influences on their structuring.[22] But beyond this, even critics of the identity/ethnicity narrative worked within the framework of identity formulation and expression.

Fourth, the ethnic conflict narrative profoundly affected the approach to peacebuilding in BiH. As Susan Woodward observes, in general terms little attention has been paid to the economic aspects of peace agreements and their implementation.[23] Economic issues typically lack the televisual drama of military security and humanitarian problems and hence fail to capture media and public attention. Unusually, IFIs were involved in shaping the peace process, promoting macroeconomic stability as a priority for BiH. But the apparent reluctance of diplomats and commentators alike to look much beyond a peace that concentrated on military security and nationality questions meant that they were ill-prepared to open a debate about economic aspects of the conflicts, let alone about the most appropriate economic policies to encourage from the outside.

As noted in Chapter 1, however, since the mid-1990s, economic variables have entered mainstream debates about regional conflict complexes. Some analysts point to localized economic rationales for the outbreak and perpetuation of war, based on opportunity and feasibility.[24] Other investigations, specifically on the political economy of Yugoslavia's disintegration, have examined the consequences of the drive on the part of the IFIs to "subordinate the Balkan peoples to global capitalism."[25] In general, however, Western commentators tended to ignore the fact that, from 1979 to 1989, Yugoslavia experienced the worst economic contraction to hit any European country since World War II.

The Economic Trajectory Toward War

Yugoslavia's integration within the global economy was instrumental in shaping the trajectory of its economic collapse prior to and during the country's dissolution. Carl-Ulrik Schierup, for example, contends that economic collapse began in the 1970s when communist and nationalist elites opted for fragmented integration into the capitalist system.[26] In Tito's last years, the formal economy entered a structural crisis as it attempted to cope with the global depression related to the Vietnam War and the oil crises.

The government sought a World Bank structural adjustment loan of U.S.$267 million in 1980 that was supposed to finance imports that would be processed for reexporting. This was accompanied by austerity measures that severely reduced domestic purchasing power.[27] With export earnings reduced because foreign markets were also in recession, and expatriate remittances static because Yugoslav workers were finding it more difficult to get work abroad, the country entered a balance of payments crisis and turned to the International Monetary Fund (IMF). The IMF agreed to postpone a U.S.$2 billion debt repayment in return for devaluation of the dinar, pricing at market rates, removal of subsidies, and a major lowering of social consumption. Paradoxically, the promotion by the IFIs of a deregulated economy required recentralization to reestablish economic discipline and secure guarantees and loan repayments. As Branka Magaš wrote at the time: "The grip which the IMF now exercises over the country's economy needed a fulcrum and found it in the increasing power of the federal state, not only over the republican and provincial centres, but also over the main levers of the economy."[28] Structural adjustment occurred just as vested interests in decentralization were consolidating power. It was the worst possible moment.[29]

The balancing of economic growth in the Federation through transfers from wealthy to poor areas was increasingly resented in the richer republics of Croatia and Slovenia.[30] Nationalist politics emerged in these wealthier areas, which the IFIs were supporting through structural adjustment to speed integration with the global economy. When structural adjustment programs were also applied in poorer areas, they began to collapse under the external demands for austerity measures.[31] Bureaucrats, politicians, and entrepreneurs now saw their role as protecting local autonomy to resist recentralization. Economic transformation in line with the dictates of capitalist integration had produced "structurally embedded economic warfare," commencing well before the physical violence.[32] The integration of party chiefs, state functionaries, and managers into the post-1974 decentralized system facilitated the "unleashing of plundering practices" by authoritarian elites, who seized the opportunities of market economics to carve up social property.[33] A prominent example, highly significant in presaging the war economy in BiH, was the collapse of Agrokomerc in Velika Kladusa, a large agricultural enterprise employing 13,000 people. In August 1987 it emerged that Agrokomerc had based its growth on false promissory notes, leaving creditors with U.S.$500 million to cover. The entire regional economy folded and about 60,000 dependents were economically marginalized.[34]

By 1985, basic industries were operating at a loss and almost half the larger enterprises had their accounts frozen because they could not service their debts: there were no funds for modernization. In 1987, Montenegro, Macedonia, and Kosovo admitted to bankruptcy. Wage cuts meant that purchasing power in Yugoslavia as a whole fell by 30 percent between 1983 and 1985. By 1990, unemployment had reached about 20 percent, and some 60 percent of the population was living at or below the poverty line.[35] A coping economy grew out of farming and small service enterprises. Corruption and black markets flourished.

At first, far from uniting ethnic groups, structural adjustment resulted in fractures that separated economic and class interests *within* ethnic groups. The ever-increasing number and strength of industrial strikes had little connection with nationality, including the miners' strike in Kosovo in February 1989, when Serbs and Albanians demonstrated together underground.[36] But by 1990, the class-based industrial unrest in Montenegro and Kosovo had merged with Serb nationalist protest. As Schierup remarks, the disintegration of institutions, together with increasing poverty, injustice, and social exclusion, stimulated authoritarian coalitions of local political elites and workers into engaging in nationalist and corporatist demands for regional autonomy.[37] Predatory regimes emerged, representing an "urge for the restoration of a strong state and paternalist protection among socially exposed population groups."[38] In the less industrialized areas, particularly, economic and social disintegration led to a strengthening of patronage bonds based on kinship and bureaucratic networks.[39] In Kosovo and the Muslim areas of Bosnia, it reinforced traditional patrimonialism (originally the *zagruda,* or clan leader, in Bosnia), in which patriarchs dominated communities and local authorities.[40]

In sum, economic stress in the region emerged from the collapse of Europe's bipolarity and Yugoslavia's unique position astride this process, and was compounded by the imposition of structural adjustment policies. Furthermore, as Xavier Bougarel argues, an essential factor in the dismemberment of BiH was the struggle for economic control from November 1990 to April 1992 as nationalists carved up the reins of economic authority.[41]

The Fuel of the War Economy

The seizure and destruction of economic resources rapidly followed the outbreak of armed conflict in April 1992. By the end of 1995, the violence in BiH had brought terrible destruction, economic dislocation, and an ethnic redistribution of assets. For BiH, it resulted in an estimated loss in direct war damage of U.S.$50–60 billion, the death of 250,000 people, the reduction of gross national product to about 25 percent of the prewar level, and the displacement of about 28 percent of the population.[42] Combatants and political elites operated "first through predatory practices to ensure control over productive resources, and then through covert and black markets to consolidate themselves."[43] As the disaggregation of the formal Yugoslav economy proceeded, so too did the consolidation of control over the shadow economy. Secessions and rebellions encouraged numerous predatory war entrepreneurs demanding a cut from smuggling. For example, the Croatian political elite, in alliance with the Italian *cosa nostra,* began wresting control over the Turkish narcotics trade from the Belgrade–Kosovo Albanian mafias.[44]

International trade sanctions imposed by the UN in 1992 contributed to the evolution of shadow economies in the region. At first imposed against all sides, Britain and the United States then specifically targeted sanctions against the Milošević regime to pressure it into stopping its support for the Bosnian Serbs, while the UN froze Yugoslav government assets in April 1993. Trade sanctions, however, could hardly be expected to work effectively against a crime-ridden economy. Milošević simply handed out licenses to cronies to supervise sanctions evasion in particular goods. Further, the effort to target the Milošević regime nurtured Serb nationalism and reinforced nationalist control over the economy and public opinion. In addition, external actors overestimated Belgrade's control over the Bosnian Serbs.[45]

Above all, sanctions fostered a thriving economy of evasion and leverage that benefited major crime syndicates and corrupt officials, and gave them every incentive to prolong both conflict and the embargo.[46] In particular, a "pax mafiosa" embracing a nonterritorial Albanian and Serb network, allowing Albanian organizations to enjoy protection in Belgrade, kept Kosovo relatively quiet until 1998 in spite of the overt repression of Albanian Kosovars. Sanctions spurred trade across the borders of Albania, Montenegro, and Kosovo, boosting incomes in the area enormously. Much of it was arranged by three luminaries from state security and secret police bureaus: Željko Ražnatović (Arkan) in Serbia, Momčilo Mandić (a member of the Karadžić government) in the RS, and Enver Hajin (murdered by a mafia rival in 1996) in Albania. About two hundred boats crossed Lake Skhoder daily in 1993–1994, with fuel-smuggling worth an estimated U.S. $1 million a day. Additionally Kosovo was a major junction on the Turkish route to ports in the Adriatic.[47] Albanian Kosovars, in collaboration with the Italian *'ndrangheta,* increasingly took control of the heroin traffic, laundering these revenues in Switzerland and financing their insurrection when the Dayton Accord failed to address their concerns. The Montenegrin capital, Podgorica, whose police chief, Vašo Bausić, was initiated into the Bari Sacra Corona Unita (Sacred United Crown of Bari), also became a safe haven for various Italian mafiosi after 1993, controlling tobacco smuggling into Italy worth U.S.$1 billion a year. One of the significant regional legacies of the Yugoslav wars, therefore, has been the embedding of Croat, Albanian, and Montenegrin-Serb trafficking corporations in the regional and European economies, among which, however, the BiH gangs remain relatively minor partners.[48]

The shadow political economies that linked Southeast Europe, and the region's ties to the global economic system, transcended both the war and the fragile peace that followed the signing of the Dayton Accord. First, the nationalist elites who had already taken the opportunities of prewar structural adjustment to control the process of dismantling social ownership plundered assets for the war effort. Economic cleansing partnered ethnic cleansing, as Bougarel notes, and reinforced the territorial carve-up.[49] Nationalist elites and the forces loyal to them began by capturing or replicating collapsed state structures, including major public industries such as Energoinvest (hydroelectricity), SIPAD (forestry), and UNIS (metals and arms). In some cases, socialist enterprises were commandeered to supply funds for the families of workers and combatants. The Zenica metal works was controlled by former communists for the benefit of the SDA. Croats took over the Mostar aluminum plant,which was then handed over to management by the HDZ. Other kinds of predatory activity included the diversion and taxation of the humanitarian aid that was sustaining an estimated 85 percent of the population.[50] In effect, the impetus to redraw community boundaries and demolish the state caused the public sphere of social and economic life to disappear. Instead, society experienced a reassertion of clientalism and patrimonialism, and the institutionalization of mafia welfare that entombed communities in a reciprocal relationship of intimidation and subsistence.

Second, the shadow economy became intricately linked with the combat economy, and these linkages continued after the peace. Indeed, the defense of Sarajevo was in the hands of gangs led by the convicts Jusuf (Juka) Prazina and Ismet Ćelo until autumn 1993, when the Bosniak professional army insisted on a crackdown.[51] While predatory gains passed their peak by spring 1994, subsistence and black market income streams developed thereafter. Serb and Croat regulars and militias received pay as well as equipment from Yugoslavia and Croatia respectively, but were also supported by local taxes and voluntary contributions. Even after the formation of the Croat-Bosniak Federation in 1994, the Herceg-Bosna "authority" levied duties on goods destined for Muslim areas and took 30 percent of the arms being supplied to the Bosnian government. Rackets multiplied and, following the price distortion of civil goods and the establishment of enclaves, black markets flourished. Saving the nation was not allowed to interfere with personal and party gain. Ideology and national identity played second fiddle to the control of economic networks, which were made both feasible by and dependent on an authoritarian political environment. Arkan's rampant Serb nationalism and butchery in Vukovar and northern Bosnia did not prevent him from giving support to Montenegrin leader Milo Đukanović, who turned against Milošević in 1997. Nor did it prevent him from being assassinated by fellow Serbs in Belgrade in 2000. Wanted by Interpol in connection with bank robberies in Western Europe, Arkan had amassed considerable wealth through criminal activities and war profiteering, including operating a black market in fuel.[52] Nationalists benefited from connections with existing networks, for example, in the state police, customs, and army in gaining key posts in the new polities. Gojko Šušak, an Ottawan businessman with army connections, became Croatia's defense minister. He also promoted nationalist projects by channeling funds through his ministry to Croat hard-liners in BiH and through his control over the mass flow of Catholic pilgrims to the shrine of Medugorje in Herceg-Bosna.[53]

Entrepreneurs such as Fikret Abdić and Arkan had prewar leverage, which they continued to exercise during and after the war. Many others were "mice" in local parlance, individuals with no previous record of racketeering, but who happened to be well placed by location or occupational position to seize opportunities to become nouveau riche. The haulage industry, especially truck driving, suddenly became a lucrative source of income as the means of distribution grew scarcer, formal accounting disappeared, smuggling was tolerated, and goods became subject to tribute when passing checkpoints. A Tuscan truck driver even became the so-called foreign minister in the Abdić enclave.[54] One of the "mice," truck driver Dinko Slezak Dika, who dealt in gold, subsequently built up a Mostar construction company reportedly worth U.S.$250 million and became part of the Jadranka Prlić group, the strongest economic and financial empire in BiH.[55] Backwater routes on the long border with Croatia in the south of Herceg-Bosna were particularly favored for smuggling and, as will be shown, subsequently remained a profitable borderland for interethnic customs-duty avoidance and money laundering.

In addition, to exact optimum gains from trafficking, the combatants and racketeers regularly cooperated across ethnic lines. For example, Croat war entrepreneurs dispatched fuel to the Bosnian Serbs in exchange for arms and ammunition supplied to the Croat Defense Council (HVO) and in return for hospital treatment and passage to safety for Croats trapped in central Bosnia.[56] Although the Croats blockaded Bosniak areas in 1993–1994, racketeers in Banja Luka and Zenica established an exchange of key goods via the summer road over Mt. Vlasić in central Bosnia—the scene of fierce fighting though the road itself was left intact. Here, too, the Serbs fired on Croat positions in exchange for lorry loads of salt from the Bosniaks,[57] while in Vareš the Serbs sold food to the Bosnian army.[58] Fikret Abdić and his Bosniak rebels imported deutschemarks with every truck convoy, collaborated with the Serb army of Krajina and General Ratko Mladić's forces, remained on good terms with Croats, and sought refuge in Zagreb when defeated by the Bosnian army. In the war for Mostar and the project to create a statelet of Herceg-Bosna, elites conducted deals while engaging in terror, and the Republika Srpska army assisted the Bosniaks in halting the Croat advance.[59] Besieged enclaves, including Sarajevo, were particularly vulnerable to profiteering. The tunnel dug under Sarajevo airport in 1993 became a lucrative business for the Bosnian First Army Corps, which controlled its access.[60] Kišeljak, located outside Sarajevo and astride key trade routes, was controlled by the Croat mafia, which did business with all sides.[61] The Sarajevo police chief accused a triethnic mafia of deliberately prolonging the siege of Sarajevo in order to profit from the black market.[62]

War termination in BiH has been attributed to the changing balance of military power, domestic political considerations (including Milošević's "betrayal" of Krajina and the Bosnian Serbs in order to protect limited gains), and the compromise of May 1994 for the 51–49 percent territorial division of BiH between the Croat-Bosniak Federation and the RS.[63] The smuggling of weapons by the United States to the Bosniaks through Tuzla airbase may have helped to change the military balance, but may also have encouraged the Bosniaks to prolong the war.[64] While such factors were certainly significant, Bougarel contends that the parties were also forced toward Dayton by inherent contradictions in prosecuting a prolonged military effort on the basis of trafficking and fragmented predatory economies. He cites, for example, tensions between regulars and paramilitaries over racketeering that weakened morale and encouraged desertions. In Banja Luka two army brigades publicly demanded the arrest of war profiteers.[65]

From Peace to "Liberal Peace"

The Dayton Accord covered a wide range of issues, but of chief relevance here are its constitutional and economic provisions, which confirmed that the price for stopping the war was to be an economically powerless central state with fragmented and overlapping authorities. An interentity boundary line separated the RS from the newly constituted Federation of Bosnia and Herzegovina (FBiH). Croat-dominated areas acted independently and were committed to re-creating the wartime statelet of Herceg-

Bosna. The eastern and western parts of the RS were joined by the narrow Posavina corridor in the north. To the north of the corridor, separated from the FBiH, were three Bosniak enclaves, one of them also separated from the others. After arbitration, the town of Brčko within the corridor became an internationally administered district, as did central Mostar. Another narrow corridor linked the FBiH to the Bosniak town of Goražde.

Each entity has its own government with control over armed forces, police, internal affairs, revenue-raising, and judiciaries. At the lower level, the RS retains municipal governments, but the FBiH has a layer of powerful cantonal government above the municipalities as well. The central state has joint functions and power-sharing with a rotating chair in a three-member presidency, a council of ministers, and a constitutional court. In addition to the provision of military security, a range of protectorate functions is performed by a welter of international agencies, overseen by the Office of the High Representative (OHR). In order to accelerate state building, the High Representative exercises special powers that include the authority to dismiss obstructive officials from their posts and to impose laws that bypass parliamentary procedures. In this way, some unitary measures have been imposed—a common currency and a currency board, car registration, common passports and citizenship laws, and a single, uniform customs territory. But the state has no independent source of income or control over macroeconomic policy. Economic transformation has to occur in a political framework reminiscent of prewar Yugoslavia: an inefficient multilayering of authority that includes about 150 ministries. To solidify and expand their wartime gains, politicians and entrepreneurs have been able to manipulate these "constitutional compromises required at Dayton to stop the war."[66]

As Schierup's analysis suggests, regional economic transformation and social change have also been contingent on a systemic adaptation by local elites to the economic strategies imposed by international actors.[67] The performance of most of the regional economies is affected not only by weak administrative infrastructures and the legacies of war, but inevitably also by the economic policies and programs of powerful external actors. Following Yugoslavia's disintegration, the new states were widely regarded as suitable cases for the application of structural adjustment policies in line with the broader vision of constructing a "liberal peace" in the region. This die was cast in BiH before the implications of such policies on regional dynamics were raised by the insurrection in Kosovo.

Since then, broader settlements—accession to the Stability Pact, integration with the European Union (EU), and membership in the World Trade Organization (WTO)—have become an integral part of the "liberal peace." This policy has been accompanied by a form of "new paternalism" or *mission civilisatrice*—in an effort to achieve radical social transformation.[68] This is not to suggest that all components of the policy have been put in place coherently and efficiently. Divergent emphases and agendas were all too evident among the international actors in BiH.[69] Nor is it to suggest that the policies of external agencies failed to adapt over time and with change of circumstance. For instance, Paddy Ashdown, who became the High Representative in 2002, appears to have been influenced by a scathing International Crisis Group report on the economy and has focused more resolutely than his predecessors on coordinating transformation to a market economy.[70] He has tackled conflict of interests among public officials through an investigation of appointees to stop those with political links from gaining a fitness certificate. In addition, in mid-2002 the OHR implemented both a "Bulldozer Strategy" to remove obstacles to business and a "Jobs and Justice Programme" as part of an economic reform agenda agreed by the BiH authorities and instituted by the IMF, the World Bank, and the EU. Job creation was declared the overriding objective, with a goal of 60,000 new private-sector jobs by the end of 2004.[71] A system of value-added tax (VAT) was also planned to unify tax collection and make fraud more difficult. At the same time, however, the means to achieve the "liberal peace" vision were becoming overstretched. The international presence began to diminish in the late 1990s. This was accompanied by shrinking donor interest in the region. Announcing that he hoped to be the last, or penultimate, High Representative, Ashdown also handed domestic elites an incentive to play a waiting game.[72]

Nowhere is the hubris and frustration of the international peacebuilding mission more evident than in BiH. Henrik Kolstrup, Resident Representative of the UN Development Programme (UNDP), expressed this when he denounced the economic situation in 2002 as "a nexus of social and economic disease, a national pathology which requires radical surgery if the patient is to be restored to health."[73] In spite of some positive economic indicators (including improved tax collection) and a successful external debt rescheduling,[74] and even allowing for the fact that official statistics underestimate economic performance—because so much activity is undeclared—the economic situation is dire without significant signs of sustainability. Ashdown provided the neoliberal diagnosis, and cure, in a nutshell:

> The economy of Bosnia and Herzegovina is in a very poor state. The absence of a fully fledged market economy, of the rule of law, of an efficient public administration, of a clear and light regulatory environment

for business and of a modern infrastructure all combine to drive away investors and exasperate entrepreneurs, who take their money elsewhere—increasingly to our competitors in the region. . . .

Things cannot go on like this. We need to transform the economy, so it becomes capable of creating jobs and generating wealth. This does not mean endless government intervention, but instead, allowing the free market to flourish. But key to a flourishing market is a stable economic environment. That is why the reforms . . . must take place against the backdrop of continued monetary stability based on the principles of the currency board, of responsibility and prudence in the management of the public finances, and on continued co-operation with the International Financial Institutions.[75]

Dysfunctional Aspects of Neoliberalism

In this section we examine the main elements of the neoliberal economic strategy that accompanied peacebuilding efforts in BiH, and their impact. In contrast to the Kolstrup/Ashdown analysis, and despite the best efforts of the external actors, it will be argued that replicating the neoliberal model and fostering regional and European integration has failed the people of BiH. This is not because elites in the shadow economy are poor entrepreneurs. On the contrary, they exhibit a sophistication that would qualify them to work on Wall Street or in the City of London, for they have adapted well to the essentials of profit seeking, asset stripping, tax avoidance, market manipulation, vertical enterprise integration, broad portfolio acquisition, and the efficient movement of financial capital. Rather, the imposition of an economic model, suspect even in advanced countries for increasing poverty, extending wealth gaps, and wrecking public services,[76] is ill suited to a poor country torn apart by war.

This is not to say that external support was not essential to help consolidate peace in the years after the Dayton Accord. However, while providing much-needed relief to the population, external support has at the same time generated dependency, partly because the conditionalities that accompanied external assistance have been inherently contradictory. On the one hand, aid has been conditional on adherence to a neoliberal strategy that does not meet social needs. On the other hand, the emphasis on counterinflationary monetarism has depressed purchasing power and economic growth in an already-impoverished society. A reliance on privatization to stimulate the economy has not produced major gains except for those local elites who were able to capture benefits from the process. Rather than building up state competence, economic deregulation and the withdrawal of the state from the economy compounds the problems of a weak central authority. Trust in foreign direct investment (FDI) to stimulate the economy is misplaced, not only because it makes little impact on growth, but also because it risks increasing volatility in production and consumption. The effort accorded to attracting private-sector investment has been inversely proportionate to the attention paid to measures that might reduce the adverse social impacts of neoliberalism. Poverty and unemployment as well as industrial and trade policy have been either neglected or treated as a kind of unavoidable collateral damage in the mission to make BiH profitable for investors.

Aid Dependency

The application of the neoliberal economic model in BiH was modified to encompass reconstruction priorities. The country assistance strategy (CAS) anticipated that reconstruction, rather than exports, would provide the motor for economic growth and recovery in the first two to three years after Dayton. Considerable attention was devoted to generating and directing external aid and cheap credit, removing obstacles to disbursement, and implementing reconstruction projects. Approximately 80 percent of the U.S.$5.1 billion in aid pledged in 1995 had been disbursed by mid-2002. In addition, the foreign presence is thought to have added a further U.S.$50–60 billion to the economy and led to an increase of about 5 percent in the size of the work force.[77]

However, economic assistance and the presence of the international community also created distortions and a persistent "dependency syndrome." First, as Susan Woodward remarks, aid has empowered certain local actors and governing authorities that the IFIs need as partners responsible for meeting loan conditions and repayments. This has also created the opportunity for those same local actors to escape ultimate responsibility for the policies that are instituted, and their effects.[78] Second, the massive international presence in BiH, as elsewhere, artificially inflated the job market, creating local "dependents" who provide labor, goods, and services. Consequently, the scaling down of the international presence has been accompanied by recession and unemployment. Third, the provision of aid has been conditional not only on compliance with the Dayton Accord, but also on adherence to three key aspects of the neoliberal agenda: monetarism, privatization, and a supportive business environment. Applied off-the-shelf from Eastern and Central Europe, these three external conditionalities, discussed in more detail below, have been key drivers of the economic transformation in BiH.

The Fetish for Macroeconomic
Stability: Impact on Growth

External assistance was conditional on maintaining macroeconomic stability, especially control of inflationary pressure. The underlying assumption was that without strict budgetary control, efficient tax collection, and structural adjustment, there would be no transition to a market-oriented economy and no extension of the IMF standby arrangement.[79] Monetarism was imposed through a currency board (the central bank) to stabilize the currency and exchange rate. This was followed by closure of the corrupt and inefficient payment bureaus, which each nationalist group had commandeered for political purposes. Their closure led to the diversion of fraudulent activities into private banks. Consolidation was introduced to reduce the number of banks, diminish state holdings in them (which fell from 59 percent in 1999 to 15 percent in mid-2002), and open them up to foreign investment. But as Dragoljub Stojanov observes, monetarism was never intended by its classical authors to apply to less developed countries, let alone countries emerging from a devastating conflict.[80] No one is suggesting that hyperinflation is beneficial, but the costs of cutting inflation to single figures in a developing economy can amount to 1–2 percent of GDP, and there is overwhelming evidence from Joseph Stiglitz and others that few, if any, gains in productivity or growth result from reducing inflation below 20 percent.[81]

Not surprisingly, monetarist policy has had adverse impacts on the BiH economy (see Table 5.1). The main manifestation of monetarism—the fixation with consolidating the financial sector and avoidance of inflation—has not been sustainable growth, but the depression of purchasing power. At a time of high unemployment, insistence on low inflation contributes to depressing potential economic growth. Growth in GDP reached 69 percent in 1996 over the estimated 1995 product, which itself, however, represented only about 25 percent of the prewar product. Further, average annual growth is predicted to fall to 4.4 percent in 2001–2005. In effect, monetarism has had a deflationary impact. For example, the high cost of borrowing (over 11 percent for business and individuals in 2002) has smothered opportunities for growth. In this respect, the shadow economy as well as the high proportion of government spending of 20–30 percent for payments to veterans and their families, although also distorting in their effects, have been a cushion against even worse distress.

Politically, the application of strict monetarist policies in BiH has precluded local ownership over macroeconomic policy and the formal economy. As a result, alternatives—such as Keynesian or state-led recovery—

Table 5.1 BiH Economic and Financial Indicators

	1990	1999	2000	2001
GDP (U.S.$ millions)	10,633	4,540	4,252	4,796[a]
GDP per Capita (current prices,				
U.S.$ millions)	2,429	1,135	1,093	1,222
FBiH		1,458	1,373	1,453
RS		821	806	873
Real GDP Growth (%) (i.e., allowing				
for inflation but not shadow activity)		9.9	5.9	5.6
FBiH		9.5	7.0	7.0
RS		11.3	2.6	1.9
Industrial Production				
FBiH		11	9	12
RS		2	6	-13
Consumer Price Index (%) at End of Year				
FBiH		-1	4.0	3.1
RS		14	12.2	5.6
Current Account Balance (U.S.$ millions)		-971	-909	-789

Source: Dragoljub Stojanov, "Poverty Reduction Strategy Paper," forum for Albania, Bosnia-Herzegovina, and the Federal Republic of Yugoslavia, Policy Notes, November 2002.

Note: a. Basic indicators for BiH in the Draft Poverty Reduction Strategy Paper revised the GDP estimate for 2001 downward to U.S.$4.5 billion.

were never an option. Macroeconomic command, including direction of the central bank, was withheld from domestic elites, who were then blamed by the external agencies for failure to implement policy.[82] It also suited the domestic politicians to hide behind the responsibility of external actors for imposing a damaging policy. Both sets of actors have exercised "responsibility evasion."

The Privatization Fix

Alongside strict fiscal and budgetary policy, the external agencies insisted that the private sector would be the main generator of growth and employment. The privatization strategy was conducted largely under the auspices of the U.S. Agency for International Development (USAID).[83] Although there were differences of emphasis among donors, including the German donor Gesellschaft für Technische Zusammenarbeit (GTZ), the UK Department for International Development (DFID), and the EU, the reification of privatization has hardly varied since 1995:

> The majority of medium-term economic growth will have to come from the extension of the service sector and the development of light industry

on the basis of private enterprises. The property now held by state firms which do not operate can be used by the private sector. What is needed here is to identify the useful parts of the state firms and to sell them through the simple and quick mechanism of privatization.[84]

Far more effort seems to be put into sweetening the business environment than employment generation or poverty reduction. For example, a postprivatization economic restructuring program sponsored by DFID, using a firm of Western consultants, offers privatized companies free diagnostics for their sluggish performance. To qualify, companies must have streamlined their employment numbers to two hundred. Whether doubts about this priority are justified or not, the implementation has been widely considered neither simple nor quick, but a disaster. By the end of 1998, only 26 of 1,600 companies in the RS and 258 of 1,600 in the Federation had prepared privatization plans.[85] By mid-2002, only 27 percent of state capital had been privatized and very few of the major strategic companies sold (raising a paltry 4.3 percent of the total value paid for in cash),[86] though about 70 percent of small and medium-sized enterprises (SMEs) in the Federation and 50 percent in the RS had been privatized. In the RS, there are 1,118 recorded enterprises. Of the 182 strategic enterprises available for open tender (veterinary stations, public utilities, heating, and power plants), only four had been sold (to Swiss, Liechtenstein, Slovak, and Lithuanian buyers) by spring 2002, with another twenty being tendered or restructured. Different systems operate for different categories of firms. One of the systems, particularly popular in the RS, was taken directly from Russia and the Czech Republic. Medium enterprises valued at over 150,000 euros in state capital were sold on the basis of vouchers for 55 percent stake, cash auction for 30 percent stake, and 5–10 percent to pension and restitution funds. The vouchers depreciated rapidly in value and were bought from poor citizens eager to raise cash by nationalist elites, who distributed some of them to their followers or used them to invest in privatized companies at full face value.[87] In consequence, the process did nothing to stimulate investment or regenerate production.

The slowness of privatization has been attributed to the lack of political and public support for a system bound to produce redundancies; the lack of legal and bureaucratic capacity and authority to deal with the issue; the early emphasis on voucher privatization and late focus on tendering; and an inability to attract foreign investors. On its own terms, therefore, the priority has not produced the returns anticipated and has not made any significant contribution to state revenues, employment, or economic growth.

Deregulation

Another main neoliberal thrust has been deregulation. Ironically, the most significant obstacle to freeing the market from protection was introduced by the Dayton Accord. Divisions between entities, the Federation cantons and the special Brčko district, made internal exchange almost a form of foreign trade as each political entity promulgated its own regulations. Nor did BiH have relevant legal, management, or accounting systems to develop a market economy. For example, foreign investors resisted purchasing the Sarajevo milk supplier Milkos because they could find no meaningful balance sheets. Obstacles to the free market have been identified as:

- Legal and bureaucratic procedures (such as laws on surveys, costs and delays affecting business registration, and the absence of commercial courts and quality controls).
- Taxation (the absence of business tax relief, employment taxes, and contributions that can account for 70 percent of a gross wage).
- Poor access to finance (high interest rates, difficulties in obtaining credits for startup projects).
- Costs of utilities (fees to utility companies, prices of telecommunications and electricity).
- The black market and shadow economy ("honest" and foreign companies cannot compete).
- Agricultural backwardness (including a lack of incentives for development and certification procedures for products for export).[88]

Accordingly, the OHR introduced the "Bulldozer Strategy" in 2002 to reduce the barriers and create a single economic space. But this is unlikely to compensate for the absence of investment in building state institutions, especially development institutions, development funds, and a responsible, accountable bureaucracy.[89] Nor will incentives for entrepreneurship protect the poor or do more than nibble at the margins of unemployment.

Striving to Rely on FDI

In the neoliberal ideology, market deregulation performs an essential function in attracting foreign direct investment, though as noted in Chapter 1, the IMF belatedly acknowledged in 2003 the detrimental effects of FDI for developing countries. In the specific case of BiH, with an estimated population of 4 million, the domestic market was small and, as a result, has struggled to attract foreign interest. In the event, FDI in BiH remained very low; only Serbia/Montenegro among the former Yugoslav territories has had a lower per capita level (see Table 5.2).

While the postwar environment and legacies of bureaucracy, corruption, and a cumbersome legal system have no doubt had an impact on deterring investment, the most significant factors that account for the relative lack of FDI in BiH are the small domestic market, the absence of domestic growth generators, low purchasing power, and limited potential for exports.

Stubborn Poverty

The peacebuilding strategy in BiH has paid little attention to the social and human consequences of the "liberal peace" vision on which it was based. Although measurement of poverty and living standards is notoriously difficult, especially in BiH where data are unreliable, the UNDP's "early warning survey" for spring 2002 suggested that poverty was widespread, serious, and rising. Some 40–49 percent in the Federation and 67–68 percent in the RS had insufficient income to cover a basic basket of consumer goods. While no groups in BiH have starved to death, one in four people in the RS survived on less than 2.5 euros a day.[90] One might reasonably

Table 5.2   Levels of Foreign Direct Investment in Southeast Europe, in euro millions

	BiH[a] (RS + FBiH)	Croatia	Slovenia	FRY (Serbia + Montenegro)	Macedonia
2001[b]	164	470	385	200	350
2000[b]	150	827	110	25	169
1999	90	1,445	144	112	27
Population (millions)	3.7 (1.4 + 2.3)	4.5	2.0	11.4 (10.6 + 0.8)	2.0
FDI (euros per million people in 2001)	44.3	104.4	192.5	17.5	175.0

Source: Information supplied by Andreas Niemann, using data from the European Bank for Reconstruction and Development, *Annual Report 2000*, excluding capital transfer for reconstruction (www.ebrd.com). The Republika Srpska Ministry of Foreign Economic Relations calculated FDI in Republika Srpska at 40.0 million KM in 1996, 61.7 million KM in 1998, 89.0 million KM in 2000, and 102.7 million KM for the first five months of 2002 (1.96 KM = 1 euro).

Notes: a. Only countrywide figures are available from international sources. Serbia and Montenegro succeeded the Federal Republic of Yugoslavia in 2002.
b. Projections/estimates.

surmise that the shadow labor market, acting as a survival mechanism, was enabling people to exist at, or just above, the general poverty level.

In response to various developmental crises, the IFIs have signaled general reforms to mitigate the harmful impacts of economic liberalization. In May 2000 the World Bank's country assistance strategy (CAS) for BiH included strengthening the social safety net. The Bank approved a credit of U.S.$14.6 million, repayable over thirty-five years, for educational development and welfare policies for the most vulnerable.[91] However, this represented only about a third of the sum committed to merely managing the privatization process.

Modification, rather than a fundamental questioning of structural adjustment, characterized the adoption of a poverty reduction strategy paper (PRSP). Supposedly driven by local conditions and requirements, and directed by local political "stakeholders," PRSPs are typically drafted at headquarters with rigid budgetary and other macroeconomic rules "distant but omnipresent."[92] There is little room for negotiation by local political elites. As such, the BiH Draft Development/Poverty Reduction Strategy of 2002 indicated that poverty reduction and employment are ancillary to the absolute necessity of enticing business and investment.[93] The only new aspects of the strategy were designed to reinforce the neoliberal agenda: convergence toward EU integration through the Agreement on Stabilization and Association, integration into the global world economic space by attracting foreign investments, and membership of the WTO. While there was reference to providing "appropriate" welfare, health, and educational systems, the PRSP contained no indication of the extent to which these sectors would be subject to market principles. Although poverty was thoroughly profiled in the main section of the report, curiously for a poverty reduction strategy the vision statement mentioned poverty only briefly and contained virtually no employment or industrial policy.

Subordinating Industry, Trade, and Unemployment

Industrial policy has been a low priority for the international agencies. Donor investment in manufacturing was a mere 2.3 percent of total Priority Reconstruction Program investment.[94] In an economy in which prewar industrial production had been highly concentrated in a dozen self-managed state companies, accounting for 35 percent of GDP,[95] their abandonment has had a disproportionate effect on the BiH economy. In the RS, industry is functioning at a third of its prewar level and aggregate reported losses in 2001 were 200 million euros.[96] The RS Directorate for Privatization believes that about one-third of all state-owned companies in the RS should go into bankruptcy and another third into liquidation, with the remainder surviving to meet most of their obligations.[97] There is no investment in the old state industries, for these are regarded as "lame ducks," too labor intensive, lacking markets, and saddled with outdated technology. Where they possessed anything of value, asset stripping has already occurred.

Under the BiH constitution, foreign trade is a federal responsibility but implementation is left to the two constituent entities. Consequently, there is no state-level institutional framework to coordinate trade policy, although, as discussed below, BiH has signed regional trade agreements and is negotiating membership of the WTO. Since it produces very little of its own fuel and manufactured consumer items, a cardinal requirement of economic integration is the stimulation of exports to pay for these imports. The country's traditional exports (timber and wood products, chemicals, processed metals, leather goods, and textiles) have generally failed to recover, in spite of the preferential status through wide tariff exemption accorded by the EU and many industrial countries. The trade deficit reached 53 percent of GDP in 1999, and although this figure subsequently declined, the value of legal imports exceeded the value of exports by four to one in 2002.[98] In January–September 2002, the export of goods and services from the Federation actually declined by 18.2 percent over the same period in 2001.[99] In part, the problem derived from price manipulation by the business cartels that control the exchange of each product. By evading tax and customs on imported goods, importers undercut local suppliers. Foodstuffs that can be grown in BiH are imported from as far away as China. Furniture manufacturers often have to reimport good-quality beechwood already sold to Italy.[100]

But the fundamental question is whether such reliance on export-led growth to satisfy market demands for cheap resources is an optimal economic strategy for an economically underdeveloped and weak state emerging from war. Membership of the WTO will at best have mixed results. The WTO enables industrialized countries to protect domestic agriculture while dumping surplus agricultural product on global markets. The rules of the Multilateral Agreement on Investment and the General Agreement on Trade in Services are designed to penalize governments that do not transfer important public services, health, education, transport, and utilities from public control to (often foreign) private companies. This elevates returns on investment above social goals. Private companies have no formal responsibility for citizen welfare or accountability mechanisms for meeting human needs—with consequences for quality and affordability.[101]

Unsurprisingly, one-third of those surveyed in BiH cited unemployment as their chief concern.[102] But employment creation had not exercised the external agencies unduly, in spite of the OHR's introduction of a "Jobs and Justice" program. To the contrary, the working assumption has been that there is excessive labor capacity and that social protection will follow market principles. This ideological rationale peddles blatant dishonesty about the choices available. According to the Economic Reform Agenda, for example: "Governments cannot create jobs. But they can create the conditions in which private enterprise can thrive and generate growth and with increased employment." Obviously, governments can and do create jobs, otherwise reforming officials would be out of work themselves, but in BiH, propaganda to the contrary has been relentless.

Employment creation came well down the list of criteria for lending by USAID in the 1990s (behind "quick start," exploitation of local raw materials, development of export potential, and exclusion of war criminals).[103] Dismissals to improve competitiveness are common and, together with new skills training, euphemistically referred to by the above-mentioned DFID consultants as "human resource change management."[104] The IMF demands "greater flexibility" in the hiring and firing of workers, and is critical of "overly generous entitlements" for maternity, employment termination, and war veterans.[105] When the Zenica steel works is privatized, half of the 2,000-member work force is expected to become redundant.[106] Moreover, although viable privatized companies may be in a better position to make redundancy payments than defunct state enterprises, they also renounce the social and welfare functions that were part of the fabric of prewar employment in Yugoslavia.

The official unemployment rate in 2002 was about 40 percent of the labor force. However, this figure is misleading because evading the registration and taxation of labor is a major industry in itself. The IMF assumes a much lower rate on the grounds that over half the unemployed work in the shadow economy, and that the true rate is a mere 17 percent.[107] Nevertheless, unemployment is still a significant drag on purchasing power and growth, and those officially employed do not necessarily get paid. The majority of the poor are employed people in families with children.[108] Although protests, strikes, and unrest are common, the *syndicats* (trade unions) lack the leverage necessary to resist or modify the neoliberal agenda. Seen as obstacles to the free market, they receive hardly any external support from donors. Paradoxically, while aligned to nationalist causes, the *syndicats* tend to be "honest" because they are not linked to the mafia.

Largely because of the hardships of war and the compounding effects of external demands for market-based restructuring, the shadow economy has no difficulty in attracting recruits. Indeed, it has played a significant role in the political economy and social transformation of postwar BiH.

Resistance in the Shadows

As we have seen, external actors approach the issue of "crime" from a legalistic perspective of capitalist regulation that delegitimizes shadow activities while simultaneously removing the state from the regulation of entrepreneurship. This paradox has enabled local elites to benefit from the externally imposed peacebuilding strategy and, in the absence of alternative means of coping or survival, to provide welfare for ordinary people. As discussed in Chapter 1, shadow economies include those economic activities that are conducted outside state-regulated frameworks and not audited by the state institutions. Further, they can be characterized as having two groups linked to each other through shadow employment, welfare, and trading: economic elites engaged in shadow trade for profit, who also exert control over the production and distribution of assets and opportunities; and elements of the general populace who participate in shadow activity as a coping or survival strategy.

Coping and Surviving in the Shadow of the Liberal Peace

Where governmental authorities have broken down, alternative shadow networks may offer alternative employment, welfare, and other means of survival. Such networks have traditionally been part of economic survival in Southeast Europe and may be considered functional and rational in conditions of economic decline.[109] Similarly, in Afghanistan, farmers and the urban poor supplement their incomes by trading or working outside legal markets.

For the majority of the populace in Southeast Europe, strategies to maintain or improve their assets include widespread moonlighting to avoid bureaucratic obstacles and financial deductions, especially taxation. Upwardly mobile young men in BiH even save to pay "entrance fees" for joining the "freemasonry" of BiH customs officials, which repays handsomely through clandestine earnings. For those living near the poverty line, whose assets are constantly threatened, barter and street selling of consumer items such as black market cigarettes and cosmetics may be essential to survival. The general populace also benefits from a U.S.-sponsored experiment in interethnic trade at the Arizona market in the Posavina corridor. Up to 25,000 people jostle on weekends to buy clandestine goods at this huge, mafia-run epitome of a "free market" that costs the government an estimated U.S.$30 million a year in lost tax revenue.[110]

In a comprehensive study of the coping and survival economies in the RS, Rajko Tomaš established that the shadow economy has had significant positive effects by increasing productivity and employment, improving the variety of goods and services, and reducing social inequalities. He estimates that it has increased RS income by more than 50 percent, and enhances "personal consumption, living standards, and overall demand." Moreover, it "also puts individuals in a position where they have to use their initiative to overcome every type of administrative obstacle . . . just to survive on the domestic and foreign markets."[111]

Moreover, in a political economy in which state institutions are weakened and many people have lost their social and economic status, neoliberalism plays into the hands of powerful elites, whose adaptation to a postconflict order is a key to understanding the shadow economy.

Elite Shadows

In BiH, elite adaptation to peace has ensured the continuation of nationalist appropriation. While military and paramilitary commandeering of spoils as part of the combat economy ended, embedded networks remained, for example, between Croat wartime militias that were controlled by soldiers and nationalists in Zagreb and Mostar. In each of the Croat and Bosniak areas of the Federation and the Serb-controlled Republika Srpska, the political organizations that took BiH into the war claimed control of resources in their ethnogeographical sectors. Not all leaders escaped retribution. Some political leaders went on trial: for example, Fikret Abdić in Croatia, and Biljana Plavšić, onetime prime minister of the RS, in The Hague. Some military and paramilitary commanders, like Željko Ražnatović (Arkan) and Jusuf (Juka) Prazina, were assassinated. But in BiH, the ruling nationalist parties extended a postwar amnesty for deserters to include "economic crimes" committed from the start of 1991 to the end of 1995, including the misuse of humanitarian aid. This immunized those politicians and wartime commanders who were otherwise vulnerable to investigation[112] and enabled thousands of others to safeguard their wartime gains and to consolidate their economic control. Command and influence in the peacetime political economy could then be exerted through clientalism, rentier fraud, corporatism, privatization processes, and continued interethnic and regional collaboration, each of which is examined below.

Clientalism. Personal and patrimonial links such as the *kum* (groom's best man) remain extremely significant as vehicles of social and economic protection and advancement. The cleric Hasan Čengić conjured funds and arms from Muslim countries and appears to have grown extremely wealthy. His control of the distribution of assets and access to economic gains has been typical of Bosniak clans that include the families of Ismet Ćelo, Alija Izetbegović, Mustafa Cerić, and Izet Hadžić.[113] Persistent clientalism also institutionalized employment discrimination against workers of other ethnic groups or who espouse political alternatives to the ruling party.[114]

Rentier fraud. Those in power can deduct rents and government revenues for their own use or for partisan gain. The main nationalist parties divided the spoils of the inefficient and costly Yugoslav payment bureaus, created in the 1950s for social bookkeeping and monopoly control over financial transactions. For example, the Bosniak payment bureau funded the election campaigns of the SDA.[115] As a huge obstacle to the development of a capital market and thus to integration into the global economy, the payment bureaus topped the "hit list" of the external donors and IFIs. But the commercial banks became just as partisan, notably the Bank of BiH, with its close links to the SDA, and the Hercegovačka Banka, with its links to the HDZ.[116] The latter was the financial tip of a political iceberg intended to create a third, Croat entity, planned in April 1999 by Franjo Tudjman and the Croat hard-line member of the BiH state presidency Ante Jelavić. Branches throughout the country were raided by the successor to IFOR, the Stabilization Force (SFOR), in April 2001, and over a million documents and 154 million convertible mark (konvertibilna mark, KM) in bank assets were seized. The Hercegovačka Banka was found to have laundered proceeds from a nationwide insurance scam and a 150 million KM oil fraud.[117] Shortly before the raid, Jelavić and other senior members of the HDZ were dismissed by the High Representative for working for Croat self-rule. Moreover, nationalist parties in the Federation controlled the cantonal financial police (subsequently absorbed into the revenue service), who were tasked with investigating corruption, money laundering, and "economic crimes." This allowed the dominant local parties to extract "revenue-raising fines" from businesses and to launch disruptive audits of opposition groups. In July 2000, Ramiz Dzaferović, director of the Federation tax authority, was removed by the High Representative for tax evasion and also for using his position to discriminate against the political opposition.[118] The head of the Elektroprivreda energy company, Edhem Bičakčić, a crony of Izetbegović, was accused of corruption long before being dismissed by the High Representative in February 2001 for diverting public funds into the SDA's coffers when he was Federation prime minister.[119]

Corporatism. What makes the shadow economy so robust in BiH is a dual corporatism: horizontal and vertical. The scale of the shadow economy is such that it could only exist through horizontal corporatism, that is, a symbiotic relationship among opportunist war entrepreneurs, organized mafia groups, and political parties in a system of mutual protection. Certainly, continuation of prewar and wartime networks among entrepreneurs, police, customs officials, and politicians shows that prohibitions against conflict of interest have counted for little in the interlocking of government and commerce. The linkage between political parties and the mafia is institutionalized and affects all political parties. Vertical corporatism signifies integrated control by political parties and entrepreneurs that link the welfare of supporters to economic empires founded on ownership of banks, hotels, casinos, and distribution, construction, and utility companies. Momčilo Mandić, one of Karadžić's wartime ministers, accumulated millions of dollars, becoming extremely rich on the proceeds of sanctions busting and also ran oil, trucking, and banking businesses afterward.[120] Mafia in the Derventa area now control lorry fleets and new petrol stations that are almost certainly a front for Karadžić and the SDS. Similarly, Jadranka Prlić (a Croat who sold oil to the Serbs during the war), became BiH foreign minister and formed business links with Niko Dodig (owner of a Medugorje-based oil company) and Marijan Primorac (a Mostar bank director). They became involved in construction projects and hotel ownership, held a monopoly in the procurement of computer equipment in Herzegovina, and acquired a holding in the Hrvatska Postanka Banka at a remarkably low price.[121]

Privatization. In their postwar mutation, war politicians and entrepreneurs may have resisted the Dayton Accord and the international agencies on political grounds, but they were also quick to exploit new economic shadow spaces created in peacetime. Among those who moved from modest circumstances to the commanding heights of economic power were Alemko Nuhanović, who owned the SAB bank that collapsed in 1998 after loans and credits made to business colleagues went unpaid,[122] and Nedim Causević, who purchased the Sarajevo Holiday Inn for approximately a tenth of its real value (though the sale was eventually annulled after investigation).[123]

There have also been opportunities for "legitimate" wealth creation among domestic elites. External support was instrumental in this regard, partly by favoring particular leaderships during the wars and partly by legitimating majority nationalists through the elections held after the wars.[124] In the economic sphere, "official" and shadow economies intersected in the distribution of state assets. Privatization was an integral component of the peacebuilding effort, but entrepreneurs and parties initially hindered the privatization drive, perceiving it as a threat to their control of the spoils. During and immediately after the war, local elites followed a "co-capitalization" model invented by the Tudjman regime in Croatia for the redistribution of government and socially owned assets.

Copied in west Mostar and other Croat municipalities, it was then adopted in Bosniak areas. Shadow boards took over enterprises prior to privatization and ensured, through contractual continuity, that existing directors would own the privatized firm. Former state enterprises were allowed to run down, any worthwhile assets were stripped, and the property sold cheaply to the shadow board in return for donations to the dominant nationalist party.[125]

From 1998 onward, elites sought to gain control of the privatization process so that they could take advantage of those donor funds that were conditional on withdrawing the state from the economy.[126] Telecommunications (including broadcasting) and energy (electricity and gas) were divided along ethnoparty lines to provide major sources of revenue for the nationalist parties and their parallel structures.[127] Paradoxically, a major privatization scandal concerning the giant Mostar aluminum plant antagonized the moderate Alliance for Change coalition, which came to power at Federation and state levels in February 2001. International executives welcomed the Alliance as an alternative to ethnonationalist politics, but then bowed to ethnic privatization. Croatia had taken over Aluminij Mostar in 1996 with an HDZ management led by Mijo Brajković. The management had it valued at U.S.$84 million, a fraction of its prewar value of U.S.$620 million, though the plant had suffered little war damage and its exports in the first year of revival reached U.S.$85 million. Brajković privatized it through a co-capitalization process, the majority of shares going to the Croat workers and management. A team of international auditors found that illegalities had occurred, but "for political and practical reasons" recommended that the ownership structure should remain undisturbed. The UK ambassador observed that the ownership structure was illegal and the company scandalously managed. Alliance politicians refused to recognize the audit and demanded that the High Representative, Wolfgang Petritsch, restore the company to the state; he claimed that he could only offer advice.[128]

Regional and interethnic collaboration. Much of the shadow economic activity in BiH has transnational and interethnic dimensions. For example, a sex industry patronized by internationals, allegedly including 30 percent of the troops stationed in Southeast Europe, is operated by gangs using the rural borderlands of Southeast Europe as holding areas for the women they traffic, before sending them on to the EU. The UN Mission in Bosnia and Herzegovina (UNMIBH) claims that only 1,000 women were trafficked through BiH. But other estimates of the number of women—mainly from the Ukraine, Moldavia, and Romania—who are trafficked through Southeast Europe as a whole and forced into the sex trade range from 175,000 to 500,000.[129] International agencies have made considerable efforts to stamp out the mafia trade in people, but collusion by local police and customs has been pervasive. It also seems likely that some of the proceeds from this and other types of trafficking filters into forms of interaction more acceptable to the international agencies.

The Croat borderlands in BiH around Stolac, Siroki Brijeg, and Herceg Novi have become a haven for transnational trafficking in drugs, cigarettes, and oil. Sometimes, Colombian cocaine arriving in Croatian ports is bartered for weapons. These borderlands have deep connections to the wartime Zagreb-Mostar military axis whose "public" goal was to break away from the FBiH. However, the extensive links that remain between this Croat network, Bosnian Serbs in Trebinje, Montenegrins, and Belgrade mafia affirm the value of interethnic and wider regional economic collaboration.[130] In Kosovo and Macedonia, the Albanian mafia has an equally powerful influence on trafficking through BiH.[131]

An important aspect of the shadow economy concerns entrepreneurs who avoid paying duties and sales tax in BiH or siphon them off to support parallel power structures. They would not be able to reap such huge profits under an international protectorate unless they possessed a sophisticated understanding of how markets work. Known sales tax fraud in the FBiH alone, from January 2001 to December 2002, cost 250 million euros, and money laundering is estimated to be worth 1.5 billion euros a year.[132] These figures do not include smuggling and customs fraud with their ancestry in wartime collaboration across ethnic divides. The undervaluation of imports in order to avoid paying customs duties costs BiH an estimated 200 million euros each year.

Two major court cases in 2002–2003 exemplified the scale of customs fraud and its interethnic dimensions. The first involved Bosniak traders based in Tuzla in the FBiH who were importing goods from Turkey, which were invoiced at 10 percent of their real value. In this instance, the documents, but not the goods, were sent to the RS customs office in Banja Luka, rather than to the Federation. The Bosniak importers paid bribes comprising a 2.5 million euro facilitation fee, plus a 5,000 euro premium for each shipment paid to authorities in Banja Luka. This meant a revenue loss to the FBiH of 15 million euros, and it is probable that these fees kept Karadžić well-funded, even though he is wanted for war crimes against the traders' compatriots.[133]

The second example involved sales tax evasion in the RS through the creation of phantom companies. The EU's Customs and Fiscal Assistance Office (CAFAO) discovered some 500 such companies, several engaged in a fuel fraud that perpetuated the wartime profiteering links between the HDZ and SDS. A small proportion of the imported fuel was unloaded legally in BiH, but invoiced to phantom companies. Most of the truck compartments were unloaded in Croatia, from which oil was smuggled into Herceg-Bosna and the rest of BiH. The proceeds were laundered at remote branches of various banks in Herceg-Bosna. Subsequently, entrepreneurs created fictitious accounts in genuine companies without these companies being aware of it. In a particularly risky variation of the fuel scam, some fuel lorries have false compartments fitted with air conditioning in which migrants transiting the region are smuggled (and allowed to smoke!).[134]

In response to the collusion of regional mafias, the UN set up a task force with Croatia and Serbia-Montenegro to detect drug and weapon smuggling, unregulated migration, and terrorism. This may be effective in limiting the role of BiH as one of Europe's prime conduits for trafficking. But a much more inclusive regional approach is necessary—bringing in Albania, Macedonia, Bulgaria, and probably Turkey—to avoid the displacement of trafficking to alternative, more northerly routes. Transnationalism in the shadow economy is, however, only one of the dynamics affecting this regional conflict complex and has been only belatedly acknowledged as a key to the sustainable transformation of Southeast Europe.

Regional Economic Transformation of Southeast Europe

Little consideration was given by the international agencies to regional peacebuilding until the Kosovo crisis broke in 1999. In fairness, the piecemeal ending of the wars in the former Yugoslavia, including the fragmentary Dayton peace agreement, was not conducive to coherent regional strategies. However, as the discussion here has highlighted, regional dimensions of the prewar, wartime, and postwar political economies are vital to understanding both the nature of the conflicts and how best to manage their legacies. Much like the conflicts of West Africa, the Yugoslav conflicts can be depicted as a matrix of localized wars that have been interlinked—as illustrated by the Kosovar Albanian irridentist incursions into Macedonia and the Presevo Valley in Serbia-Montenegro in December 2000.

Commentators have urged some kind of "New Deal" or Marshall Plan for the region. Petritsch, former High Representative in BiH and EU Special Envoy to Kosovo, argues with hindsight: "I think a comprehensive regional approach from the outset—a 'grand design' for the Balkans—

c Community began as a mutually protective
mains to this day, not least in the EU's highly
In this light, one of three paths might be fol-
st Europe: (1) insistence on the neoliberal pre-
nally before regional integration occurs; (2)
bypass regionalism in pursuit of independent
orting a protectionist model based on regional
to, but not immediately convergent with, the EU.
e in the form of a customs union could nurture
a regional market, its creation must depend on the
nstitutions to revisit the dominant economic ideol-
n in the light of economic stress in Latin America,
elsewhere in the periphery of core capitalism.

between the two prongs of Europe's approach
mid-2003. The shape of the Stability Pact for South-
rry and its promotion as a prerequisite for EU mem-
y to lead to an authentic, locally owned, regional eco-
tion, the EU Stabilization and Association Agreements
may prove divisive and undermine the prospects for
n over the medium to longer term. First, although there
ption that all countries in the region would eventually
nembership, clearly the ripest cherries (such as Slovenia)
. In addition, while reasons for this approach may include
n of a higher level of integration with the region than
prresponding processes for improving relations and extend-
 with the Mediterranean or the former Soviet Union, EU
regional economic harmony as a requirement for wider inte-
also be seen as a way of keeping the region at arm's length.

s and Recommendations

ntext of the liberal peace project, processes of globalization ham-
ibility of less developed countries to manage their own economic
ment. This is especially true of postconflict and aid-dependent
es such as BiH. Dragoljub Stojanov's diagnosis indicates that for
rmation from a war to a peace economy, from a self-managed to a
t economy, and from aid dependency to a sustainable economy, too
reliance was placed on liberalizing foreign trade and capital move-
ts (so that there is a net outflow), on the free market and privatization,
on FDI in promoting economic growth. Attempting to promote export-
growth without increasing production other than by using expensive

would have helped. . . . The only unifying idea in Bosnia and Herzegovina is indeed Europe."[135] In fact, the EU established a Consultative Task
Force (CTF) in 1998 to confer with and advise domestic interests about
measures that would harmonize BiH development and secure the return of
refugees, a particular preoccupation of EU countries. Benn Stiel and
Susan Woodward have advocated EU expansion, including admission to
the eurozone and granting special trading arrangements "without
strings."[136] But already the KM, having been originally pegged to the
deutschemark, became de facto pegged to the euro at the start of 2002, and
there was little prospect of the EU dropping conditionality. The EU is a
Lord of the Strings. Its raison d'être is to integrate through regional harmonization on EU terms, which include allowing free trade in both directions that would further harm domestic production by exposing the
region's vulnerability to competition and trade imbalances.

The Stability Pact for Southeast Europe

In the wake of the war in Kosovo, the EU proposed a Stability Pact with
the purpose of establishing a comprehensive regional platform for stability and development. It encompasses the regional states of Albania, BiH,
Bulgaria, Croatia, Hungary, Romania, Slovenia, the former Yugoslav
Republic of Macedonia (FYROM), and Turkey. Along with Canada,
Japan, Russia, the United States, IFIs, and various international organizations, these countries signed the pact in Cologne on June 10, 1999. The
EU appointed a special coordinator to promote the pledge of the signatories to cooperate on security issues, human rights and democracy, and economic reconstruction and development. Strategic stabilization and cooperation within the region were regarded as the prerequisite for integration
into Euro-Atlantic institutions. In the Zagreb Declaration of November 24,
2000, the EU, Albania, Yugoslavia, FYROM, BiH, Croatia, and Slovenia
placed European integration in the context of regional collaboration, reconciliation, and democratic development. Regional participants at the
Sarajevo summit in July 1999 had been expected to drive their own
intraregional relations. Good-neighborliness was a key issue, but so too
was macroeconomic stabilization and restructuring of the economies. For
the IFIs, the long-term prospect of European integration, if not the short-
term reality, was a form of economic discipline, an incentive and rationale to increase the pace of economic reform.[137]

There is certainly a powerful case for regional economic integration
because of the deeply embedded transborder connections that have exacerbated economic deprivation, poverty, shadow economies, and conflict.

As we suggest for West Africa, regional peace agreements would promote a holistic approach to positive peace and also avoid displacing shadow economic activity elsewhere in the vicinity. Moreover, from an economic perspective, the Stability Pact can better address the problems of the small national markets, which, with the exception of Slovenia, lack capital, have weak institutions, and struggle with chronic balance of payments deficits, high unemployment, and increasing poverty. They could pool resources and benefit from economies of scale. However, politicians in BiH seem less interested in the Stability Pact's potential to foster greater security than in its potential to compensate for the fall in external funding from other sources. They also seem concerned about its threat to national sovereignty.[138]

The extent to which regional integration will be conditioned by an insistence on the part of donors, who have promised U.S.$40 billion to the pact, on replicating the neoliberal agenda remains open to question. These funds will not go far and are liable to increase the region's foreign debt burdens because the aid would be in the form of loans.[139] The Stability Pact's mission statement specifies "creating vibrant market economies based on sound macro economic policies, markets open to greatly expanded foreign trade and private sector investment . . . developing strong capital markets and diversified ownership, including privatization."[140] Perhaps this leaves the door open for a more nuanced approach than in earlier prescriptions for neoliberal reform, but the Stability Pact lacks specific indications as to how economic growth is to be achieved. Would the members be allowed to develop protectionist and interventionist solutions to address the underemployment of resources? For some critics of current policy, if the Stability Pact requires countries to maintain currency convertibility, pegged to the euro, with anti-inflationary unemployment policies, participation in it would be a waste of time.[141]

The influence of the Stability Pact on domestic policies in the region, while still uncertain, is likely to be weak. Apart from a few exceptions, such as the Sava River Commission, an agreement between Slovenia, Yugoslavia, Croatia, and BiH at the end of 2002 to jointly manage the Sava Basin, there seems to be little substantive or strategic linkage between the goals of the pact and domestic economic programs. Other bilateral agreements on trade, for example, have been concluded outside the pact, while the reconstruction activities of the Organization for Security and Cooperation in Europe (OSCE) and UN Mission in Kosovo have been conducted without reference to the pact. Consequently, the pact remains largely a mechanism for coordinating donor support and fund distribution and, like the EU-linked Stabilization Process, makes little concession to social needs.[142]

Stabilization and As...

In parallel with the S...
region a Stabilization...
framework to harmonize...
aid program, Community...
and Stabilization (CARD...
reconstruction and refugee...
works; sustainable, market...
transnational, and regional c...
March 2000 with eighteen ke...
abolishing the payment bureau...
to be accomplished before an...
Ministry for European Integrati...
Road Map was substantially comp...
ever, takes precedence over the d...
tractually binding, requiring candi...
the thirty-one chapters of the *acq...*
Macedonia had signed up to the proc...

Herein lies the first of several tens...
mentary since each state has particular...
economic convergence. Slovenia is due...
BiH remains under international execu...
achieve a coherent regional policy when S...
region. There are few incentives for more c...
nia to assist, rather than exploit, the less co...

A second source of tension arises from t...
optimistic view, both sovereignty and intrasta...
politically potent by the sharing of sovereign...
European integration. Territorial boundaries be...
more fluid because the state is less meaningful...
way, particularly in the case of BiH. On the oth...
associated with the status of borders and entities...
ous status of Kosovo, constitutionally part of Se...
autonomous international protectorate, is a potential...
flict that could prevent and disrupt regional relat...
neoliberal agenda is not working domestically, there...
doubt that it would work regionally. Restructuring is in...
process that takes several years to surmount before ne...
are likely to work, with privatization a long and expensi...

As the origins of the EU model demonstrate, integrati...
sible in conditions of economic expansion and growth. Th...

foreign and domestic capital was equally problematic.[143] Two key determinants of economic sustainability were either simply not considered or consciously ruled out on a mixture of practical and ideological grounds: (1) building institutions with funding made available for recurrent spending; and (2) generating production and bolstering purchasing power. The role of the state and its institutions, as well as its industrial, labor, and social policies, have been neglected relative to making the country safe for private investors.[144] If the neoliberal development paradigm had been fully implemented, it would have produced an even leaner state. BiH would have been among the poorest countries that on average spend on government only about half the proportion of GDP that is spent by EU states.[145] What lessons may be drawn from this analysis?

Strengthening Institutions

Deciding the economic model for a devastated country, before building its institutions, has put the cart before the horse. As Woodward argues, donors are more willing to fund reconstruction projects than public institutions and political structures, or to provide core and recurrent budgets in public services.[146] In practice, more than eight years after the signing of the Dayton peace accord, BiH still lacked the power to formulate and implement independent monetary, fiscal, price, and foreign-exchange-rate policies, and policies regarding privatization, incomes, and social welfare.[147]

Integrating Economic Policies into Peace Processes

The experience of BiH suggests that the isolation of economic policies for reconstruction from peace processes simply does not work. As commentators have suggested, economic regeneration and peace processes have been nurtured as if children of different families.[148] Placing privatization in the hands of the ideologically driven agency USAID not only proved to be a farce, with the United States suspending the process in spring 2000, but was also divorced from other elements of peacebuilding—even from the OHR's remit to reform the economy. Above all, policies of economic revival need to be integrated with the needs of the population as a whole and not driven by the ideological fixations of outsiders. In 2002, BiH was in the unenviable situation of having imposed from outside another transfixed High Representative, Paddy Ashdown, a former Royal Marine shipped in to complete a Thatcherite revolution that he had vigorously opposed in his own country. At the very least, external agents need to undertake sui generis economic impact assessments based on a range of options that include Keynesian pump-priming and dirigisme.

Creating Social Capital

Even without a subvention on the scale of a Marshall Plan, a form of recovery strategy that boosts production and purchasing power is necessary to create social capital. Making borrowing less expensive and keeping price inflation to a 20 percent maximum would have provided a necessary stimulus to consumption, savings, and domestic investment. In the orthodox canon, minimal rates of tax and a dramatic lowering of duties on goods would be expected to stimulate investment and diminish the black market. But the poor do not pay tax, nor do they rely on the state to fund social benefits, as few government revenues are earmarked for this purpose. In these conditions, curtailing shadow economic activities and the livelihoods they provide would also hurt the poor. More effective would be a lowering of the employment tax to stimulate registered employment and thereby spread the tax burden among more people and maintain state income. Development based on a fiscal policy that stimulates borrowing to build production capacity, strict government control of imports while liberalizing those vital for processing and trade, and devaluing the currency only to the point that it allowed a competitive exchange rate would offer an alternative route to growth, as Stojanov suggests.

In this respect, transforming the decrepit state industries represents a particularly difficult problem. No one contemplates putting them all back on a permanent, state-managed antebellum footing: such a solution would no longer be possible, even if it had been an option in 1996. However, not all state-owned enterprises are lost causes, especially those in the timber, mineral, and aluminum production sectors. Blanket insistence on denying the state the opportunity to make them productive and competitive, in whole or in part, and to develop an industrial strategy, has almost certainly resulted in lost production and reduced employment and purchasing power.

Substituting the Shadow Economy

Controls over the shadow economy need to be linked to policies that address the reasons why it is functional. It is essential to acknowledge the distinctions in the shadow economy between the entrepreneurial activities closely linked to mafia-scale operations and the coping/survival mechanisms among the general populace, and to recognize the extent to which the poor depend on the shadow economy. In the absence of social safety nets, unregulated economic activity and shadow markets are essential coping mechanisms. The dog of neoliberalism continues to chase its tail of "crime" because control measures are asymmetrical, criminalizing shadow economies while leaving economic authorities free to legalize policies that engender social and economic strain on vulnerable populations. An emphasis on crime control ignores the role of free markets in weakening social cohesion and political authority, in removing social safety nets, and in providing opportunities for corruption. Particularly in postconflict contexts, regional political economies are unlikely to emancipate the populations from clientalism and mafia welfare without providing for social needs through government employment creation and social spending.

Fostering Regional Reconstruction

The long-neglected regional dimension of postconflict reconstruction might be addressed through the formation of a regionwide payments and customs union. As with the original European Payments Union and the European Community after World War II, this would concede that mutual protection to replace national protection is a reasonable starting point, rather than aiming to engineer the integration of uncompetitive war-torn economies on the basis of complete free trade. A regional payments and customs union could work toward the abolition of import duties between the members but maintain common tariffs, though gradually lowered, against selected imports for a period of, say, ten to fifteen years against nonmembers. Proceeds from the collection of the latter could be distributed among the members on an equitable basis with a portion retained centrally to finance the union's budget. The arrangement should be compatible with separate fiscal, exchange-rate, and currency systems, and be accompanied by the retention of nontariff barriers to protect particularly sensitive sectors such as agriculture.

It can be argued that a customs union would have to pitch external tariffs at a sufficiently high level to protect the least-efficient producers. Nonetheless, in combination with currency devaluation and a production policy to subsidize sectors that will grow as demand rises, such an arrangement could also make it easier to manage the demise of ailing industries. Losses from trade diversion on account of the external tariff would be relatively small because the members of any southeast Europe union have economies, with the possible exception of Slovenia's, that are significantly different from the EU's and those of other core capitalist areas, while not being so different within the union as to discourage mutual cooperation. The overall effect would be to foster production using currently underemployed resources, expand the size of the local market, offer economies of scale and intraregional specialization, foster competition in a relatively equitable context (the members falling within a narrow range of development stages), and increase bargaining power in dealing with other economies. Most significant would be the salutary impact on borderlands, which would cease to be no-go areas for governments, but would gain from "licensed" industrial location in proximity to neighboring markets.[149]

Reconceptualizing the Economic Space

A more radical departure could be to reconceptualize the economic space in Southeast Europe to take advantage of opportunities that arise from globalization processes. A conventional, state-bounded political economy is supposed to forge a spatial connection between people and economy in pursuit of national goals, determining a country's status in international trade.[150] However, maintaining this is problematic where civil war has created contradictory structures, substate identities have developed, and economic doctrine proposes global markets and a borderless consumer world driven by the imperatives of the liberal peace.[151] Yet, globalizing dynamics are accompanied by radical economic restructuring freed from territorial concerns, as evidenced by offshore economies, tax-free havens, flags of convenience in shipping, telecoms, data-inputting, service centers, and software design. Local and regional economic communities cease to be embedded in national economic space, instead linking and competing with economic communities in other states.[152] Delinkage from a national political economy, clearly evident in the shadow economy of BiH, fosters the creation of new internal boundaries. But the emergence of new political configurations from regional conflict complexes, in which the social and economic dynamics of war do not tally with past models of state-making, may also engender new opportunities.[153] Export-processing and free trade zones now account for a quarter of the world's manufacturing (mostly assembly plants for components made elsewhere).[154] Clearly this type of integration requires the cultivation of sophisticated management, banking capacity, and servicing skills, requisites that have not been apparent to the external agencies in their strategic thinking. BiH as an entrepôt and free trade zone might, however, become part of its sustainable future.

Conclusion

The dynamics of postconflict transformation create reactions and resistances, whether dialectical or elliptical and fragmentary. Any economic model is liable to have flaws; the important thing is to acknowledge and deal with them. In general, however, external agencies have neglected the negative effects of imitation and disregarded the inapplicability of the neoliberal model to war-torn states.[155] The model of reconstruction intro-

economies. Most significant would be the salutary impact on borderlands, which would cease to be no-go areas for governments, but would gain from "licensed" industrial location in proximity to neighboring markets.[149]

Reconceptualizing the Economic Space

A more radical departure could be to reconceptualize the economic space in Southeast Europe to take advantage of opportunities that arise from globalization processes. A conventional, state-bounded political economy is supposed to forge a spatial connection between people and economy in pursuit of national goals, determining a country's status in international trade.[150] However, maintaining this is problematic where civil war has created contradictory structures, substate identities have developed, and economic doctrine proposes global markets and a borderless consumer world driven by the imperatives of the liberal peace.[151] Yet, globalizing dynamics are accompanied by radical economic restructuring freed from territorial concerns, as evidenced by offshore economies, tax-free havens, flags of convenience in shipping, telecoms, data-inputting, service centers, and software design. Local and regional economic communities cease to be embedded in national economic space, instead linking and competing with economic communities in other states.[152] Delinkage from a national political economy, clearly evident in the shadow economy of BiH, fosters the creation of new internal boundaries. But the emergence of new political configurations from regional conflict complexes, in which the social and economic dynamics of war do not tally with past models of state-making, may also engender new opportunities.[153] Export-processing and free trade zones now account for a quarter of the world's manufacturing (mostly assembly plants for components made elsewhere).[154] Clearly this type of integration requires the cultivation of sophisticated management, banking capacity, and servicing skills, requisites that have not been apparent to the external agencies in their strategic thinking. BiH as an entrepôt and free trade zone might, however, become part of its sustainable future.

Conclusion

The dynamics of postconflict transformation create reactions and resistances, whether dialectical or elliptical and fragmentary. Any economic model is liable to have flaws; the important thing is to acknowledge and deal with them. In general, however, external agencies have neglected the negative effects of imitation and disregarded the inapplicability of the neoliberal model to war-torn states.[155] The model of reconstruction intro-

economies while leaving economic authorities free to legalize policies that engender social and economic strain on vulnerable populations. An emphasis on crime control ignores the role of free markets in weakening social cohesion and political authority, in removing social safety nets, and in providing opportunities for corruption. Particularly in postconflict contexts, regional political economies are unlikely to emancipate the populations from clientalism and mafia welfare without providing for social needs through government employment creation and social spending.

Fostering Regional Reconstruction

The long-neglected regional dimension of postconflict reconstruction might be addressed through the formation of a regionwide payments and customs union. As with the original European Payments Union and the European Community after World War II, this would concede that mutual protection to replace national protection is a reasonable starting point, rather than aiming to engineer the integration of uncompetitive war-torn economies on the basis of complete free trade. A regional payments and customs union could work toward the abolition of import duties between the members but maintain common tariffs, though gradually lowered, against selected imports for a period of, say, ten to fifteen years against nonmembers. Proceeds from the collection of the latter could be distributed among the members on an equitable basis with a portion retained centrally to finance the union's budget. The arrangement should be compatible with separate fiscal, exchange-rate, and currency systems, and be accompanied by the retention of nontariff barriers to protect particularly sensitive sectors such as agriculture.

It can be argued that a customs union would have to pitch external tariffs at a sufficiently high level to protect the least-efficient producers. Nonetheless, in combination with currency devaluation and a production policy to subsidize sectors that will grow as demand rises, such an arrangement could also make it easier to manage the demise of ailing industries. Losses from trade diversion on account of the external tariff would be relatively small because the members of any southeast Europe union have economies, with the possible exception of Slovenia's, that are significantly different from the EU's and those of other core capitalist areas, while not being so different within the union as to discourage mutual cooperation. The overall effect would be to foster production using currently underemployed resources, expand the size of the local market, offer economies of scale and intraregional specialization, foster competition in a relatively equitable context (the members falling within a narrow range of development stages), and increase bargaining power in dealing with other

Creating Social Capital

Even without a subvention on the scale of a Marshall Plan, a form of recovery strategy that boosts production and purchasing power is necessary to create social capital. Making borrowing less expensive and keeping price inflation to a 20 percent maximum would have provided a necessary stimulus to consumption, savings, and domestic investment. In the orthodox canon, minimal rates of tax and a dramatic lowering of duties on goods would be expected to stimulate investment and diminish the black market. But the poor do not pay tax, nor do they rely on the state to fund social benefits, as few government revenues are earmarked for this purpose. In these conditions, curtailing shadow economic activities and the livelihoods they provide would also hurt the poor. More effective would be a lowering of the employment tax to stimulate registered employment and thereby spread the tax burden among more people and maintain state income. Development based on a fiscal policy that stimulates borrowing to build production capacity, strict government control of imports while liberalizing those vital for processing and trade, and devaluing the currency only to the point that it allowed a competitive exchange rate would offer an alternative route to growth, as Stojanov suggests.

In this respect, transforming the decrepit state industries represents a particularly difficult problem. No one contemplates putting them all back on a permanent, state-managed antebellum footing: such a solution would no longer be possible, even if it had been an option in 1996. However, not all state-owned enterprises are lost causes, especially those in the timber, mineral, and aluminum production sectors. Blanket insistence on denying the state the opportunity to make them productive and competitive, in whole or in part, and to develop an industrial strategy, has almost certainly resulted in lost production and reduced employment and purchasing power.

Substituting the Shadow Economy

Controls over the shadow economy need to be linked to policies that address the reasons why it is functional. It is essential to acknowledge the distinctions in the shadow economy between the entrepreneurial activities closely linked to mafia-scale operations and the coping/survival mechanisms among the general populace, and to recognize the extent to which the poor depend on the shadow economy. In the absence of social safety nets, unregulated economic activity and shadow markets are essential coping mechanisms. The dog of neoliberalism continues to chase its tail of "crime" because control measures are asymmetrical, criminalizing shadow

foreign and domestic capital was equally problematic.[143] Two key determinants of economic sustainability were either simply not considered or consciously ruled out on a mixture of practical and ideological grounds: (1) building institutions with funding made available for recurrent spending; and (2) generating production and bolstering purchasing power. The role of the state and its institutions, as well as its industrial, labor, and social policies, have been neglected relative to making the country safe for private investors.[144] If the neoliberal development paradigm had been fully implemented, it would have produced an even leaner state. BiH would have been among the poorest countries that on average spend on government only about half the proportion of GDP that is spent by EU states.[145] What lessons may be drawn from this analysis?

Strengthening Institutions

Deciding the economic model for a devastated country, before building its institutions, has put the cart before the horse. As Woodward argues, donors are more willing to fund reconstruction projects than public institutions and political structures, or to provide core and recurrent budgets in public services.[146] In practice, more than eight years after the signing of the Dayton peace accord, BiH still lacked the power to formulate and implement independent monetary, fiscal, price, and foreign-exchange-rate policies, and policies regarding privatization, incomes, and social welfare.[147]

Integrating Economic Policies into Peace Processes

The experience of BiH suggests that the isolation of economic policies for reconstruction from peace processes simply does not work. As commentators have suggested, economic regeneration and peace processes have been nurtured as if children of different families.[148] Placing privatization in the hands of the ideologically driven agency USAID not only proved to be a farce, with the United States suspending the process in spring 2000, but was also divorced from other elements of peacebuilding—even from the OHR's remit to reform the economy. Above all, policies of economic revival need to be integrated with the needs of the population as a whole and not driven by the ideological fixations of outsiders. In 2002, BiH was in the unenviable situation of having imposed from outside another transfixed High Representative, Paddy Ashdown, a former Royal Marine shipped in to complete a Thatcherite revolution that he had vigorously opposed in his own country. At the very least, external agents need to undertake sui generis economic impact assessments based on a range of options that include Keynesian pump-priming and dirigisme.

Stabilization and Association Process

In parallel with the Stability Pact, the EU offered each country in the region a Stabilization and Association Process (SAP) as a contractual framework to harmonize standards on a range of issues. The lure was an aid program, Community Assistance for Reconstruction, Democratization, and Stabilization (CARDS). The priorities of CARDS include aid for reconstruction and refugee returns; institutional and lawmaking frameworks; sustainable, market, and social development; and international, transnational, and regional cooperation. BiH adopted an EU Road Map in March 2000 with eighteen key conditions (such as the adoption of laws abolishing the payment bureaus and guaranteeing human rights) that had to be accomplished before an SAP could be considered. BiH opened a Ministry for European Integration, and although subject to delays, the Road Map was substantially completed by the end of 2002. An SAP, however, takes precedence over the domestic laws of candidates and is contractually binding, requiring candidates to draw up positions on each of the thirty-one chapters of the *acquis communitaire*. Only Croatia and Macedonia had signed up to the process by 2002.

Herein lies the first of several tensions. The process is inherently fragmentary since each state has particular problems and a different level of economic convergence. Slovenia is due to enter the EU in 2004, whereas BiH remains under international executive authority. It is difficult to achieve a coherent regional policy when SAPs divide rather than unite the region. There are few incentives for more convergent states such as Slovenia to assist, rather than exploit, the less convergent ones.

A second source of tension arises from the issue of sovereignty. In the optimistic view, both sovereignty and intrastate divisions are rendered less politically potent by the sharing of sovereignty implied by regional and European integration. Territorial boundaries become less significant and more fluid because the state is less meaningful to nationalist groups anyway, particularly in the case of BiH. On the other hand, the uncertainty associated with the status of borders and entities in BiH and the ambiguous status of Kosovo, constitutionally part of Serbia but practically an autonomous international protectorate, is a potential source of further conflict that could prevent and disrupt regional relations. Finally, as the neoliberal agenda is not working domestically, there is good reason to doubt that it would work regionally. Restructuring is initially a dislocating process that takes several years to surmount before neoliberal principles are likely to work, with privatization a long and expensive process.

As the origins of the EU model demonstrate, integration becomes feasible in conditions of economic expansion and growth. Though often forgotten, the European Economic Community began as a mutually protective system, the legacy of which remains to this day, not least in the EU's highly protected agricultural sector. In this light, one of three paths might be followed in relation to Southeast Europe: (1) insistence on the neoliberal preconditions being met nationally before regional integration occurs; (2) allowing national SAPs to bypass regionalism in pursuit of independent entry to the EU; (3) supporting a protectionist model based on regional needs and initially parallel to, but not immediately convergent with, the EU. Although the last of these in the form of a customs union could nurture domestic production for a regional market, its creation must depend on the willingness of external institutions to revisit the dominant economic ideology of global integration in the light of economic stress in Latin America, Southeast Europe, and elsewhere in the periphery of core capitalism.

The relationship between the two prongs of Europe's approach remained unclear in mid-2003. The shape of the Stability Pact for Southeast Europe was blurry and its promotion as a prerequisite for EU membership was unlikely to lead to an authentic, locally owned, regional economic bloc. In addition, the EU Stabilization and Association Agreements for each country may prove divisive and undermine the prospects for regional integration over the medium to longer term. First, although there is a clear assumption that all countries in the region would eventually qualify for EU membership, clearly the ripest cherries (such as Slovenia) are picked first. In addition, while reasons for this approach may include the anticipation of a higher level of integration with the region than through the corresponding processes for improving relations and extending free trade with the Mediterranean or the former Soviet Union, EU insistence on regional economic harmony as a requirement for wider integration can also be seen as a way of keeping the region at arm's length.

Prospects and Recommendations

In the context of the liberal peace project, processes of globalization hamper the ability of less developed countries to manage their own economic development. This is especially true of postconflict and aid-dependent countries such as BiH. Dragoljub Stojanov's diagnosis indicates that for transformation from a war to a peace economy, from a self-managed to a market economy, and from aid dependency to a sustainable economy, too much reliance was placed on liberalizing foreign trade and capital movements (so that there is a net outflow), on the free market and privatization, and on FDI in promoting economic growth. Attempting to promote export-led growth without increasing production other than by using expensive

would have helped. . . . The only unifying idea in Bosnia and Herzegovina is indeed Europe."[135] In fact, the EU established a Consultative Task Force (CTF) in 1998 to confer with and advise domestic interests about measures that would harmonize BiH development and secure the return of refugees, a particular preoccupation of EU countries. Benn Stiel and Susan Woodward have advocated EU expansion, including admission to the eurozone and granting special trading arrangements "without strings."[136] But already the KM, having been originally pegged to the deutschemark, became de facto pegged to the euro at the start of 2002, and there was little prospect of the EU dropping conditionality. The EU is a Lord of the Strings. Its raison d'être is to integrate through regional harmonization on EU terms, which include allowing free trade in both directions that would further harm domestic production by exposing the region's vulnerability to competition and trade imbalances.

The Stability Pact for Southeast Europe

In the wake of the war in Kosovo, the EU proposed a Stability Pact with the purpose of establishing a comprehensive regional platform for stability and development. It encompasses the regional states of Albania, BiH, Bulgaria, Croatia, Hungary, Romania, Slovenia, the former Yugoslav Republic of Macedonia (FYROM), and Turkey. Along with Canada, Japan, Russia, the United States, IFIs, and various international organizations, these countries signed the pact in Cologne on June 10, 1999. The EU appointed a special coordinator to promote the pledge of the signatories to cooperate on security issues, human rights and democracy, and economic reconstruction and development. Strategic stabilization and cooperation within the region were regarded as the prerequisite for integration into Euro-Atlantic institutions. In the Zagreb Declaration of November 24, 2000, the EU, Albania, Yugoslavia, FYROM, BiH, Croatia, and Slovenia placed European integration in the context of regional collaboration, reconciliation, and democratic development. Regional participants at the Sarajevo summit in July 1999 had been expected to drive their own intraregional relations. Good-neighborliness was a key issue, but so too was macroeconomic stabilization and restructuring of the economies. For the IFIs, the long-term prospect of European integration, if not the short-term reality, was a form of economic discipline, an incentive and rationale to increase the pace of economic reform.[137]

There is certainly a powerful case for regional economic integration because of the deeply embedded transborder connections that have exacerbated economic deprivation, poverty, shadow economies, and conflict.

As we suggest for West Africa, regional peace agreements would promote a holistic approach to positive peace and also avoid displacing shadow economic activity elsewhere in the vicinity. Moreover, from an economic perspective, the Stability Pact can better address the problems of the small national markets, which, with the exception of Slovenia, lack capital, have weak institutions, and struggle with chronic balance of payments deficits, high unemployment, and increasing poverty. They could pool resources and benefit from economies of scale. However, politicians in BiH seem less interested in the Stability Pact's potential to foster greater security than in its potential to compensate for the fall in external funding from other sources. They also seem concerned about its threat to national sovereignty.[138]

The extent to which regional integration will be conditioned by an insistence on the part of donors, who have promised U.S.$40 billion to the pact, on replicating the neoliberal agenda remains open to question. These funds will not go far and are liable to increase the region's foreign debt burdens because the aid would be in the form of loans.[139] The Stability Pact's mission statement specifies "creating vibrant market economies based on sound macro economic policies, markets open to greatly expanded foreign trade and private sector investment . . . developing strong capital markets and diversified ownership, including privatization."[140] Perhaps this leaves the door open for a more nuanced approach than in earlier prescriptions for neoliberal reform, but the Stability Pact lacks specific indications as to how economic growth is to be achieved. Would the members be allowed to develop protectionist and interventionist solutions to address the underemployment of resources? For some critics of current policy, if the Stability Pact requires countries to maintain currency convertibility, pegged to the euro, with anti-inflationary unemployment policies, participation in it would be a waste of time.[141]

The influence of the Stability Pact on domestic policies in the region, while still uncertain, is likely to be weak. Apart from a few exceptions, such as the Sava River Commission, an agreement between Slovenia, Yugoslavia, Croatia, and BiH at the end of 2002 to jointly manage the Sava Basin, there seems to be little substantive or strategic linkage between the goals of the pact and domestic economic programs. Other bilateral agreements on trade, for example, have been concluded outside the pact, while the reconstruction activities of the Organization for Security and Cooperation in Europe (OSCE) and UN Mission in Kosovo have been conducted without reference to the pact. Consequently, the pact remains largely a mechanism for coordinating donor support and fund distribution and, like the EU-linked Stabilization Process, makes little concession to social needs.[142]

duced to protect the people of BiH from future conflict appears to have done little to alleviate social stress and has probably contributed to it. In the protectorates of BiH and Kosovo, war entrepreneurs and patrimonial elites interacting with international bodies and external capitalist states have adopted a socially detrimental economic model. James Wolfensohn, president of the World Bank, conceded in 2002 that such a one-size-fits-all model introduced from outside has not endured. But his two-part solution contained a contradiction: (1) creating an investment climate that encourages the private sector, and (2) empowering and investing in poor people.[156] As critics such as Zygmunt Bauman note, however, the shrinkage of the public space seems to do little to empower the poor.[157]

In their efforts to make these economies conducive to shareholding and private profit, external actors have engendered an incoherent policy by which the goal of state building is at cross-purposes with the program of withdrawing the state from the economy. Intervention stems from seeing "the other" as a dysfunctional, war-wrecked statist economy, and from attempts to wear down the resistance of local war entrepreneurs to modify their "criminal," corporatist systems. The inhabitants are deemed unable to determine their futures without paternalistic guidance and rules of governance determined from the outside. The withdrawal impetus comes from representing integrative economies as those that "legitimise reductions in welfare spending and the privatisation of essential services," leading to differentiation between those able to participate in the liberalized global order and the excluded poor, unemployed, inflexible, and uncompetitive.[158]

The dominant representation of troubled political economies in this region is that they are products of a socialist past, ethnic wars, local peace "spoilers," and "criminality." By contrast, the role of external actors has been depicted as beneficent, if occasionally misguided in its particulars. The strategic direction in which the region is being pushed politically and economically is rarely questioned, perhaps because most of the analysis emanates from within and around an overarching framework of political economy, the liberal peace, against which progress is registered. Thus there has been a tendency to depict failures to measure up to the liberal peace as inadequacy on the part of the populations, rather than as problematic issues inherent in the paradigm itself.

Notes

1. Wolfgang Petritsch, "The Fate of Bosnia and Herzegovina," in Christophe Solioz and Svebor Dizdarević, eds., *Ownership Process in Bosnia and Herzegovina* (Baden-Baden: Nomos Verl. Ges., 2003), p. 25. The EU took over the job of

police monitoring in BiH from the UN at the start of 2003 and the new High Representative, Lord Paddy Ashdown, became the EU's representative.

2. Introduction to "Development Strategy BiH: PRSP," *Poverty Reduction Strategy Paper,* draft for public discussion, Sarajevo, December 2002. Like all BiH statistics, this must be treated cautiously.

3. Ibid. (italics added).

4. "Basic Economic Indicators for BiH," *Poverty Reduction Strategy Paper,* p. 7.

5. Charles Tilly, "War Making and State Making as Organised Crime," in P. Evans, D. Reuschemeyer, and T. Skocpol, eds., *Bringing the State Back In* (Cambridge: Cambridge University Press, 1995); Charles Tilly, *Coercion, Capital, and European States, A.D. 900–1992,* rev. ed. (Oxford: Blackwell, 1990).

6. As explained in Miranda Vickers, *Between Serb and Albanian: A History of Kosovo* (London: Hurst, 1998).

7. Modernizers in the federal government of Ante Marković subsequently introduced the Polish model of neoliberal "shock therapy" in late 1989. Susan L. Woodward, *The Balkan Tragedy: Chaos and Dissolution After the Cold War* (Washington, DC: Brookings Institution, 1995), pp. 86,100.

8. Miroslav Hadžić, *The Yugoslav People's Agony: The Role of the Yugoslav People's Army* (Aldershot: Ashgate, 2002), p. 264.

9. Established by UNSC Resolution 734 (1992) of February 21, 1992.

10. For a useful detailed account, see Laura Silber and Allan Little, *The Death of Yugoslavia,* 2nd ed. (London: Penguin, 1996).

11. United Nations, *Report of the Secretary-General Pursuant to General Assembly Resolution 53/35 (1998) Srebrenica Report,* UN Doc. A/54/549, 1999.

12. Ibid.

13. Paul Shoup, "The Bosnian Crisis in 1992," in Sabrina Petra Ramet and Ljubisa S. Adamovic, eds., *Beyond Yugoslavia: Politics, Economics, and Culture in a Shattered Community* (Boulder, CO: Westview Press, 1995), p. 155.

14. Robert D. Kaplan, *Balkan Ghosts: A Journey Through History* (New York: Vintage Departures, 1993); Misha Glenny, *The Fall of Yugoslavia: The Third Balkan War* (Harmondsworth: Penguin, 1993); comments by Daniele Conversi in Branka Magaš and Ivo Zanić, eds., *The War in Croatia and Bosnia-Herzegovina, 1991–1995* (London: Frank Cass, 2001), p. 322, n. 5.

15. James Gow, *Triumph of the Lack of Will: International Diplomacy and the Yugoslav War* (London: Hurst, 1997).

16. See, for example, Christopher Bennett, *Yugoslavia's Bloody Collapse* (London: Hurst, 1995); Silber and Little, *The Death of Yugoslavia,* pp. 131–132; and Mihailo Crnobrnja, *The Yugoslav Drama* (London: I. B. Tauris, 1996).

17. Beverly Crawford and Ronnie Lipschutz, "Discourses of War: Security and the Case of Yugoslavia," in Keith Krause and Michael Williams, eds., *Critical Security Studies* (Minneapolis: University of Minneapolis Press, 1997). See also Lene Hansen, *Western Villains or Balkan Barbarism? Representations and Responsibility in the Debate over Bosnia* (Copenhagen: University of Copenhagen, Institute of Political Science, 1998).

18. See Brancko Milinković, ed., *Hate Speech* (Belgrade: Center for Antiwar Action, 1995); and James Gow, Richard Paterson, and Alison Preston, eds., *Bosnia by Television* (London: British Film Institute, 1996).

19. David Campbell, *National Deconstruction: Violence, Identity, and Justice in Bosnia* (Minneapolis: University of Minnesota Press, 1998), p. 129.

20. Ibid., pp. 116–119.

21. Jan Oberg, *Preventing Peace: Sixty Examples of Conflict Mismanagement in Former Yugoslavia Since 1991* (Lund: Transnational Foundation for Peace and Future Research, November 1999), point 4.

22. Branka Magaš, *The Destruction of Yugoslavia: Tracking the Breakup, 1980–92* (London: Verso, 1993); Marijan Korosić, *Jugoslavenska kriza* (Zagreb: Naprijed, 1988); Vjeran Katunarić, *Dioba Drustva* (Zagreb: Drustvo Hrvatske, 1988); Branko Horvat, *The Political Economy of Socialism: A Marxist Social Theory* (New York: M. E. Sharpe, 1972); Josip Zupanov, *Peasants, Politics, and Social Change in Yugoslavia* (Stanford, CA: Stanford University Press, 1955).

23. Susan L. Woodward, "Economic Priorities for Successful Peace Implementation," in Stephen Stedman, Donald Rothchild, and Elizabeth Cousens, eds., *Ending Civil Wars: The Implementation of Peace Agreements* (Boulder, CO: Lynne Rienner, 2002), pp. 183–214.

24. Paul Collier, "Economic Causes of Civil Conflict and Their Implications for Policy," World Bank, June 15, 2000, www.globalpolicy.org/security/issues/diamond/wb.htm.

25. See, for example, James Petras and Steve Vieux, "Bosnia and the Revival of U.S. Hegemony," *New Left Review* no. 218 (July–August 1996): 3–25; Woodward, *Balkan Tragedy*, pp. 58–72; and Carl-Ulrik Schierup, ed., *Scramble for the Balkans: Nationalism, Globalism, and the Political Economy of Reconstruction* (Basingstoke: Macmillan, 1999).

26. Carl-Ulrik Schierup, "Prelude to the Inferno: Economic Disintegration and Political Fragmentation of Socialist Yugoslavia," *Migration* no. 5 (1993): 5–40; Wayne S. Vucinich, "Nationalism and Communism," in Wayne S. Vucinich, ed., *Contemporary Yugoslavia: Twenty Years of Socialist Experiment* (Berkeley: University of California Press, 1969), pp. 236–284.

27. Rita L. Chepulis, "The Economic Crisis and Export-Led Development Strategy of SFR Yugoslavia: In Between Possibilities and Limitations," paper presented at the Mediterranean studies seminar "Models and Strategies of Development," Dubrovnik, April 1984. See also David A. Dyker, *Yugoslavia, Socialism Development, and Debt* (London: Routledge, 1990); and Sabrina Petra Ramet, *Balkan Babel: The Disintegration of Yugoslavia from the Death of Tito to Ethnic War,* 2nd ed. (Boulder, CO: Westview Press, 1996), pp. 9–43.

28. Magaš, *Destruction of Yugoslavia*, p. 97.

29. Oberg, *Preventing Peace*, point 16.

30. Dijana Pleština, "Democracy and Nationalism in Croatia: The First Three Years," in Ramet and Adamovic, *Beyond Yugoslavia*, p. 126.

31. Woodward, *Balkan Tragedy*, p. 62.

32. Schierup, "Prelude to the Inferno," p. 8.

33. Francesco Strazzari, "Between Ethnic Collusion and Mafia Collusion: The 'Balkan Route' to State Making," in Dietrich Jung, ed., *Shadow Globalization, Ethnic Conflicts, and New Wars: A Political Economy of Intra-State War* (London: Routledge, 2003), p. 142.

34. Magaš, *Destruction of Yugoslavia*, p. 111.

35. Ibid., pp. 96–97. See also George Macesich, ed., with Rikard Lang and Dragomir Vojnić, *Essays on the Yugoslav Economic Model* (New York: Praeger, 1989).

36. Magaš, *Destruction of Yugoslavia*, p. 179.

37. Carl-Ulrik Schierup, *Migration, Socialism, and the International Division of Labour* (Aldershot: Avebury, 1990), pp. 244–256; Carl-Ulrik Schierup, "The Spectre of Balkanism," in Schierup, *Scramble for the Balkans*, pp. 36–39.

38. Schierup, "Spectre of Balkanism," pp. 7–8 (italics in original).

39. Schierup, *Migration*, p. 232. In this he follows Korosić, *Jugoslavenska kriza;* and Boris Young, "Nothing from Nothing Is Nothing: Privatisation, Price Liberalisation, and Poverty in the Yugoslav Successor States," in Schierup, *Scramble for the Balkans*, pp. 152–153.

40. M. K. Skulić, *Uzroci sadašnje ekonomske krize un SFRJ* (Belgrade, 1982), cited in Schierup, *Migration*, p. 244. See also, Jens Stilhoff Sørensen, "The Threatening Precedent: Kosovo and the Remaking of Crisis," MERGE Paper on Transcultural Studies, 2/99 (Norrköping: University of Umeå, 1999).

41. Xavier Bougarel, *Bosnie: Anatomie d'un conflit* (Paris: La Découverte, 1996), p. 122.

42. Žarko Papić, "The General Situation in B-H and International Support Policies," in Žarko Papić, et al., *International Support Policies to SEE Countries: Lessons (Not) Learned in Bosnia-Herzegovina* (Sarajevo: Open Society Fund/Soros Foundation, 2001), p. 5; "Poverty Profile in Bosnia and Herzegovina," *Poverty Reduction Strategy Paper*, p. 5.

43. Strazzari, "Between Ethnic Collusion and Mafia Collusion," p. 142.

44. The U.S. Drug Enforcement Agency estimated in 1997 that the Kosovo Albanian mafia's finances were worth treble the GDP of the Albanian state, cited in ibid.

45. Woodward, *Balkan Tragedy*, pp. 293–294. Other commentators claim that sanctions did affect Serbia's support for the RS. See David Cortright and George A. Lopez, *The Sanctions Decade: Assessing UN Strategies in the 1990s* (Boulder, CO: Lynne Rienner, 2000), pp. 67–68.

46. David Cortright and George A. Lopez, *Sanctions and the Search for Security: Challenges to UN Action* (Boulder, CO: Lynne Rienner, 2002), p. 98.

47. Strazzari, "Between Ethnic Collusion and Mafia Collusion," p. 145.

48. A special criminal investigator in Republika Srpska told us in late 2002 that he would have no stomach for doing the same job in Croatia or Serbia.

49. Bougarel, *Bosnie*, p. 125.

50. Ibid.

51. Peter Andreas, "Criminalized Conflict: The Clandestine Political Economy of War in Bosnia," *International Studies Quarterly* (forthcoming).

52. Steven Erlanger, "Belgrade Silent on Serb 'Hit,'" *International Herald Tribune*, January 17, 2000, pp. 1, 7; Gariel Partos, cited in "Arkan Murder 'Prevents Justice,'" *BBC News*, news.bbc.co.uk, January 16, 2000.

53. Luca Rastello, *La Guerra in casa* (Turin: Einaudi, 1998), pp. 63–77, cited in Strazzari, "Between Ethnic Collusion and Mafia Collusion," p. 150.

54. Strazzari, "Between Ethnic Collusion and Mafia Collusion," p. 143.

55. Neven Katunarić and Marijan Puntarić, "Prlić i partnari sada Peru Robu u Pistom Moru Makarske Rivijere" [Prlić and his partners now launder money in

the clean sea of Makarska River], *Slobodna Dalmacija* (Split), September 24, 2001 [OHR trans.].

56. Marijan Puntarić, "Tri Hercegovacka kralja ulija" [Three Herzegovinian kings of oil], *Slobodna Dalmacija,* September 21, 2001 [OHR trans.].

57. Statement by Brigadier-Genenal Jovan Divijak, Republic of Bosnia Army (ret.), in Magaš and Zanić, *War in Croatia and Bosnia-Herzegovina,* p. 249.

58. Tim Judah, *The Serbs: History, Myth, and the Destruction of Yugoslavia* (New Haven, CT: Yale University Press, 1998), pp. 248–249.

59. N. Bjelaković and Francesco Strazzari, "The Sack of Mostar, 1992–1994: The Politico-Military Connection," *European Security* 8, no. 3 (1998): 74–75.

60. Andreas, "Criminalized Conflict."

61. Silber and Little, *Death of Yugoslavia,* p. 296.

62. Cited in Bougarel, *Bosnie,* p. 126.

63. Norman Cigar, "Serb War Effort and Termination of the War," in Magaš and Zanić, *War in Croatia and Bosnia-Herzegovina,* pp. 200–235.

64. Richard J. Aldrich, "America Used Islamists to Arm the Bosnian Muslims: The Srebrenica Report Reveals the Pentagon's Role in a Dirty War," *The Guardian* (London), April 22, 2002, special report on Yugoslavia war crimes.

65. Bougarel, *Bosnie,* p. 130. See also Marie-Joëlle Zahar, "Militia Motivations in Peace Negotiations: Lessons from Bosnia," paper presented at the annual meeting of the International Studies Association, Washington, DC, February 16–20, 1999.

66. UNDP, *Human Development Report: Bosnia and Herzegovina 2002* (Sarajevo: UNDP, 2002), p. 99.

67. Schierup, "Spectre of Balkanism," p. 12.

68. See generally, David Chandler, "The Responsibility to Protect? Imposing the Liberal Peace: A Critique," in Alex Bellamy and Paul Williams, eds., *Peace-keeping in Global Politics* (London: Frank Cass, 2004); William Bain, *Between Anarchy and Society* (Oxford: Oxford University Press, 2003), chap. 6; and Roland Paris, *At War's End: Building Peace After Civil Conflict* (Cambridge: University of Cambridge Press, 2004).

69. Nebojsa Vukadinović, "Economies d'après-guerre entre reconstruction et transition," *Relations Internationales et Stratégiques* 28 (Winter 1997): 47–62; Elizabeth M. Cousens and Charles K. Cater, *Toward Peace in Bosnia: Implementing the Dayton Accords* (Boulder, CO: Lynne Rienner, 2001); Margaret Cobble, "The Political Economy of Post-Conflict Transition in Bosnia and Herzegovina," unpublished manuscript, University of Plymouth, Department of Politics and International Relations, 2000.

70. International Crisis Group (ICG), *Bosnia's Precarious Economy: Still Not Open for Business,* report no. 115 (Sarajevo: ICG, August 7, 2001).

71. OHR Economic Task Force Secretariat, *Newsletter* 5, no. 3 (October 2002).

72. Paddy Ashdown, "Inaugural Speech," OHR press release, May 27, 2002, www.ohr.int.

73. Henrik Kolstrup, UNDP Resident Coordinator, foreword to *Human Development Report: Bosnia and Herzegovina 2002,* p. 3. In Kolstrup's own country, Denmark, politicians had just harnessed a "pathology" of racism against immigrants to win an election.

74. By early 2003 the budget deficit had been reduced from 10 to 4 percent of GDP, and a rescheduling of U.S.$2.5 billion by the World Bank and the London and Paris clubs, with a term date of 2042, was expected to be easily managed by BiH.

75. OHR, "Our Reform Agenda," July 31, 2002, www.ohr.int.

76. Of the numerous critiques of neoliberal globalization, see Zygmunt Bauman, *Globalisation: The Human Consequences* (Cambridge: Polity, 1998).

77. Papić, "General Situation in B-H," p. 10; interviews with OHR economic advisers, Sarajevo, December 12, 2002.

78. Woodward, "Economic Priorities," p. 206.

79. International Monetary Fund (IMF), *Bosnia and Herzegovina: Selected Issues and Statistical Appendix* (Washington, DC: IMF, June 26, 2000), p. 12; IMF, "IMF Completes Final Bosnia and Herzegovina Reviews, Approves U.S.$119 Million Credit Tranche," *News Brief* no. 01/46, May 25, 2001.

80. Dragoljub Stojanov cites Michael Porter's *The Competitive Advantage of Nations* (New York: Free Press, 1990) to support an argument that BiH has not reached a stage of capitalism that can dispense with a direct government role in developing home industry. Dragoljub Stojanov, "Bosnia-Herzegovina Since 1995: Transition and Reconstruction of the Economy," in Papić et al., *International Support Policies*, pp. 59–62.

81. Joseph Stiglitz and David Ellerman, "New Bridges Across the Chasm: Macro- and Micro-Strategies for Russia and the Other Transitional Economies," *Zagreb International Review of Economics and Business* 3, no. 1 (May 2000): 41–73; Felipe Larrain and Andres Velasco, "Exchange Rate Policy in Emerging-Market Economies: The Case for Floating," National Bureau of Economic Research Working Paper, Princeton University, April 2001, cited in Stojanov, "International Financial Institutions and the Financial Stability in B&H (Federation of B&H)," paper presented at the conference "International Financial Institutions and Sustainable Development," Media Centre, Belgrade, December 2002.

82. UNDP, *Human Development Report,* p. 99.

83. For more extensive discussion, see Timothy Donais, "The Politics of Privatization in Post-Dayton Bosnia," *Southeast European Politics* 3, no. 1 (June 2002): 3–19.

84. World Bank, European Commission, and European Bank for Reconstruction and Development, *Bosnia and Herzegovina on the Road to Recovery,* 1996, cited in Stojanov, "Bosnia-Herzegovina Since 1995," pp. 50–51.

85. "Private Sector Development," progress report of the Private Sector Development Task Force Secretariat, Sarajevo, September 1999.

86. "Privatization," *Poverty Reduction Strategy Paper,* p. 5.

87. Donais, "Politics of Privatization."

88. Report of a meeting with local businessmen (SME sector) in Banja Luka on December 4, 2002, organized with the support of the RS Chamber of Commerce, Association of Employers, and the RS Craftsman's Chamber.

89. Dragoljub Stojanov, "Understanding B&H Reform," paper presented at the conference "Serbia and Monte Negro on the Way to EU," Belgrade, December 2002.

90. UNDP, *Early Warning System: Bosnia and Herzegovina,* quarterly report, April–May 2002, p. 16.

91. "Bosnia-Herzegovina: World Bank Announces Assistance Strategy," UN Wire, May 25, 2000, www.unfoundation.org.

92. Interview with World Bank official, Sarajevo, December 12, 2002.

93. "Introduction," Poverty Reduction Strategy Paper.

94. International Crisis Group, Why Will No-One Invest in Bosnia-Herzegovina, report no. 64, Sarajevo, April 21, 1999.

95. Dragoljub Stojanov, "Bosnia and Herzegovina: Economy in the Process of Transition, Five Years Later," in Solioz and Dizdarević, Ownership Process, p. 91.

96. Information from Andreas Niemann, OHR, Banja Luka, based on the RS government's report on the situation of the RS industry as discussed in the RS National Assembly, May 10, 2002.

97. Ibid., based on work by the RS Directorate for Privatization.

98. OHR Economic Task Force Secretariat, Newsletter 5, no. 3 (October 2002). The trade deficit was regarded as manageable in some circles, but see Stojanov, "Understanding B&H Reform"; and Žarko Papić, "Ownership Versus Democracy: Lessons (Not) Learnt in Bosnia and Herzegovina," in Solioz and Dizdarević, Ownership Process, p. 78.

99. Stojanov, "Understanding B&H Reform."

100. Interview with Professor Rajko Tomaš, Banja Luka University, December 10, 2002; comment by director of timber company SIPAD, seminar, Banja Luka, November 2002.

101. Caroline Thomas, Global Governance, Development, and Human Security (London: Pluto Press, 2000), p. 90.

102. UNDP, Early Warning System, p. 16.

103. Interview with Dr. Mike E. Sarhan, director of the Economic Restructuring Office, USAID, Sarajevo, September 16, 1999.

104. Management consultant seminar, Banja Luka, November 2002.

105. IMF, Bosnia and Herzegovina, pp. 14, 17.

106. OHR, BiH Media Roundup, Sarajevo, August 31, 2001.

107. IMF Staff Report, February 2002.

108. "Poverty Profile in Bosnia and Herzegovina," Poverty Reduction Strategy Paper, p. 8.

109. Christopher Corpora, "The Gas Station Blues in Three Parts: The Effects of Organized Crime on Stability and Development in Southeast Europe," paper presented at the ISA conference, New Orleans, March 23–27, 2002.

110. Andreas, "Criminalized Conflict."

111. Rajko Tomaš, Analysis of the Grey Economy in Republika Srpska (Banja Luka: UNDP, March 1998), p. x.

112. Andreas, "Criminalized Conflict."

113. "Hoće li Bakir Izetbegović odgovarati pred sudom?" Dani (Sarajevo), August 6, 1999, p. 16; "Abeceda korupcije," Dani (Sarajevo), August 27, 1999, pp. 16–21.

114. Agnes Picod, "Discrimination in Employment," background paper, OHR, Sarajevo, January 1999.

115. USAID, Payments Bureaus in Bosnia and Herzegovina: Obstacles to Development and a Strategy for Orderly Transition, final draft (Sarajevo: Economic Reconstruction Office, February 15, 1999), pp. 90, 101; International Advi-

sory Group, *Functional Analysis and Strategic Implementation Plan: Transformation of the Payment Bureaus in Bosnia and Herzegovina*, Sarajevo, July 1999.
116. "Abeceda korupcije," pp. 16–21.
117. Adrian Rausche, "International Direct Intervention Responses to Clandestine Political Economies: The Hercegovacka Bank Case Study," paper presented to the workshop "Clandestine Political Economy of War and Peace," Thomas J. Watson Institute for International Studies Global Research Program, Brown University, May 6, 2003.
118. "Removal of Ramiz Dzaferović," OHR press release, July 28, 2000; ICG, *Bosnia's Precarious Economy*, p. 11, annex B.
119. "A gdje su indijanci, Kauzlarichu?" *Dani* (Sarajevo), August 27, 1999, pp. 16–21; "High Representative Removes Former Prime Minister Edhem Bičakčić," OHR press release, February 26, 2001.
120. Christopher A. Corpora, "Three Actions That Staggered a Giant: Is There Hope for Transforming Former Yugoslavia's Clandestine Political Economy?" paper presented to the workshop "Clandestine Political Economy of War and Peace," Thomas J. Watson Institute for International Studies Global Research Program, Brown University, May 6, 2003.
121. Prlić was subsequently deputy minister for trade and economic affairs. The chair of the House of Peoples called for his removal after a financial audit of the Foreign Ministry discovered that illegal activities had occurred in 2000. The Prlić empire is estimated to be worth U.S.$1.3 billion. BiH Media Roundup, Sarajevo, October 18, 2001; Katunarić and Puntarić, "Prlić i partnari."
122. "Bosnia's Corrupt Elite Grow Fat on Human Cargo," *The Observer* (London), January 27, 2001; ICG, *Bosnia's Precarious Economy*, p. 32.
123. Donais, "Politics of Privatization," p. 7.
124. See Michael Pugh, "Protectorate Democracy in South-East Europe," Copenhagen Peace Research Institute Working Paper, June 2000.
125. Interview with James Lyon, ICG, Sarajevo, September 29, 1999. For Eronet and the HDZ, see ICG, *Bosnia's Precarious Economy*, p. 26.
126. Žarko Papić, "Ethička privatizacija: Neograničene mogućosti prevare" [Ethnic privatization: Unlimited possibilities for cheating], *Dani* (Sarajevo), August 6, 1999, pp. 20–21.
127. For example, the SDA controls utilities such as the PTT, Elektroprivreda, and Energoinvest. *Dani* (Sarajevo), August 6, 1999, pp. 16–19; European Stability Initiative (ESI), "Taking on the Commanding Heights," Berlin, May 3, 2000.
128. UK ambassador Graham Hand in "Privatizacija Aluminija je potpuno kriminalna" [The privatization of Aluminij is completely criminal], *Dani* (Sarajevo), August 2001; "German Daimler Chrysler Wants to Purchase Aluminij Mostar," *Jutarnji List* (Zagreb), August 28, 2001; "Politicki rat buziran na Mostarski Aluminijum" [Political war over the Mostar-based Aluminij], *Večernji List* (Zagreb), August 31, 2001; "Scimnjiva privatizacija Aluminijuma" [The suspicious privatization of Aluminij], *Nacional* (Zagreb), September 6, 2001.
129. "OSCE Examines Forced Prostitution," UN Wire, April 27, 2001; 80 percent of the women are from Moldova and Romania. UNMIBH Special Press Conference, "Anti-Trafficking Project and Introduction to the Special Trafficking Operations Program (STOP)," July 26, 2001, UNMIBH, Sarajevo; UNMIBH,

"Efforts Against Organized Crime and International Terrorism Within BiH and Regionally," Special Representative of the Secretary-General, unpublished paper, Sarajevo, par. 7; Jamie Wilson, "£110,000 Payout for Sacked Whistleblower," *The Guardian* (London), November 27, 2002. The Bijeljina Ministry of Interior, Department of Foreigners, was systematically facilitating trafficking of women. UNMIBH, "Efforts Against Organized Crime," par. 15; "OSCE Examines Forced Prostitution"; Audrey Gillan, "Sex Abuse Scandals Tarnish Work of Aid Agencies in Africa," *The Guardian* (London), April 20, 2002, pp. 20–21.

130. "Croatia and Bosnia-Herzegovina: Powerful Political-Military Networks," *Geopolitical Drug Newsletter* no. 8 (Nantes, France) (May 2002): 1–3.

131. The Albanian bosses, protected by the new political leader in Tirana, Fatos Nano, acquired dominance when the diversion of trafficking to the southern Albanian ports of Saranda and Vlora offered a more convenient outlet to the sea and to hard currency markets combined with the militarization of the Kosovar Albanian struggle, which Nano now fervently supported. Strazzari, "Between Ethnic Collusion and Mafia Collusion," p. 147.

132. Customs and Fiscal Assistance Office (CAFAO), *Revenue Loss from Tax and Customs Fraud in BiH Identified by CAFAO*, internal document, u/eg/ CAFAOGeneral/revenue 260902 (Sarajevo: CAFAO, December 13, 2002). However, in the first seven months of 2002, customs and tax revenue increased by 17 percent in the Federation and by 39 percent in the RS over the previous year.

133. Interview with senior CAFAO official, Sarajevo, December 13, 2002. The Federation also has nine duty-free zones (whereas the whole of the EU only has thirty), into which goods are supposed to be imported for reexport without distribution in the country. The goods often vanish.

134. Interview with CAFAO official, Sarajevo, December 12, 2002. In late 2002 the author encountered a student working in a traditional Sarajevo cafe who testified that a Turk and a Tunisian present at the rear of the premises were smuggling seven to eight people a month from Turkey through Sarajevo, but he did not wish to approach the BiH police, because "they could not be trusted."

135. Petritsch, "Fate of Bosnia and Herzegovina," pp. 18, 25.

136. Benn Steil and Susan L. Woodward, "A European New Deal for the Balkans?" *Foreign Affairs* 78, no. 6 (November–December 1999): 95–105; B. Granville, "Time for a Rescue: Balkans' 'Marshall Plan,'" *The World Today* 55, no. 7 (1999): 7–9.

137. World Bank, *The Road to Stability and Prosperity in South Eastern Europe: A Regional Strategy Paper* (Washington, DC: World Bank, March 2000), par. 127, p. 16.

138. Žarko Papić, "The SEE Region and Stability Pact," in Papić et al., *International Support Strategies*, p. 26.

139. Martin Walker, "Balkan Nations Could Join EU," *The Guardian* (London), April 9, 1999, p. 5.

140. Stability Pact, the Cologne Declaration, June 10, 1999, Part III, art. (10).

141. Stojanov, "Bosnia and Herzegovina: Economy in the Process of Transition," p. 105.

142. Papić, "SEE Region and Stability Pact," pp. 26–28; East-West Institute and European Stability Initiative, *Democracy, Security, and the Future of the Stability Pact for South Eastern Europe: A Political Framework*, Berlin, April 4,

2001; ESI, "Western Balkans 2004: Assistance, Cohesion, and the New Bound-aries of Europe—A Call for Policy Reform," Berlin, November 3, 2002, p. 11.

143. Stojanov, "Bosnia-Herzegovina Since 1995," p. 46.

144. On the World Bank's priorities and social policy reform, see Paul Stubbs, "'Social Sector' or the Diminution of Social Policy? Regulating Welfare Regimes in Contemporary Bosnia-Herzegovina," in Papić et al., *International Support Strategies,* pp. 102–104. On analysis of social capital as a contribution to the Poverty Reduction Strategy Paper, see Xavier Bougarel, *Bosnia and Herze-govina: Local Level Institutions and Social Capital Study,* vol. 1 (Washington, DC: World Bank, ECSSD, June 2002).

145. Stefan Andréasson, "Neoliberalism and the Creation of 'Virtual Democ-racy' in the Global South," paper presented at the International Studies Associa-tion annual convention, New Orleans, March 24–27, 2002.

146. Woodward, "Economic Priorities," pp. 183–214.

147. Stojanov, "Bosnia-Herzegovina Since 1995," p. 46.

148. Alvaro de Soto and Graciana del Castillo, "Obstacles to Peacebuilding," *Foreign Policy* 94 (Spring 1994): 72.

149. Branko Horvat, *Theory of International Trade: An Alternative Approach* (Basingstoke: Macmillan, 1999), pp. 136–149, 170–171.

150. Angus Cameron and Ronen Palan, "The Imagined Economy: Mapping Transformations in the Contemporary State," *Millennium: Journal of Interna-tional Studies* 28, no. 2 (1999): 271–274, 279.

151. Gearóid Ó'Tuathail, Andrew Herod, and Susan Roberts, "Negotiating Unruly Problematics," in Andrew Herod, Gearóid Ó'Tuathail, and Susan M. Roberts, *Unruly World? Globalization, Governance, and Geography* (London: Routledge, 1998), pp. 1–24.

152. Cameron and Palan, "Imagined Economy," p. 171.

153. Klaus Schlichte, "State Formation and the Economy of Intra-State Wars," in Jung, *Shadow Globalisation,* pp. 27–44.

154. Cameron and Palan, "Imagined Economy," p. 171.

155. Biljana Vankovska, "Rule of Law and Democratic Control of Armed Forces in the Post–Cold War International Setting," paper presented at the Inter-national Studies Association annual convention, New Orleans, March 24–27, 2002.

156. Development Committee, "Note from the President of the World Bank," DC2002-0007/Rev1, April 12, 2002.

157. Bauman, *Globalisation.*

158. Cameron and Palan, "Imagined Economy," pp. 269–271.

6

Controlling War Economies: A Critique of the "Liberal Peace"

The preceding case studies have analyzed the role of economic factors and the regional economic dimensions of war economies in particular contexts. This chapter examines more thematically the interaction between war economies and external responses. A growing interest in the political economy of conflict has led to a corresponding interest in the development of initiatives aimed at restricting economic activity that prolongs violence or undermines either conflict prevention or peacebuilding. These have taken both particularistic and generic forms. The former include controls on conflict trade such as the commodity sanctions imposed by the UN on the Union for the Total Independence of Angola (UNITA) and the Revolutionary United Front (RUF), as well as the development of a global certification scheme for conflict diamonds. However, the attempt to address the dynamics of conflict trade can also be understood as part of a generic model of globalization that extends beyond narrow regulation to incorporate a much wider range of problems and threats deemed to emanate from the developing world. Control strategies developed to address the economic dimensions of violence reflect what Paul Rogers refers to as the Western strategy of "liddism"—attempting to keep the lid on growing insecurity without addressing the core reasons for dissent.[1] These strategies attempt to insulate the developed world from the negative effects of poverty, war, drug addiction, and crime in the developing world, while simultaneously preserving the essential elements of a neoliberal version of globalization.

This same system, however, also plays a significant role in exacerbating these problems. We have noted that the interventionist policies of international financial institution (IFI) austerity programs contributed significantly to the permissive conditions for state decline and conflict in Sierra Leone and Bosnia and Herzegovina (BiH) in the first place. Further, the introduction of the neoliberal model to forge transformation in post-conflict situations has been problematic in all three cases—Afghanistan, Sierra Leone, and BiH—suggesting that this aspect of the liberal peace is unsuitable for economies emerging or struggling to emerge from conflict.

Liberal Peace and Governance
for the Developing World

As observed in Chapter 2, the attempt to discipline the "periphery" into the adoption of appropriate forms of what Mark Duffield terms "liberal peace" is connected with the reconceptualization of underdevelopment as a security issue: "The focus of new security concerns is . . . the fear of underdevelopment as a source of conflict, criminalized activity and international instability . . . the idea of underdevelopment as dangerous and destabilising provides a justification for continued surveillance and engagement."[2] Liberal peace and governance, for Duffield, encompasses an element of "riot control" in the form of "global poor relief" to encourage conflict prevention and resolution. But it also serves to discipline poor states into adopting the dominant models of neoliberal economic and political governance and aims at a social transformation within states that changes both the balance of power between groups and the very attitudes and beliefs of societies.[3] This is not to deny that such modes of intervention are in fact often advocated by actors with a genuine concern to alleviate conflict and suffering. Moreover, to the extent that such reforms genuinely aim to bring about effective and accountable states, they can be said to be addressing one of the prerequisites essential for sustainable peace and development.

However, the problem is that meaningful solutions to underdevelopment and conflict are, at best, watered down in the process of political bargaining between the interests of the underdeveloped world and the interests of the immeasurably more powerful developed world. Moreover, the stranglehold that the matrix of neoliberal economics, democracy, and individualism has on the philosophy of intervention means that solutions within this framework are simply taken for granted as part of an order that is self-evidently correct and even natural. As in the film of the same name, solutions outside of "The Matrix" are almost inconceivable and certainly considered to be illegitimate. Ironically, however, the same neoliberal drive for free trade, open borders, and deregulation prescribed under the tenets of the liberal peace also provides the permissive conditions for conflict in the economically vulnerable countries and for the deterritorialized network trade of conflict entrepreneurs. This occurs in three ways.

First, at the global level, the dominance of neoliberalism, coupled with its selective application, has largely served to compound existing global inequalities. Thus, poor countries have been faced by creditor demands for reforms in economic governance that have opened up their markets to predation from outside investors. While external economic actors such as multinational corporations (MNCs) sometimes bring a range of economic and social benefits, and while many may even operate more enlightened wage and labor policies than local actors, it is also the case that the opening of vulnerable domestic markets to outside competition frequently has negative effects. Thus, in Haiti, trade liberalization implemented under the auspices of the International Monetary Fund (IMF) and World Bank has led to steep cuts in import tariffs on rice, opening the market to highly subsidized imports from the United States. This has had an adverse impact on rural incomes in a country where 80 percent of the rural population lives below the poverty line.[4] Similarly, West African cotton exporters are estimated to lose U.S.$250 million a year as a direct result of U.S. subsidies to its own industry. For countries like Burkina Faso and Mali, where cotton accounts for more than one-third of export earnings, the losses represent roughly three times the savings provided through debt relief.[5]

These effects have been exacerbated by the selective application of the neoliberal agenda. Thus, markets in which producers in the periphery have a comparative advantage are subject to a variety of protectionist measures on the part of Western governments. Indeed, Oxfam has estimated the total cost of Western trade barriers imposed on agricultural products at over U.S.$100 billion—more than double the total amount of aid provided to poorer countries.[6] Moreover, these countries face difficulty in adding value to their products as tariffs escalate according to the level of processing undergone.

Consequently, the structure of the official global economy often serves to marginalize those in the economically vulnerable countries. At worst, this exacerbates social stresses such as poverty and inequality that contribute to the risk of war. At best, it creates a context in which participation in shadow economic activities becomes a means by which those excluded from or relegated to the periphery of the global economy can reincorporate themselves into its workings. For instance, in Angola it has been estimated that as little as 10 percent of the country's gross national product is produced through the formal economy,[7] while in Afghanistan 80 percent of the economy and 30–50 percent of the population have been involved in some aspect of the drug trade.[8]

Second, local and global deregulation, coupled with the high-technology revolution, improvements in transport technology, and increased migration, have facilitated the development of local, regional, and global trade networks that sustain both the legitimate and illegitimate conflict trade. Overland transport networks have improved markedly in the developing world since the 1980s, while developments such as containerization have simultaneously lowered the unit cost of trade and made it more anonymous.[9] As David Held and his colleagues have further noted, the cost of sea freight, air transport, and transatlantic communication have all fallen significantly over the last seventy years.[10] Similarly, post–Cold War military reductions have released aircraft and other vehicles into deregulated private and commercial use. In the long-haul market, decommissioned aircraft from the Soviet military fleet have created a direct link between remote airfields in conflict zones and the international trade networks of both the formal and the informal global economy.[11]

At the same time, the move to a more open trading system has facilitated the interpenetration of local, regional, and global markets. The proportion of the world's economies operating broadly open trade policies has risen significantly since the 1980s, while the proportion of world output accounted for by exports rose from 7 percent in the 1950s to as much as 17 percent by the 1990s.[12] Furthermore, the growth in global financial markets (more than U.S.$1.5 trillion is now exchanged daily in world markets[13]) has not only made it easier to launder money, but has made it correspondingly more difficult for investigators to discern illegitimate from legitimate transactions.

Third, as noted in the preceding chapters, the requirement of neoliberal reform as a condition of accessing IFI funds has frequently had the effect of exacerbating domestic inequalities and social stresses. Rather than aiding economic stability and conflict prevention, all too often the effect has been to hasten the slide to conflict and make the challenge of postconflict peacebuilding that much more difficult. In El Salvador, for instance, the stringent fiscal policies of the IFIs have been held responsible for hindering development of the new National Civilian Police and the land transfer program, both of which were essential elements of the UN's peacebuilding strategy.[14] Building on this point, we now examine the problems inherent in applying generic neoliberal precepts to postconflict contexts.

Implications for Transformation

Transformation strategies based on the neoliberal model of political economy have been shown in the preceding case studies to be particularly unsuitable to war-torn societies. This is largely because they confront the pressures of multiple transition affecting governmental, political, social, and economic spheres, and recovery from conflict. These are not simply cases of transformation from one political system to another or from one economic system to another. To observe that societies emerge from civil conflict with civil public institutions debilitated, with the "official" economy and infrastructure wrecked, with war entrepreneurs in a strong position to claim spoils, and with the general population struggling to survive, is to state the obvious. What is not so obvious is why external assistance, and in some situations such as BiH, direct neopaternal governance, should be predicated and conditional on a particular model of political economy. The model is unsuitable for many reasons.

First, the notion that "one size fits all" is a demonstrably flawed approach. Attempts to graft holus-bolus a neoliberal model of political economy into recovery programs disregards the crucial relevance of local contexts. As discussed with regard to Afghanistan, a lack of understanding of the history and social networks that underpin the country's political economy has led to a rigid and false conception of what is legitimate and illegitimate economic activity. Consequently, inappropriate frameworks are devised that hinder recovery and deny opportunities for sustainable growth. This not only perpetuates economic injustice and warlord governance, but also exacerbates tensions between groups competing for assistance and scarce resources. Stability and peace in these circumstances is likely to be short-lived once the presence of international forces is removed.

Second, the neoliberal model places a low priority on institution building as part of peacebuilding, as opposed to an emphasis on securing military cease-fires. Indeed, the ideology of "small" government, and reduced public resources and the privatization of socially owned assets, weakens already weak states. The implications derived from the case studies are that states emerging from conflict are not equipped with effective administrative, authoritative, and coercive capacities. By depriving states of their formative roles in generating economic growth and strategic planning for economic development, the effect of donor economic policies and liberal governance is to systematically contribute to low state capacity. One might say that liberal peace is achieved at the cost of development. The negative impact is not merely economic, however. Prescriptions for a minimal state also compromise the state's ability to command the loyalty of its population and to govern its territory effectively, particularly its borderlands. In the cases of protectorate governance, as in BiH, this model fosters dependency on aid and employment with international agencies, while simultaneously limiting the ownership and responsibility of local institutions and officials for what happens. Both sides engage in denial:

the international agencies blame local vested interests for corruption and incompetence; local patrimonial elites hide behind international agencies to evade responsibility.

The model emphasizes macroeconomic stability that is absolutely at odds with sustainable recovery. The precepts of monetarism, designed to ensure equilibrium in the absence of an interventionist state, have deflationary effects that go beyond the need to curb any potential for hyperinflation. Restraints on public expenditure place a ceiling on the role of the state in managing the economy through strategic industries, employment creation, and distributive justice. As Susan Woodward has noted of IFI intervention in postconflict countries: "Policies of macroeconomic restraint prevent the public expenditures that are essential to peace, such as building a new, competent civilian administration, financing demobilization, and providing social infrastructure. . . . Orthodox stabilisation policies also tend to increase and exacerbate social inequalities."[15] In the short-term, this may prevent timely recovery and reduce development options. But the implications may not stop at embedding a system of flawed social justice. The long-term consequence of monetarism in these environments is likely to be a shadow economy that leaves society once again vulnerable to violent conflict.

Liberal governance gives priority to structural adjustment on the basis of privatization, foreign direct investment (FDI), and deregulated markets. Implementing these principles has had deleterious effects not only on prewar economies but also on postwar transformations, and for similar reasons. First, privatization rewards war entrepreneurs with spoils of peace. Rather than co-opting them into institution building, privatization can legitimate parallel economic activity outside institutional control, as noted in BiH, where this process has gone furthest. Here, it has perpetuated corruption and forms of governance that foment popular grievance. Second, the argument that privatization and foreign direct investment will provide employment and economic growth is less than convincing. As indicated in Chapter 1, the IMF now cautions that FDI can make poor economies vulnerable to financial crisis, which, as in Albania, can trigger domestic conflict. Privatization has had some effect in redistributing the existing level of employment in BiH, but it has had nowhere near the positive impact on family incomes as has participation in the shadow economy. Modified structural adjustment in the form of poverty reduction strategies relies on the same hoary old formula: curbed government spending, privatization, FDI, and the free market, with a bit of extra cash for retraining and education thrown in. The implications of structural adjustment for the prewar economies of West Africa and the former Yugoslavia have already been spelled out as a contributory cause in their respective trajectories toward violent conflict. There is little reason to be optimistic that the cycle will not be repeated.

As applied to address shadow economies, the model is also problematic. More effective economic policing to eliminate "illegal" activities neglects the function performed by shadow economies for substantial sections of the population. Here, a double jeopardy is at work: effective policing deprives households of work and income, while structural adjustment removes the ability of the state to provide alternative means of coping and survival. The immediate consequence is the persistence of poverty and new and inventive forms of "criminality." In the medium and longer terms, the systemic consequences are the institutionalization of structural violence and conflict.

Finally, by focusing on the territory within state borders, while rendering it more easily penetrated by the global economy, the model ignores the regional economic dimensions of conflict. Although the World Bank has now acknowledged that Afghanistan's peripheries are in need of dedicated economic attention, although the Stability Pact for Southeast Europe has been in place since 1999, and although some conflict trade controls have a regional dimension in West Africa, there are still no comprehensive policy approaches to the transformation of regional conflict complexes that will significantly reduce their potential for future conflict. Indeed, if the Stability Pact is used to open the borders of Southeast Europe to vigorous competition from outside, the economic situation in each country could easily worsen, feeding grievances that could lead to a renewal of conflict.

The scale and intensity of war economies can be understood partly as a simple response to the opportunities for profit-making presented by the interconnected networks of globalization. It is also partly a consequence of deprivation and/or elite adaptation to the demands of external creditors in a context in which regional and global transfers of goods, people, and money have been facilitated by dynamics of the global trading system. Finally, it is partly a consequence of the way in which wars create acute imperatives to develop mechanisms of financing that are able to exploit the opportunities of a networked global shadow economy.

Viewed in this light, initiatives to address the economic dimensions of conflict by improving economic governance inside postconflict states essentially represent an attempt to address the *symptoms* of a dysfunctional global order—and are often, as in BiH and Kosovo, undertaken by the agents of that self-same order. Control strategies designed to tackle combatant "greed" by interrupting or eliminating linkages between resources and conflict need to be seen in the same light.

Control Strategies

Current and emerging control strategies include transparency initiatives, voluntary codes of conduct, the use of IFI conditionality, and formal regulations. These initiatives can be categorized in a variety of ways. For instance, they can be characterized according to whether they have been developed at the national, regional, or global level. However, even global regulations inevitably have impacts at the national and regional levels and vice versa. An alternative method of categorizing such initiatives might be in terms of their functional focus—for example, drug interdiction, curbing the trade in rough diamonds, or combating money laundering or terrorist financing. Given the role such control measures play in the policy of "liddism," however, a more useful approach is to categorize them according to three levels of purpose and scope in relation to liberal peace: governance initiatives, prophylactic control, and control-lite.[16]

Governance Initiatives

The first of the control strategies involves the use of donor conditionality to promote peace and improved political and economic governance. Like other control strategies, this represents an extension of the liberal peace project and also leads to greater external intervention in the governance of developing world states. Paradoxically, the new measures of liberal intervention continue to be pursued even as similar initiatives elsewhere have been criticized for being counterproductive. For example, donors are beginning to recognize that linking aid to direct reductions in military expenditures without also ensuring local ownership of budgetary decisions is unlikely to work. Indeed, such conditionality may simply foster corrupt practices and undermine transparency by encouraging off-budget military expenditures.[17] At the same time, and as will be noted below, concern about the unaccountable use of natural resource revenues to fund defense expenditure has led to revenue-sharing initiatives, such as the Chad/Cameroon pipeline project noted below, that aim to limit the ability of governments to use these revenues to finance military expenditure. Thus, while the strategy has changed, the goal of imposing external management of domestic decisions on the allocation of resources to defense remains much the same.

What forms, then, are these governance initiatives taking? In one sense, of course, adherence to the macroeconomic fundamentals of neoliberalism, at either the global or the domestic level, is frequently justified in terms of the positive benefits it produces for peace by fostering growth, interdependence, and democracy. Thus, at one level, initiatives to refashion the domestic economies of aid supplicants can be understood as part of the attempt at conflict prevention and/or resolution—privatization as peace-building, in effect.

Linkage has also been made between economic reform and stability, not only with respect to the domestic economies of specific countries, but also with reference to regional initiatives. External aid has been used to lever economic and governance reforms following the rationale that this promotes both growth and sustainable peace. Thus, as its name suggests, the Stability Pact for Southeast Europe, as discussed in Chapter 5, is an integral element in the attempt both to consolidate fragile peace and to prevent the transmission of instability to other countries in the region. Similarly, the New Partnership for African Development (NEPAD) uses promises of aid, debt cancellation, and market access to leverage reforms in economic and political governance. In part, the aim is simply to promote growth. But underlying the program is an assumption that growth and development will also promote peace and stability in a continent in which large parts are perceived as suffering from endemic conflict. Indeed, this linkage is reflected in the fact that NEPAD has a dedicated "Peace and Security" component.[18]

In addition to such general programs of reform, however, current concern over the role of economic resources in financing war or excessive military expenditures has also led to the development of new liberal peace initiatives specifically aimed at addressing this linkage. This includes the IMF's "oil diagnostic" in Angola, agreed as part of a staff-monitored program that provides the basis for further IFI lending to the country. The diagnostic monitors oil revenues to a government that has faced widespread allegations over the "illicit" diversion of public funds to finance arms purchases and the luxury lifestyles of senior officials[19]—although it has been criticized by nongovernmental organizations (NGOs) for not going far enough.[20] A further example is the model developed in the Chad/Cameroon oil pipeline project, a social revenue-sharing agreement between the governments of Chad and Cameroon, NGOs, and an international oil consortium, under the auspices of the World Bank. According to the terms of the agreement, oil revenue from Chad's Doba region will be deposited into an offshore escrow account and supervised by a "stakeholder committee" made up of a Chadian NGO, a trade union, members of the Parliament, and the Supreme Court. Under a national revenue management plan, the government is committed to allocate 80 percent of its share of oil revenue to finance poverty reduction and development and 15 percent to finance recurrent state expenditure. The remaining 5 percent is earmarked for development in the oil region.[21] However, questions remain over the commitment of the government to abide by the agreement. In particular, critics have pointed to a November 2000 purchase of arms using U.S.$4.5 million of a U.S.$25 million bonus the government received from the oil companies. The extent to which the deal is replicable in other countries has also been questioned, although East Timor, which is beginning to develop its own oil fields, has reputedly expressed interest in a similar scheme.[22]

Prophylactic Control

Prophylactic control strategies are designed to address the problems that war and informal economies are perceived to export to the "zones of peace"[23] in the West—for example, drugs, asylum seekers, and sex workers. However, rather than attempting to transform the state from within, the emphasis here is on creating a cordon sanitaire around the "unruly" world. The aim is to prevent transmission of the "virus of disorder"[24] to the developed world. The most extreme example is, perhaps, U.S. military aid to Colombia, variously justified as part of the U.S. war on drugs and, subsequently, the war on terror. Not only is U.S. support for Plan Colombia problematic in itself, but it also ignores both global and local economic dynamics, such as the way that falling global prices for legal commodities have encouraged farmers to plant more lucrative coca crops. In this sense, U.S. military aid to Colombia represents an attempt to address the symptoms (guerrillas and drug production) rather than the cause—because even recognizing the cause, let alone dealing with it, is too problematic. Alternative approaches, such as eliminating the subsidies and trade barriers that protect Western farmers, represent a much greater threat to the established order of the capitalist world than any narcoterrorist. The option of allowing the poor world to deploy the same subsidies and trade protections as have many states of the rich world is even more of a challenge. As the U.S. General Accounting Office (GAO) noted without any trace of irony: "Without interdiction and eradication as disincentives, growers are unlikely to abandon more lucrative and easily cultivated coca crops in favor of less profitable and harder to grow licit crops or to pursue legal employment."[25]

But Plan Colombia is merely the most extreme version of prophylactic control. Other examples abound. For instance, measures undertaken by the UN Drug Control Program (UNDCP) in Central Asia have been criticized for focusing on interdiction, border control, and strengthening law enforcement agencies rather than on harm reduction.[26] This approach has been damned not only as hypocritical—as the domestic strategies of many developed states do in fact emphasize harm reduction—but also as ineffective.[27] Similarly, the UK provides funding to Caribbean countries to train coast guards and marine police units to better intercept drug consignments from a region estimated to account for 65 percent of the cocaine entering Europe.[28]

Control-Lite

The third common strategy reflects a recognition that actors or trading structures of the developed world may be complicit in or facilitate the transmission of disorder, whether through actively supplying arms or money to armed groups or through acting as a magnet for disorder by the consumption of illicit drugs and conflict goods or participation in the illicit sex trade. At heart, however, control-lite represents a form of tokenism that serves to mask the failure to undertake the more fundamental reforms to the structures of global economic and political governance that are required if the varied security threats supposedly transmitted from the "unruly" world really are to be addressed. Control-lite is characterized by two types of tokenism, often in the same initiative: a focus on rogues and the imposition of nominal controls.

Focus on rogues. The first is a regulatory focus on a specific aspect of a much larger problem: "pariah weapons," "rogue companies," or "rogue commodities" in the case of conflict trade. With conflict trade there is a tendency for control initiatives to focus around particular rogue actors (UNITA, the RUF) or particular rogue products (most notably the trade in rough diamonds), leaving other commodities free of formal restrictions — whether oil in Angola or coltan in the Democratic Republic of Congo (DRC). Indeed, even action taken against a rogue product or country has tended, in practice, to be highly selective. Thus, until May 2003, timber was excluded from the list of items subject to sanction in Liberia because of objections by China and France, the largest importers of Liberian timber. Likewise, both Uganda and Rwanda have benefited from the regional trade in conflict diamonds from the DRC, in which they support rebel movements.[29] Despite this, neither country has been the subject of UN Security Council sanctions. In contrast, Liberia has experienced an embargo on its diamond exports because of its role in acting as a conduit for RUF diamonds in the war in Sierra Leone — a war that has now formally ended. It is hard to avoid the conclusion that the main reason for this apparent inequality of treatment relates to the fact that Uganda and Rwanda remain in favor with key UN Security Council members, such as Britain and the United States, while Charles Taylor was given the status of rogue or pariah. Similarly, while the Taliban regime was demonized for its role in the heroin business (even though it had virtually managed to eliminate such activity by the time the United States launched military action following the events of September 11, 2001), the Northern Alliance's involvement in drug and emerald trading was studiously overlooked, as was the complicity of other states in the region.

Imposition of nominal controls. The second type of tokenism could be described as "control–very lite," and is characterized by the development of nominal controls and regulations for the activities of Western economic actors with operations in conflict zones, such as weapons suppliers and oil and diamond companies. To be sure, controls developed against rogue actors and conflict commodities are often quite weak, but this weakness stems from poor implementation. In contrast, nominal controls against corporate actors from the developed world are weak by design. For instance, the European Union (EU) code on arms sales, like current initiatives on light weapons, is an example of an attempt to impose controls on the supply and sale of a broad range of weapons, but is more notable for the softness of its regulatory touch. For instance, the EU code has not prevented the UK from marketing nuclear-capable planes to India or from arranging major defense deals with South Africa despite the latter's crushing social problems and the allegations of corruption that have dogged these transactions. Even regarding those controls that appear rigorous, the reality is somewhat different. For instance, the Ottawa Treaty, on land mines, is notable for the paucity of verification measures and the absence of any meaningful costs for defection or noncompliance. This contrasts sharply with the disciplinary mechanisms that are in place to enforce adherence to the core principles of neoliberalism. For instance, in 1999 British Airways was fined £4 million for breaching EU competition rules. Its crime was to offer extra commission to travel agents who increased the airline's ticket sales.[30] The costs for utilizing land mines or trading in coltan from the DRC or oil from Sudan are, at worst, only to reputation.

Control-lite in operation. Several examples of the control-lite approach are worth noting. First, transparency initiatives have been developed which use the "naming and shaming" of states and MNCs to urge compliance in sanctions enforcement. To some extent, such initiatives have merit in that they aim both to deter shadow trade through shedding light on it and (potentially) to provide an evidentiary basis for more substantive action. Likewise, they represent an attempt to rectify deficiencies in local and global governance, particularly with respect to the issue of corruption. At the same time, however, transparency initiatives also represent a way of appearing to address a problem, while avoiding developing mechanisms that actually would have regulatory teeth for economic actors in the developed world. Indeed, as with all control-lite initiatives, such strategies are deemed acceptable precisely because they do not imply fundamental reform of the neoliberal fundamentals of the global economy.

One example of a transparency initiative is the anticorruption "publish what you pay" (PWYP) campaign, motivated in part by concern about the use by unaccountable regimes of "signature bonus payments" from resource extraction companies to fund arms purchases in countries like Angola. In some respects, the goals of this campaign are quite innovative, in that its ultimate objective is to make listing of companies on stock markets contingent upon transparent publication of all payments to national governments, with the economic penalty being a loss of investor access. The aim, then, is to lever MNC transparency as a way of promoting state transparency, thereby exposing and deterring corruption. However, the goal of changing actual behavior relies merely on the indirect pressure that comes from public scrutiny, first of multinational extractive companies, and second of state officials in host countries. Moreover, the record of other transparency initiatives such as the UN Arms Register, suggests that, in the absence of effective regulation to actually punish errant behavior and in a context where the incentives to perpetuate such behavior may be strong, simply shedding light upon an activity may not be a sufficient disincentive. Indeed, the act of publication sometimes provides a veneer of legitimacy—as has occurred in the UK with respect to the government's introduction of an annual report on arms exports, allowing actors to claim that openness is itself a demonstration of purity, irrespective of the actions they are being open about. Furthermore, while the essentials of the PWYP campaign have now been incorporated in the Extractive Industries Transparency Initiative (EITI) being promoted by the UK government, it has also been watered down. In particular, under current proposals, the emphasis is on a voluntary compact, rather than a mandatory one, and the mechanisms for monitoring have been diluted,[31] leading some skeptics to label it the "Blair Which? Project." Thus, to date, even the "publish what you pay" campaign has not yet succeeded in achieving its goals.

The most significant transparency initiative has been the UN's adoption of independent Expert Panels to monitor compliance with sanctions and/or the role of "illicit" resource exploitation in a number of conflicts, including Angola, Sierra Leone, Liberia, and the DRC. While such panels have been very successful in raising awareness of the issues, their effect has been limited in a number of respects. First, they are currently established on an ad hoc basis rather than institutionalized as a standard response to any conflict. Second, while in some cases, such as Angola and Liberia, the reports of Expert Panels have reinforced the commitment to impose sanctions, in others reports have not had the same impact. Notable here is the UN Security Council's demurral of an Expert Panel recommendation to impose sanctions against combatants in the DRC. In addition, when reports have resulted in action, it has tended to be targeted at the "unruly" world and the arenas of conflict, particularly rebel groups. Actors in the developed world have largely escaped formal sanction. Thus, for instance, some thirty-two Belgian companies have been named in UN reports as having imported diamonds under false declaration. Other than a letter of reprimand, however, none has been subject to any sanction.[32]

The control-lite approach is also reflected in a number of initiatives to develop voluntary codes under which firms commit themselves to abide by certain ethical trading practices. Examples include the Wolfsberg Principles, under which a number of major banks have committed themselves to take action against money laundering; the UN's Global Compact; the U.S.-UK Voluntary Principles on Security and Human Rights, agreed by a number of companies in the extractive and energy sectors; and the Organization for Economic Cooperation and Development (OECD) Principles of Corporate Governance.[33] The nonbinding nature of voluntary codes makes them more attractive to industry and thus increases the likelihood of adoption and the potential scope of their coverage. Self-regulation also solves some of the enforcement problems experienced by states or multilateral organizations when trying to apply formal regulations.[34] It might also be argued that voluntary codes have the potential to prevent the pathologies of the developed world from destabilizing the weak states. The problem with this latter argument, however, is that the voluntarism implied by such schemes tends to result in acts of tokenism that do not go much beyond a level of regulation acceptable to the most reluctant and foot-dragging partner. Crucially, of course, such schemes also tend to lack monitoring and enforcement provisions, a feature that substantially erodes their effectiveness. Indeed, this does nothing to address the existing difficulties involved in overcoming the collective action problems of competitive economic actors—as, reputational costs aside, defection does not incur penalties and may even offer commercial advantages. For example, only five of the major U.S. multinationals have joined the UN's Global Compact,[35] while a number of signatories to both the Global Compact and the OECD Principles have also been criticized for their complicity in "illicit" resource exploitation in the conflict in the DRC.[36]

A third example of the control-lite approach is regulatory initiatives that significantly impact on the operations of developed state firms, most notably the global certification scheme for rough diamonds. This arose out of the Kimberley Process, the name given to a series of meetings that ultimately brought some fifty-two trading and producer states, NGOs, and businesses together to develop a scheme to prevent the trade in "conflict diamonds." The Kimberley Process itself represented a response to NGO campaigns over the way in which the shadow trade in rough diamonds has funded conflict in countries such as Angola, Sierra Leone, and the DRC. For instance, in some years UNITA earned as much as U.S.$700 million per annum from sales of conflict diamonds.[37] The formally stated aim of the Kimberley Process was to develop a scheme that would prevent, or at least curtail, the trade in conflict diamonds. Kimberley participants finally agreed on the modalities of a scheme in March 2002 and formal implementation began in January 2003.

The scheme itself consists of four main elements. First, there is a requirement for standardized control in producer countries, from mine to the point of export. The second element is a certification process in which exported rough diamonds are moved in sealed packages and equipped with a Kimberley Process certificate detailing specific data for the diamonds therein (e.g., country of origin, carat weight/mass, exporter and importer). This is received and documented by customs officials in the importing country. Third, a voluntary system of industry warranties aims to start with the first import of rough diamonds into a processing country and will continue to track them along the supply chain, as long as they remain in their rough state. The fourth element is a commitment to the regular publication of standardized statistics on production, export, and import. The absence of such standardized statistical data in the past has made identification of suspicious trading activity difficult.

In theory, countries failing to comply with the essential elements of the scheme can be excluded from trading with participants.[38] However, as currently envisaged, the scheme suffers from significant weaknesses. The definition of "conflict diamonds" is narrowly focused on "rough diamonds used by rebels or their allies to finance conflict aimed at undermining legitimate governments."[39] This excludes rough diamonds traded by governments unless, as in the case of Liberia, they are acting as proxies for rebels in another state. Government diamonds from the conflict in the DRC are not deemed conflict diamonds and are thus not subject to action under Kimberley. Including trade by recognized governments would have had the effect of potentially opening up a much wider range of developed states and allies, such as Israel, to allegations of trading in conflict diamonds. In the spirit of control-lite, the regime's function seems to be to discipline actors defined as "rogues" and "radicals" in the dominant security narratives of the major powers, rather than to address the trade in conflict diamonds per se. The focus on rough diamonds may also provide scope for actors in conflict to evade controls simply by establishing their own cutting and polishing centers—as Rwanda is currently doing for the diamonds it is taking from the DRC—making it relatively easy for conflict entrepreneurs to evade Kimberley controls.

The integrity of the scheme depends on effective controls from the mine to the first point of export in producer countries. However, as noted in the chapter on Sierra Leone, a combination of weak state capacity and pervasive corruption has meant that rebel diamonds have already been laundered through official certification processes or smuggled out through regional shadow trading networks. The introduction of a certification scheme in Sierra Leone may, in fact, have made it *easier* to launder diamonds, as it has obviated the need for complicated smuggling through other countries. This highlights the requirement for developed states to support capacity-building and anticorruption measures among producer states.[40] The text agreed in March 2002 failed to address this issue specifically, though the European Commission, for instance, is planning to invite bids for assistance from the European Development Fund. In early 2003, the issue of administrative support for implementation of the Kimberley scheme remained controversial. Indeed, lobbying by a number of governments ensured that the final text contained no reference to a secretariat, while proposals tabled by the European Commission to divide administrative tasks between a number of bodies have been criticized for potentially denuding the certification regime of an effective implementation mechanism.[41] Finally, there is no mechanism—apart from a full plenary debate—to determine an applicant's suitability for membership in the scheme or for monitoring member states' national controls. Review missions can only be triggered by "credible indications of significant noncompliance," but have to be authorized at the annual plenary of all participants. It also requires the assent of the country under consideration, as all decisionmaking is undertaken by consensus.[42] A system of states volunteering to be inspected has been discussed, but it is unclear whether states such as Russia and China, which originally objected to inspections, will accept such a principle even if they themselves are not formally required to submit to it.

The Utility of Regional Initiatives

Given that one of the central concerns of this study involves the regional dimensions of conflict, it is useful to evaluate the merits of regional-level control initiatives. First, regional mechanisms to address the link between economic agendas and conflict have, to date, been relatively underdeveloped. In part, this reflects the acute security dilemmas that exist between states embedded in regional conflict complexes; in part, it reflects a lack of institutional capacity. But it also underscores the relative neglect of the regional dynamics of conflict, in particular their economic dimensions, by both research and policy. Moreover, where initiatives have been developed, they tend to represent regional versions of existing global strategies. Thus the Economic Community of West African States (ECOWAS) has established a Drug Control Unit, which is tasked with formulating regional drug control programs. Members of ECOWAS have also adopted a security mechanism that includes a call for improved cooperation in early warning, conflict prevention, peacekeeping operations, and curtailing cross-border crime and the trafficking in small arms.[43] Similarly, the Caribbean Financial Action Task Force (CFATF), which has been established to develop a common approach to the problem of the laundering of drug money in the region, is modeled on the OECD's Financial Action Task Force (FATF).[44]

Such regional initiatives suffer from some obvious drawbacks. Just as global initiatives tend to reflect the interests of the major powers, so regional initiatives risk being constructed to serve the interests of regional hegemons. In addition, to the extent that regional actors are complicit in the very shadow economies they are supposed to be addressing, the incentive to deliver anything more than tokenistic measures to address problems such as the trade in conflict diamonds, illicit arms, and drugs or money laundering, may be weak. Furthermore, regional initiatives to address the economic dimensions of conflict can become a substitute for firmer, more effective action at the global level. Alternatively, they can become further vehicles for the capitalist cores to extend the regulatory arena of liberal peace initiatives in the world peripheries. Thus, regional initiatives to address the economic agendas in conflict are unlikely, in themselves, to constitute an alternative possibility for a more effective and more transformative approach to the political economy of violence.

However, action at the regional level does have advantages that international policy might usefully seek to build upon. First, and most obvious, given the strong regional dimensions in the political economy of contemporary violence, regional organizations by definition represent a particularly appropriate forum in which to address such dynamics. They may also be more responsive both to the local problems created by regulation and the adaptive reactions or evasion strategies of conflict entrepreneurs. Regional-level initiatives may be just as likely to be influenced by vested interests as initiatives at either the domestic or the global level, but the problem could be tackled through stronger cooperative partnership arrangements with international organizations and by empowering civil society monitoring, as noted below.

Second, regional-level action in the undeveloped world has the potential, through collective action, to create a more balanced forum in which the geography of regulation can be negotiated. One possible example is the way in which the NEPAD Subcommittee on Peace and Security has taken steps to promote a minimum standard for MNCs operating in the region.[45] The aim is to prevent multinational companies and foreign countries from contributing to conflict and corruption through the exploitation of natural resources. Potentially, such a forum for African states may increase their negotiating power with respect to outside actors, although this is not guaranteed—the rigor of these kinds of initiatives risks being watered down either by outside pressure or by internal competition for inward investment that creates a rush to the regulatory bottom.

Regional-level initiatives also have the capacity to produce more far-reaching responses to specific problems, particularly when local actors have a more direct and immediate experience of them. For instance, although honored more in the breach, the Organization of African Unity's Convention for the Elimination of Mercenarism in Africa, which entered into force in 1985, is the only international instrument in force that is specifically applicable to mercenary activity. At the very least, therefore, it provides a baseline against which local states can be judged. In contrast, the 1989 UN International Convention Against the Use, Financing, and Training of Mercenaries has not yet entered into force.[46] Similarly, in 1996 the Organization of American States adopted the first international convention targeting corruption. Indeed, the convention is more encompassing than either the U.S. Foreign Corrupt Practices Act or the OECD convention on bribery that entered into force in 1999.[47]

Regional mechanisms may also contain other potentials that have remained largely unexplored. As already noted, regional-level initiatives often replicate global or developed-state initiatives to address a particular issue. Alternatively, they address activity that has been labeled as "illicit" or that has been problematized in the economic and security discourse of the major powers. What is significant about such discourses is that they reflect the economic and power interests of dominant global actors. Thus, what is construed as "illicit" or "criminal" economic activity is as much a function of these power relations as it is of any objective harm that particular types of economic activity produce. For instance, British piracy in the Elizabethan era was undertaken with royal sanction. Similarly, when China banned the sale of opium by the British East India Company, the British prime minister of the day, Lord Palmerston, dispatched a naval squadron to bombard Canton and other ports.[48] In contrast, British prime minister Tony Blair contributed British troops to the overthrow of the Taliban regime. While the motivation for this was largely a function of the so-called war on terrorism, a supplementary justification was to address the role of Afghanistan in the drug trade. Such developed state determinations of what constitutes "criminality" and "illegitimate" conflict trade not only represent an oversimplification of a complex issue, but may also produce counterproductive policies. Yet again, this is an example of the skewed ideological matrix surrounding issues of development and security. Regional-level initiatives may offer an opportunity for local actors to construct alternative representations of the political economy of conflict and to develop novel regulatory mechanisms to address such issues. In this sense then, they have an unrealized potential to develop far more radical and more transformational approaches to the economics of violence. Whether this potential can be realized is another question.

Regional-level action also presents a greater opportunity for local civil society actors to influence agendas. Currently, local civil society in the developing world, while often quite vibrant, suffers from unequal power relations in their dealings with Western NGOs and donors, and domestic governments. Collective civil society action at the regional level has the potential to offset both of these disadvantages. These regional groupings, therefore, have the potential to provide civil society in the undeveloped world with a more effective voice on issues related to the political economy of violence.

Moreover, given the acute regional security dilemmas that hinder state-to-state cooperation in areas such as West Africa or Southeast Europe, regionwide civil society action has the potential to foster common bonds of understanding and erode mistrust at the grassroots level, processes that ultimately can influence government action. A model here is that of the European Nuclear Disarmament movement during the Cold War and the Helsinki Citizens Assembly. Regional-level variants of such groups, which concern themselves not only with human rights or arms reduction but also with the political economy of peacebuilding, may have an as yet relatively untapped potential to foster a political economy of peacebuilding from below.[49] Moreover, these groups can also promote debate and provide forums for the semiofficial exploration of cooperation initiatives that governments may be wary of voicing in public.

In addition, regional-level civil society action to address the political economy of violence has the potential to be particularly beneficial precisely because it is a topic on which the voice of civil society is generally given less credence. While the potential of local NGOs to contribute to peacebuilding is often lionized by external actors, this tends to be with respect to issues such as human rights, gender, or good governance. This is largely because such groups are deemed to have direct experience of issues such as human rights abuse and thus are considered to have both a moral and an empirical claim to knowledge. In contrast, despite the profound effects it has on ordinary people's lives, the political economy of postconflict peacebuilding is often treated as a set of technical issues concerned with balancing inflation and other indicators of macroeconomic stability, issues more amenable to solution by knowledgeable technocrats. Regional-level action and coordination by local civil society groups may help to address this problem in a number of ways. First, the creation of groupings at a regional level can facilitate civil society recognition. The politics of pressure-group influence is an area where both size and breadth matter. Second, and following from recognition, such groupings may have greater potential to attract the kind of funding that will enable the research and other activities necessary to generate local expertise on the regional economic dynamics of conflict and peacebuilding. Third, regional civil society groupings are less likely to be hampered by the statist or functional restrictions and sclerotic bureaucracies that limit the perspectives of multilateral agencies and hinder their capacity to effectively deal with the adaptive mutation of shadow economies. Thus they have the potential to provide a perspective that transcends borders and issue areas in precisely the way that actors in the shadow economy do, and with the same adaptive speed of the criminal networks. Effectively funded regional-level civil society groupings can thus make a claim to knowledge that would give them a voice in policymaking. One notable example is the Centre National d'appui au Développement et à la participation populaire (CENADEP) in the DRC, a federation of civil society groups with regional allies that has sought, through research and advocacy, to bring attention to the issue of resource exploitation in the Great Lakes regional conflict complex.

This is not to idealize the potentials inherent in civil society action. As has occurred to some extent in Sierra Leone, civil society groups sometimes can be dominated by a narrow core of activists. Thus the voice of civil society can sometimes simply reflect the opinions of a relatively narrow band of opinion formers. Worse still, civil society groups can also act as a front for particular government or industry interests. To some extent, however, even these problems may be ameliorated by the requirements of intergroup coordination at the regional level.

Conclusion

The growing focus on the role of economic agendas in regional conflict complexes and the way the trade in resources has been used to fund militarism have resulted in pressure for the development of a range of initiatives aimed at curtailing such linkages. To date, however, the set of measures that has emerged reinforces the level of intervention in the economic governance of states in the periphery, while largely failing to address either the fundamental inequalities inherent in the global trading system or even the networked trading activities of shadow economies. Indeed, the way in which such initiatives are applied tends to both reflect and reinforce existing global inequalities. Thus the underdeveloped world has become the object of strategies of deep reform, sanctioned by aid conditionality and/or an arena of prophylactic control. At the same time, initiatives that significantly impact on Western firms and economies are marked either by voluntarism or by the lightest of regulatory touches. This is particularly apparent when one contrasts the weakness of the mechanisms available to enforce adherence to regulatory initiatives such as those on arms or conflict diamonds with those available to enforce compliance with the free trade principles of neoliberalism. Finally, while regional-level initiatives to address the political economy of violence are certainly not a panacea, they nevertheless offer a number of potential options for addressing this issue, not the least of which is reflected in the very fact that such political economies do have strong regional dimensions.

Notes

1. Paul Rogers, *Losing Control: Global Security in the Twenty-First Century* (London: Pluto Press, 2000).

2. Mark Duffield, *Global Governance and the New Wars: The Merging of Development and Security* (London: Zed Books, 2001), p. 7.

3. Ibid., p. 15.

4. Oxfam, *Rigged Rules and Double Standards: Trade, Globalization, and the Fight Against Poverty* (Oxford: Oxfam, 2002), p. 141.

5. Okoth F. Mudhai, "Exploring the Plausibility of the New Inclusive Partnership Development Agenda for Africa," paper presented at the British International Studies Association conference, LSE, London, December 16–18, 2002, p. 8.

6. Oxfam, *Rigged Rules and Double Standards,* p. 96.

7. Duffield, *Global Governance and the New Wars,* p. 141.

8. International Crisis Group (ICG), *Central Asia: Drugs and Conflict,* ICG Asia Report no. 25 (Brussels: ICG, November 26, 2001).

9. John MacKinlay, *Globalization and Insurgency,* Adelphi Paper no. 352 (Oxford: Oxford University Press for the International Institute of Strategic Studies, 2002), pp. 15–29.

10. David Held, Anthony McGrew, David Goldblatt, and Jonathan Perraton, *Global Transformations: Politics, Economics, and Culture* (Cambridge: Polity Press, 1999), p. 170.

11. MacKinlay, *Globalization and Insurgency,* pp. 15–29.

12. Held et al., *Global Transformations,* pp. 165–170.

13. Susan Willett, "Introduction: Globalization and Insecurity," in Susan Willett, ed., "Structural Conflict in the New Global Disorder: Insecurity and Development," *IDS Bulletin* 32, no. 2 (April 2001): 1.

14. Robert C. Orr, "Building Peace in El Salvador: From Exception to Rule," in Elizabeth M. Cousens and Chetan Kumar, with Karin Wermester, eds., *Peacebuilding as Politics: Cultivating Peace in Fragile Societies* (Boulder, CO: Lynne Rienner, 2001), pp. 167–168.

15. Susan L. Woodward, "Economic Priorities for Successful Peace Implementation," in Stephen John Stedman, Donald Rothchild, and Elizabeth M. Cousens, eds., *Ending Civil Wars: The Implementation of Peace Agreements* (Boulder, CO: Lynne Rienner, 2002), p. 193.

16. This represents a refinement of the argument presented in Neil Cooper, "Dealing with War Economies: Control-Lite as a Substitute for Real Reform," in Jurgen Brauer, Paul Dunne, David Gold, and John Tepper Marlin, eds., *ECAAR Review 2002* (New York: Economists Allied Against Arms, 2002), pp. 45–56.

17. Department for International Development (DFID), *Security Sector Reform and the Management of Military Expenditure: High Risks for Donors, High Returns for Development,* report of an international symposium sponsored by the DFID, London, February 15–17, 2000 (London: DFID, 2000).

18. International Peace Academy, *Policies and Practices for Regulating Resource Flows to Armed Conflict* (New York: International Peace Academy, 2002) p. 11.

19. Global Witness, *All the President's Men: The Devastating Story of Oil and Banking in Angola's Privatised War,* March 2002, www.oneworld.org/globalwitness.

20. Human Rights Watch, *The Oil Diagnostic in Angola: An Update,* a backgrounder by Human Rights Watch (Washington, DC: Human Rights Watch, 2001).

21. Phillipe Le Billon, Jake Sherman, and Marcia Hartwell, *Controlling Resource Flows to Civil Wars: A Review and Analysis of Current Policies and Legal Instruments* (New York: International Peace Academy, 2002), p. 39.

22. International Peace Academy, *Options for Promoting Corporate Responsibility in Conflict Zones: Perspective from the Private Sector,* IPA Meeting Report (Jake Sherman, rapporteur), New York, April 2002, pp. 7–8.

23. M. Singer and A. Wildavsky, *The Real World Order: Zones of Peace and Zones of Turmoil* (Chatham, NJ: Chatham House, 1993).

24. Timothy Luke and Gearóid Ó'Tuathail, "On Videocameralists: The Geopolitics of Failed States, the CNN International, and (UN)governmentality," *Review of International Political Economy* 4, no. 4 (1997): 709–733.

25. U.S. General Accounting Office (GAO), *Drug Control: Efforts to Develop Alternatives to Cultivating Illicit Crops in Colombia Have Made Little Progress and Face Serious Obstacles,* GAO-02-291 (Washington, DC: GAO, February 2002).

26. United Nations International Drug Control Program, *Strengthening Drug Control and Crime Prevention Capacities in the Central Asian States,* July 2001.

27. Mathew Fielden and Jonathan Goodhand, "Beyond the Taliban? The Afghan Conflict and United Nations Peacemaking," *Journal of Conflict, Security, and Development* 1, no. 3 (2001): 5–32.

28. UK Foreign and Commonwealth Office, "FCO Funded Training Results in Drug Seizures in the Caribbean," press release, March 31, 2003.

29. United Nations, *Final Report of the Panel of Experts on the Illegal Exploitation of Natural Resources and Other Forms of Wealth of the Democratic Republic of the Congo*, S/2002/1146, 2002, www.globalpolicy.org/security/docs/minindx.htm.

30. "BA Fined £4 Million for Illegal Trading," *The Guardian* (London), July 15, 1999.

31. Report of the Extractive Industries Transparency Initiative (EITI) Workshop, February 11–12, 2003, www.dfid.gov.uk/News/News/files/eiti_intro.htm.

32. Ian Smillie, *Dirty Diamonds: Armed Conflict and the Trade in Rough Diamonds*, FAFO Report no. 377 (Oslo: Fafo Institute for Applied Social Science, 2002), p. 44.

33. Le Billon, Sherman, and Hartwell, *Controlling Resource Flows to Civil Wars*.

34. International Peace Academy, *Economic Agendas in Armed Conflict: Defining and Developing the Role of the UN* (New York: International Peace Academy, March 2002).

35. Oliver Williams, "Major U.S. Companies Doubt Global Compact Credentials," *Business Day*, April 22, 2003, www.bday.co.za/bday/content/direct/1,3523,1330151-6096-0,00.html.

36. United Nations, *Final Report of the Panel of Experts on the Illegal Exploitation of Natural Resources in the Democratic Republic of the Congo*.

37. Global Witness, *A Rough Trade: The Role of Companies and Governments in the Angolan Conflict* (London: Global Witness, 1998).

38. General Accounting Office, *International Trade: Critical Issues Remain in Deterring Conflict Diamond Trade*, GA-02-678 (Washington, DC: GAO, June 2002), p. 18.

39. *Essential Elements of an International Scheme of Certification for Rough Diamonds, with a View to Breaking the Link Between Armed Conflict and the Trade in Rough Diamonds*, Kimberley Process Working Document no. 1/2002, www.globalpolicy.org/security/issues/diamond/index.htm. See also UN Resolution GA55/56, January 2001, p. 29, www.globalpolicy.org/security/issues/diamond/index.htm.

40. Fatal Transactions, *Implementing Kimberley: Stopping the Blood Diamond Trade to Europe*, report of the European Union Expert Meeting, March 7, 2002 (Amsterdam: Fatal Transactions, April 2002), p. 5.

41. Ibid., pp. 7–18.

42. Ian Smillie, *The Kimberley Process: The Case for Proper Monitoring*, Diamonds and Human Security Project, Occasional Paper no. 5 (Ottawa: Partnership Africa Canada, 2002).

43. Comfort Ero, Waheguru Pal Singh Sidhu, and Augustine Toure, *Towards a Pax West Africana: Building Peace in a Troubled Sub-Region*, report on IPA-ECOWAS, September 27–29, 2001, Abuja Seminar (New York: International Peace Academy, 2001), p. 16.

44. Le Billon, Sherman, and Hartwell, *Controlling Resource Flows to Civil Wars*, p. 20.

45. International Peace Academy, *Policies and Practices for Regulating Resource Flows*, p. 11.

46. Ibid., p. 42.

47. Ibid., p. 24.

48. Oxfam, *Rigged Rules and Double Standards,* pp. 25, 32.

49. Mary Kaldor, *Europe from Below: An East-West Dialogue* (London: Verso, 1991).

7

Conclusion: Toward a
New Agenda for Transforming
War Economies

This book has drawn attention to the limited nature of existing research on civil conflicts, a consequence of the way that such conflicts have been represented as retreats into ethnic or religious "barbarism." It has also noted the limits of research on war economies, especially in relation to regional conflict complexes and postconflict transformation strategies. Of course, surveying the landscape of war economies is hardly an exact science. Conflict propels economic activity toward the shadows of survival, subsistence, and subterfuge, and disrupts measurement and data collection. But as well as creating difficulties for the researcher, the rough terrain opens up opportunities to examine shadow linkages across borders and how regional economic, political, military, and social dynamics impact on the character of armed conflict. Such analysis challenges the dual fixations with global and national security, for conflict complexes are arenas not only where national and global factors interact, but also where state authorities collapse and borderlands become critically important determinants of peace and stability.

This has led us to review the political and social purposes of war-induced economic activity and to conclude that many features of the resistance to a destiny mapped for war-torn societies by rigid free market policies endure and adapt into peacebuilding. Indeed, one of the tests that war-torn societies invariably confront is the contingency of the help they receive, assistance that is predicated on their acceptance of a model of economic development favored by postindustrial donor states and international financial institutions (IFIs). The expectation that the political economy of a war-torn society should conform to an external model has been shown to be problematic. Our conclusions are that the representation of war economies as "abnormal" or "illegal" underestimates their rationality, their functionality, and their resilience. This is not to deny that predation engenders alienation and dissent and thus leads to the mobilization of alternative values and institutions that may rebel against the political economy of war and, as in Bosnia and Herzegovina (BiH), produce incentives to sue for peace. Nevertheless, war economies clearly create problems for postconflict transformation.

The predominant model of political economy in the liberal peace also produces problems. Alternative forms of political economy, tailor-made for particular postconflict contexts, but placing more emphasis on social needs, are available and feasible if policymakers are prepared to look outside the neoliberal paradigm of transformation. Our overall conclusion, then, is that the externally derived paradigm of free market development is a highly problematic if not counterproductive response to the challenges posed by war economies. Indeed, not only is this model inappropriate for postconflict situations generally, but it is also particularly ill suited to counter the vicissitudes of predation and corruption engendered by war. Among other things, it fails to understand the role of shadow economies, the need for comprehensive regional approaches to security and development, and the need for strong state institutions with the authority and capacity to protect vulnerable populations, provide essential public goods, and generate economic growth.

The chapter begins by drawing out the major lessons of the cases for postconflict transformation and for addressing their regional dimensions. This discussion is followed by recommendations for the kinds of alternative policies that might be pursued.

Lessons from the Cases

The case studies have indicated the importance of understanding the economic trajectories of war, the key role played by regional networks in the political economy of war, and the challenges posed by the legacies of war economies for effective transformation strategies.

Distinctive Features

Each case has distinctive features in its political economy, implying different challenges for transformation as well as a requirement for situation-specific policy responses. Each is in a different stage of the conflict cycle. In Afghanistan, the security situation remains extremely fragile. With warlords in control of much of the country beyond Kabul, there is little sign of a durable peace emerging. While in better shape than Afghanistan, Sierra Leone remains prey to incursions and skirmishes and depends for its security on the presence of UK troops and the largest current deployment of UN peacekeepers. Actual or potential insurgent activity remains at relatively high levels, both within these states and across their regions, requiring government and foreign forces to be on high states of alert. BiH is at the heart of a now quiescent regional conflict complex, and the war economy as such has mutated into the exertion of clientalist controls and influence over the spoils of peace. While the Dayton Accord (and in Kosovo military-technical agreements), backed by a foreign military, police, administrative, and judicial presence, have produced structurally flawed political arrangements, they have nonetheless allowed for enduring cease-fires, sufficient to enable extensive peacebuilding activity.

The cases also differ in terms of their geopolitical constraints. Central Asia remains economically peripheral but has become strategically crucial to the U.S. "war on terror." Afghanistan's political regime was forcibly changed by external intervention, creating a new geostrategic dynamic within the region, in which the United States supplies arms and other forms of military aid to authoritarian but "friendly" neighbors such as Pakistan, Uzbekistan, and Kyrgyzstan. Southeast Europe is strategically important for the EU and NATO, requiring the continued presence of foreign troops. Its fragmentation and unresolved sovereignties and its role as a crossroads of trafficking and migration make BiH a neuralgia spot in close proximity to a relatively prosperous and stable Western Europe. In West Africa, the UK and France have traditional interests that have prompted military intervention, but the region poses no direct strategic threat to either. Unlike the other cases, however, West Africa does possess valuable natural resource endowments that are accorded a legitimate role in world trade, including diamonds and timber. Southeast Europe has a few resources of value but also serves as a conduit of drug smuggling and human trafficking. The relatively high level of education and marketable technological skills of the population encourages a "brain drain." Likewise, Afghanistan has few resources, and its most valuable crop, poppy, is regarded as "illegitimate" in the world trading system. These differences present different challenges.

Compared to other conflicts, Afghanistan has been underfunded by donors, and 6 million people remain economically vulnerable, as noted in Chapter 3. War and shadow economies continue to thrive in the regional borderlands of Central Asia. Indeed, Jonathan Goodhand has questioned the label "postconflict" as applied to the Afghan political economy. In particular, it is clear that while military commanders and mafia elites engage in shadow activities that prey on the vulnerability of the poor and deprive the state of revenues, they are also supporting an economy on which the majority of the population depends. The poorest sections of the community have few options but to engage in rational coping and survival strategies, including growing and dealing in the opium poppy. Afghanistan continues to lack a strong, credible, centralized state with a monopoly of violence that has the capacity to offer incentives, welfare, and effective security as alternatives to warlord rule and the "illicit" economic pursuits that enable warlords to thrive. The strong implication is that peace will remain elusive for some time to come.

A primary lesson, therefore, is that Afghanistan will require a significant increase in the scope of international security provision beyond Kabul, curbs on arms trading by external powers to the region, and greatly increased external funding to transform governing institutions so that they can provide social protection and offer incentives to entrepreneurial elites to engage in state-building economic activities. Given the cross-border linkages that sustain combat, shadow, and coping economies, a second set of priorities, more developmental in design, is to address these regional interactions. These efforts should not be limited to improving policing and more effective controls over cross-border trades; they should also entail massive increases in government spending and international investment in regional infrastructure, in the first instance, to develop communications, trade, power, and water supplies. A third set of transformation initiatives, also to foster development and poverty reduction, but ultimately to reduce dependency on provincial warlords, is to provide investment in a system of agricultural incentives to make alternatives to the monoculture of opium attractive.

In the case of Sierra Leone in West Africa, the narrative of conflict has given economic agendas a prominent role. Even as this mode of analysis has yielded some useful insights into the dynamics of the political economy of the regional conflict complex, it has obscured others. In particular, the dominant narrative of predatory rebels has neglected both the complicity of the state in the shadow economy and the long-standing regional networks and traditions of parallel trade that created bottom-up structural incentives for participation in "illicit" exchange prior to the outbreak of civil war. The networks developed to facilitate this shadow trade were readily adapted to military ends by conflict entrepreneurs as well as by patrimonial elites. Prior to the conflict, the state was already severely debilitated by the effects of the economic changes demanded by the IFIs. First, successive rulers were able to use IFI demands for reductions in public expenditure and state-directed development to eliminate inconvenient economic regulation and to reinforce their personal authority, mediated through networks of patrimonial welfare. Second, the application of cuts in state expenditure, the advent of privatization, and the elimination of subsidies for key commodities exacerbated people's alienation from the state and increased their dependency on shadow economic activity.

The primary lesson here is that securing peace in the West African conflict complex requires a regionwide conflict resolution process that addresses the phenomenon of displacement and the fueling of conflict that occurs through the transnational movement of weapons and mercenaries in particular. Here also, the challenge is to regulate the trade in lucrative natural resources, driving it into the "legal," formal economy. Steps have already been taken to address the conflict trades in this region, but they need to be strengthened. In particular, funding needs to be provided to increase the capacity of regional states to cooperate in monitoring and in licensing economic activity. A control regime also needs to be more equitable in its impact, curtailing the demand side in the developed world for goods that fuel conflict. Protectionist economic policies on a regional basis could be encouraged, including the provision of subsidies for agriculture, not only to channel coping and survival strategies and regional development into the formal economies but also to empower public institutions.

Largely because of the dominant discourses relating to ethnic identity and congenital Balkan instability, analyses of the wars in the former Yugoslavia have generally ignored the economic drivers of this conflict complex. In the first instance, however, the disintegration of Yugoslavia was partly the consequence of the pressures that the IFIs exerted on a highly brittle federal system that had undertaken economic decentralization. Paradoxically, the wars fostered the process of state disintegration, even while keeping open profitable channels across ethnic lines. Indeed, in the post-Dayton peace, shadow economies have thrived by exploiting the incongruities of differential regulatory regimes. Another misleading discourse has been current. The postconflict economy is depicted as corrupt, dysfunctional, war-wrecked, and statist; by contrast, external actors are commonly portrayed as disinterested observers and beneficent agents of intervention. This underestimates the sophistication and positive aspects of the shadow economy on the one hand, and the deleterious effects of neoliberal policies on the other. External policies that seek the withdrawal of the state from the economy have done little to free the vast majority of the populations from their dependence on "illicit" survival and coping mechanisms, and may have increased it.

In contrast to the other two cases, BiH and Southeast European countries do possess established or formative bureaucracies that operate with a degree of effectiveness, though often for narrow party or patrimonial interests. A primary challenge of transformation to sustainable peace is to lift the dead hand of macroeconomic stability, privatization, and FDI, and equip ministries and local authorities with the means to plan and implement state intervention for generating production and consumption power that would reduce the size of the shadow economies. Southeast Europe has an option of regional economic integration, and in the long term, of eventual integration with the contiguous, magnetically attractive European Union (EU). The Stability Pact for Southeast Europe has been an attempt at comprehensive regional peacebuilding, but has not yet addressed key issues of the level and purpose of integration, or the precise form it would take. A consequence of making support for such a formation contingent on the adoption of free market policies (as indicated in the pact's basic principles), and of monetarist policies (in line with EU accession requirements), is likely to be a prolongation of poverty and mafia welfare. If, on the other hand, a regional formation had, as its *initial* rationale, an element of mutual protection *against* the vulnerabilities of EU integration—for example, through the development of a regional customs union—then such a bottom-up, building-block approach would not only cushion societies against economic instability, but also eventually prove compatible with the concept of a peaceful Europe of the regions.

Common Elements

Despite differences in their levels of development and their different natural resource endowments, the three cases also exhibit in common the military, political, social, and economic elements of regional conflict complexes discussed in Chapter 2. They feature many of the permissive conditions for regional conflict complexes—including pressures for structural adjustment, the economic marginalization of borderlands, weak central state authorities, poor regional security integration, and economic mechanisms that give rise to shadow economies. They all face the challenge of multiple transitions: from war to peace or relative peace, from command to open economies, and from collapsed states to nascent state systems. Their postconflict economies all feature intensive smuggling and trafficking activities and the existence of autonomous borderlands that facilitate this. It is almost no exaggeration to describe Afghanistan and BiH as borderlands in their own right. They all lack a strong state system (though the multiplicity of authorities in BiH suggests too much governance rather than too little) and each features patrimonial and clientalistic forms of political economy. And all evince significant levels of shadow economic activity either in the form of entrepreneurial and mafia profiteering or in the form of coping strategies. Moreover, all three cases demonstrate the persistence of shadow networks into the postconflict period and their flexibility in adapting to the exigencies of liberal peace strategies.

A further shared feature is the ambivalent role in war and postconflict transformation played by shadow economies. They bequeath a mixed legacy for peacebuilding. On the one hand, shadow economies are arenas for entrepreneurial elites to exploit the comparative advantages that arise from the mix of corruption, weak governance, and porous borders and to divert these assets to the prosecution of war. On the other hand, they also serve broad welfare needs, providing shortcuts through bureaucracy and a defense against state corruption and neglect that allow more efficient economic transactions and, in more dire economic and security circumstances, enabling people to cope and survive. Certainly, the social functions of families, clans, and occupational networks can spread cultures of nepotism and cartelism. But capitalism is itself hardly immune from market fixing and criminality.[1] Shadow economies and their profiteers have been stigmatized as major obstacles to the favored model of peacebuilding. But transformation to a peace economy will not be eased by their criminalization and marginalization, because these shadow systems are not separate from the larger economic forces of globalization. Indeed, they are an integral part of the global economy. A neglected but significant challenge for postconflict transformation, then, is to overturn the routine assumption that shadow economies are simply local pathologies that are antithetical to welfare.

Finally, these three cases highlight the inapplicability of neoliberalism to war-torn states. This model of political economy—introduced through international administration, the conditionality of international donor assistance, and the propaganda of the triumph of free markets—often fails to serve those who, of necessity, depend on foreign aid and forms of economic "crime" to get by. This may not be the intention of interventionists but rather a form of "collateral damage" that is nevertheless inherent in the dominant neoliberal model of political economy. It is, however, contradictory to insist on policies of reliance on macroeconomic stability, external investment, and privatization that weaken social cohesion and the economic role of the state, while at the same time bemoaning the existence of shadow economies, widespread poverty, and the fragility of state institutions. The model is particularly ill suited to war economies because it promotes state weakness and social inequality in conflict-weakened states, where populations are already economically dislocated, marginalized, and dependent on aid or shadow economies for their survival. The impact of the neoliberal model on social cohesion, governance, and therefore peace in vulnerable or war-torn societies is profound. It places the onus of insurance against economic failure on people already impoverished by conflict, while depriving the state of options in economic planning that could address the problem of borderlands that have been empowered by war. Furthermore, it contributes to making economies that were exposed to structural adjustment, and then precariously adjusted for war, vulnerable to further economic crisis. Yet proponents of this model of development and reconstruction continue to rationalize these shortcomings and deny the possibility of alternatives.

Recommendations

This section outlines proposals that might connect a regional approach to the predicaments of war-torn societies confronting the demands of neoliberalism. While not prescriptive in the sense of offering detailed policy recommendations (which would need to be tailored to particular cases and regions), it suggests a set of alternative approaches that, taken together, envisage a more radical and bottom-up approach to peacebuilding in two broad ways. First, the proposals start from a recognition of the economic agendas and social needs of war-torn states and impoverished communities. Rather than approaching transformation from the perspective of a particular economic orthodoxy, we proceed from an acknowledgment of the sui generis nature of the political economies of postconflict societies. In addition, we recognize the duality of predatory and homicidal warlord and mafia activity that often also provides functional benefits. Second, the recommendations are guided by a concern to foster genuine local ownership of both the substance and processes of postconflict transformation.

Neutralizing Warlords and Mafiosi

Various strategies might be adopted to deal with warlords and mafiosi: co-option, elimination by policing, Keynesian policies of economic development, and "functional neglect." All of these strategies are problematic. Co-option involves compromise with and the legitimation of warlords, some of whom may be guilty of war crimes. As demonstrated by the abortive effort to secure peace in Sierra Leone by offering the lucrative office of minister of mining and gems to Revolutionary United Front (RUF) leader Foday Sankoh, this strategy does not always work. But even where it does, the predictable result is peace at the price of justice and accountable government. Criminal policing of shadow economies in the absence of broader economic and social incentives to attract participation in the formal economy is likely to stimulate further adaptation and displacement rather than eliminate shadow economic behavior. Policies of state-regulated economic expansion, while more promising in the longer term, are unlikely to address the immediate challenges of postconflict reconstruction. "Functional neglect" is predicated on the assumption that profit-seeking warlords are essentially protocapitalists who, given the right conditions, will ultimately become respectable businessmen and use accountants to avoid taxes. However, like co-option, this strategy of calculated neglect can undermine efforts to secure rule of law. It has to be emphasized that although warlords and mafiosi may have a functional role in providing employment and welfare for allies and followers, this has to be balanced against their records as ruthless predators and exploiters, often engaged in egregious pillaging, human rights abuse, and war crimes. There is no simple solution to the dilemmas that this situation poses. Judgments regarding appropriate strategies will depend to some extent on the political context; a judicious mix of all of the above may be necessary. Nevertheless, the success or failure of the mix will also depend on complementary social, political, and economic reforms undertaken at the national, regional, and global levels that address the economic agendas that drive conflict and compromise postconflict peacebuilding. For example, part of the strategy of dealing with post-Taliban opium dealers in Afghanistan should involve attempts to better address the demand for heroin on the streets of London and New York. Drawing on our analysis in the preceding chapters, we now turn to summarizing the kind of approaches that might be adopted.

Improving the Design and Implementation of Sanctions

As already noted, sanctions on arms or conflict goods are unlikely to prevent illicit trade in the absence of broader frameworks of economic and social support within and for states. Indeed, shadow trade networks evince a remarkable ability to adapt to new geographies of regulation created by sanctions. Furthermore, the application of sanctions tends not to target actors engaged in conflict or egregious behavior per se, but rather those with insufficient diplomatic, economic, or strategic weight to effectively oppose restrictions on their arms or conflict trade. In other words, the likelihood of sanctions being applied is largely a function of political relationships between UN Security Council (UNSC) members and potential targets. The failure to consistently apply sanctions not only undermines their effectiveness in terms of scope, but also compromises the moral authority of the UNSC when urging the international community to rigorously apply those sanctions it does introduce. Furthermore, in the absence of broader and more rigorous regulation of the global trade in arms and other potential conflict goods, sanctions can simply become another variant of prophylactic control and control-lite strategies, whereby specific offenders or types of trade are targeted but other conflict-inducing activities are either unregulated or regulated in a tokenistic way. Even where sanctions are introduced, the arrangements for monitoring and implementation are generally inadequate. In the current international context, then, sanctions on specific actors are, at best, an example of the policy of "liddism" noted in earlier chapters—an attempt to keep the lid on international instability without seriously addressing the broader structures of the economic system and the trade in arms and conflict goods that contribute to conflict more generally. At worst, sanctions represent a form of tokenism that is expected (and arguably designed) to fail.

Despite these flaws, however, there are a number of reforms to the current sanctions regimes that might usefully improve their operation. Most significant, there is a need for what might be termed a "Brahimi condition" for the introduction of sanctions. The Brahimi report on UN peacekeeping argued that missions should not be authorized by the Security Council until the UN had received sufficient funding and troop commitments from member states.[2] Similarly, certain conditions should be met both prior to the introduction of sanctions by the UNSC (and, indeed, by other bodies such as the EU) and as a condition of their continued maintenance.

First, the introduction of sanctions on conflict goods should be conditioned upon the prior completion of a feasibility study on the likely effect and effectiveness of sanctions as well the measures needed to ensure implementation. For instance, one of the (hotly disputed) claims over the introduction of timber sanctions on Liberia was that a measure designed to punish the Taylor regime would adversely impact the livelihoods of innocent civilians in the Liberian timber industry.[3] A prior feasibility study could assess the accuracy of these kinds of claims. Similarly, sanctions are currently introduced in the full knowledge that weak commitment and/or weak capacity for implementation within a target region make them destined to fail. Any feasibility study would therefore need to assess both the likely effectiveness of sanctions and the measures necessary to ensure effective implementation. In the latter case, this might include initiatives such as the introduction of monitors on the ground and capacity-building support for neighboring states to better institute sanctions. Precedents for such initiatives already exist: for instance, the Sanctions Assistance Missions (SAMs) employed under the European Union's Yugoslav sanctions.[4] But these types of initiatives need to be institutionalized. The Stockholm Process, for making targeted sanctions more effective, has also recommended that the UNSC include in the mandates of UN peacekeeping and observer missions a requirement to report sanctions violations.[5] Finally, the feasibility study should also be tasked with considering the economic impact of sanctions on neighboring states that may lose trade or incur costs in implementation. Where the economic impact is substantial, a precondition for the introduction of sanctions should be a requirement for the provision of compensation. This is more likely to encourage rigorous application among frontline states.

Second, any sanctions actually introduced should include a requirement for regular impact assessments. These would examine the ongoing effectiveness of sanctions and their implementation, the ways in which shadow networks have adapted to evade sanctions, and the counterproductive impacts on innocent communities, while also recommending measures to improve the operations of a sanctions regime. To some extent, this already occurs via the ad hoc mechanism of the UN Expert Panels. However, as discussed further below, the Expert Panels need to be institutionalized, as does the coverage of their remit.

Third, consideration should be given to either imposing secondary sanctions or a substantial financial penalty in cases of established complicity in significant violations of sanctions by other economic and political actors.[6]

Institution Building and State Direction

States that lack capacity to manage the economic dimensions of postconflict reconstruction need greater assistance, primarily in institution building and in meeting the recurring costs of governance until domestic revenue systems are adequate and sustainable. The suitability for postconflict settings of the neoliberal concept of the minimal state (for which governance is largely confined to maintaining a monopoly of violence, passing legislation, and regulating private enterprise) needs to be reviewed. Such minimalism appears to depress economic growth while enabling borderlands and shadow economic networks to resist central authority. Strategies and funding to develop and support governing institutions, in ways that reflect the context of history and social relations, are necessary to develop the state's capacity to protect its people and provide incentives to invest in social and economic development. External support for improved military, police, and customs control will be insufficient without simultaneous support for state authorities to develop more interventionist fiscal, trade, and agricultural and industrial policies. Social networks and sectors that support and are supported by shadow economies are unlikely to be broken without the provision of "pump-priming" growth and employment creation (as occurred to a limited extent in the U.S. New Deal in the 1930s), substitution for mafia welfare, and the institutionalization of genuine and robust forms of transparency and accountability in public governance. This will entail a broader remit for state-managed development, particularly as it concerns economic protection of the poor and high-level economic planning. That this is technically and politically feasible in postwar contexts has been demonstrated time and again from reconstruction after World War II to the reconstruction of Vietnam. Thus, escape from "The Matrix" to dislodge the current orthodoxy, reform the world trade system, and reconstitute the structures and programs of the IFIs is at least conceivable. We are not recommending the wholesale adoption of command economies that would reinvent corruption, black markets, and shadow economic activity. Many countries, including Sweden, France, and Japan, have adopted dirigiste economic strategies at various times without compromising political pluralism, transparency, and accountability.

Promoting Regional Economic Development

A regional approach offers an alternative perspective that existing analyses barely touch upon. In the case of Afghanistan and Central Asia, regionally coordinated policies are likely to remain focused on the regulation and control of illicit trafficking, with perhaps some attention to regional arrangements for the return and resettlement of refugees. However, there is an evident need for a more considered policy commitment to the development of regionwide trade and infrastructure cooperation to create better alternatives to regional shadow networks that can undermine peace and development. In the case of West Africa and Southeast Europe, a regional strategy of economic development could be more intensively pursued, not only to improve regulation but also as a means of mutual protection in the process of transformation from war to peace economies. As war-torn countries will not be able to fund such arrangements, international aid donors will not only have to provide the money but also have to begin conceptualizing the regional dimensions of their peacebuilding strategies. Without a regional approach to economic exchange, the exploitation of the regulatory borderlands is likely to continue and national control solutions are likely to be fruitless.

A regional approach would be useful not only to exercise regulation and control over shadow economies, but also to develop social and human development standards. Even in Southeast Europe, this will probably not happen for the next ten years, but the equivalent of the EU's Social Charter, tailored to fit the different context of Southeast Europe, would be a starting point, with perhaps reciprocal arrangements for the movement of labor. The process could begin bilaterally and continue in piecemeal fashion. Additionally, the benefits of a relatively well-protected economic union could provide the incentive for the countries of Southeast Europe to consider development policies and social legislation that leave open the possibility of mutuality and reciprocity. ECOWAS in West Africa may also have potential to develop standards of a common regional social and economic policy. As with other initiatives we have proposed for the region, these might also help to mute security dilemmas by fostering a process of peace from below. Indeed purely "national" solutions also imply a denial of opportunities for civil society movements to act transnationally in taming the hubris of particular external economic models.[7]

Promoting Regional Protection

A regional approach could also go beyond the limitations of the liberal peace by offering a degree of protection against neoliberalism's most harmful impacts. The thrust of international policy in regard to regionwide initiatives, though limited in scope, is usually based on assumptions about macroeconomic stability and opening up markets for foreign investment. For the majority of the population in fragile postconflict economies, this rigor is rather like rubbing salt into war wounds. Instead, regionalism can be considered as a mechanism to protect these economies from current policies that have the effect of reducing purchasing power, increasing unemployment, and limiting production—at least until they show signs of sustainability. As discussed in Chapter 6, regional frameworks such as ECOWAS and the Balkans Stability Pact could pursue economic integration on the basis of protection behind common customs and trade policies. To some degree, this would invert the prophylactic control strategies, discussed in Chapter 3, that aim to stop refugees and illicit goods coming to the affluent world by adopting strategies to stop neoliberal economics from further debilitating postconflict economies. In principle, this approach is obviously feasible; this was precisely how the European Coal and Steel Community and European Economic Community started out. Moreover, protective regionalism could help to foster value-added production. In West Africa, the regional integration of the producers of diamonds and other primary products might allow these industries to achieve economies of scale, which would make the creation of value-added manufacturing processes more feasible. Instead of exporting raw coffee beans, Côte d'Ivoire could develop finished coffee production. Likewise, diamond polishing could be established on a regional level in the Mano River region, instead of sending rough diamonds to outside manufacturing centers that currently reap the benefits attached to the added value derived from finishing processes.

Mitigating Displacement

While we acknowledge that improved controls alone will achieve little in regions where trade channels are multiple and easily shifted, regionalism could also provide a way of mitigating the logic of displacement. Currently, the mental map of external peacebuilders stops at a nation's borders. Yet as these cases demonstrate, informal economic networks exploit differentials in tax rates, currency convertibility, customs duties, and policing across borders. Peacebuilders need to be sensitive to the fact that a concentration on economic reconstruction within the state, transformation to a market economy, and disciplinary regulation often has the effect of shifting shadow economic activities into neighboring territory or along alternative routes. By tackling controls at the regional as well as the global and national levels, a holistic approach to regulation is possible, and evasion and adaptation through relocation becomes more difficult for the entrepreneurs of shadow trade. The case of Sierra Leone highlights the need for more effective regional management of conflict trade. In this respect, eliminating differentials in the regional regulatory environment, particularly for the trade in diamonds, would offer governments in the region a way of coping more effectively with the phenomenon of conflict and shadow trade, and thereby offer an additional incentive for cooperation.

More Effective Regulation

The contemporary focus on national and global regulation neglects the opportunity to deepen the conflict goods control regime. Current agendas for controlling conflict trades rely on voluntarism, nominal controls, and "transparency," neglecting the need for more robust forms of implementation and monitoring. The control agenda is also asymmetrical, concentrating on the curbing of war economies locally, while overlooking their symbiotic relationship with global aid, trade, and investment. While the nongovernmental organization (NGO) Global Witness occasionally names Western companies complicit in conflict trade, at the formal regulatory level there is at best a patchy collection of national industry codes. Regional organizations and initiatives could be mechanisms for translating control-lite agendas into more effective forms of regulation based on closer economic relations within regions. Particular regions facing a common challenge, such as mercenary activity, may be more willing to tackle the problem regionally than globally. Sanctions regimes could also be regionally resourced and funded to make them more stringent, through a common framework for customs, policing, economic intelligence, and monitoring.

Regional Analyses

Information gathering, analysis, and monitoring on a regional basis would not only contribute to regulation but also to improved understanding of the regional dimensions of war economies and the challenges they pose for economic development. Various measures can be stimulated under this rubric.

Conflict impact assessments. While it is currently fashionable to emphasize the importance of conflict impact assessments when designing development strategies, in reality this concept is rarely implemented. However, it would also be useful to expand such assessments to incorporate a regional dimension that would encourage an awareness that peacebuilding initiatives in the economic sphere may simply displace conflict and trafficking to other locations.

Transparency and monitoring initiatives. In addition to being established only on an ad hoc basis, UN Expert Panels, currently at least, have only been created to investigate the trade in arms and conflict goods that supports war in a specific state (Angola, Sierra Leone, the Democratic Republic of Congo [DRC]) and/or the implementation of an embargo against a specific state (Liberia). This has not precluded their examination of the regional networks that support specific wars such as that in the DRC. However, this is not the same as specifically examining the political economy of regional conflict complexes, particularly where outright war and/or the risk of war are exhibited in a number of states in such a complex. Expert Panels could be established to examine the country manifesting open hostilities, and also the region as a whole with a view to tracing and regulating networks that not only sustain war in one country but also that contribute to the maintenance of the regional conflict complex more generally. For instance, the International Crisis Group (ICG) has argued that the UN Expert Panel on Liberia should be transformed into a regional reporting and monitoring mechanism with a mandate encompassing the whole of West Africa and with a remit to examine the web of traders and businesses that supply weapons both to and within the region.[8]

NGO networks and interest groups. Given that the bureaucratic processes of intergovernmental organizations tend to be slow and cumbersome, consideration should be given to funding local NGO networks and interest groups that span regions. For instance, support could be given for the development of regional linkages between trade unions and employers organizations. Another example could be support for forums of academic economists, perhaps partnered by international NGOs, such as the International Crisis Group and Global Witness, that already have a capacity to collect information and produce analysis quickly at the regional level.

Regional institutes. Support to regional academic institutes, perhaps partnered by external institutes to offer intellectual and disciplinary development and professional witness to any local intimidation, would be another way of encouraging independent analysis of the impact of both conflict on regional economies and the political economy of peacebuilding.

Regional Settlements for Durable Peace

As discussed in Chapter 6, peace agreements currently tend to be reached separately and successively, even in cases where conflict in one country is embedded in a wider regional conflict complex. Given the multiple political, economic, military, and social dynamics that underpin such complexes, and given the tendency of both shadow networks and conflict itself to shift to neighboring states in response to international action, it may be more appropriate to seek regional settlements for durable peace. Although the multiplicity of actors and agendas might make regionwide agreements more difficult to achieve, integrating regional peacebuilding measures to deal with the multidimensional dynamics of war economies would achieve more effective transformations. Such settlements should include aspects of the recommendations noted above and allow local actors to develop initiatives that are responsive to particular conditions in each region. For example, the specific challenges of peacebuilding and economic transformation in borderlands may require the development of innovative approaches that take into account cross-border economic, cultural, and political factors.

Further Research

None of these recommendations entails sailing into completely uncharted waters. In broad outline, they have been used in other times and in other contexts. Obviously, simple transposition from one context to another—for example, imposing West European principles of integration into Central Asia—will not work, any more than the neoliberal economic template for postindustrial societies at peace works for undeveloped and fragile states emerging from conflict. We take for granted the necessity of local adaptation. For example, any measures related to Keynesian pump-priming by a state would need to reflect the natural, human, and institutional resources available, domestically, regionally, and globally. The changing global context, in which state sovereignty is diminishing and transnational networks are expanding, offers new opportunities for the reconfiguration of the state and of governance. In some respects BiH seems well placed to take advantage of the deterritorialization of economic activity in the global economic system. But such a reinvention of the BiH political economy would, paradoxically, also require determined political planning and direction. Moreover it assumes a more radical pace of political, economic, and social change than currently appears likely. It is more plausible to postulate for all three cases a rebalancing of public and private production, distribution, and exchange within a strong territorial authority until full-fledged regional integration is attained.

Perhaps most obvious, because we have provided perspectives of the political economy of conflict in only three regional conflict complexes, this sort of analysis could be deepened by research into the specific security architecture and economic dynamics of other regions. Work on the complex of the Sahel, Sudan, and Ethiopia has been undertaken, notably by Mark Duffield. But other complexes, in Central and Latin America, South Asia, the DRC–Great Lakes, and the Middle East, might also be investigated.

Further research on the regulatory policies of Western states would also be valuable, as these policies tend to be developed on an ad hoc basis, and on the national rather than the international level. This lack of coordination leads to inconsistent and counterproductive policy initiatives, notably in the arms trade.

More research on the actors involved in conflict complexes is needed. For instance, we know little about the way that regional and global diasporas resist, adapt to, or are co-opted into postconflict transformation. As they often exert a powerful influence on the fate of peace processes, their potential in contributing to the creation of political economies of peace needs to be better understood and encouraged. Evidence from Uganda and Ethiopia points to the crucial role of entrepreneurial returnees in reinvigorating local economies in contexts of postconflict recovery. And in cases of ongoing conflict, diaspora support can be vital to the coping and survival economies. Indeed, the Somali diaspora has provided more financial support for Somalis at home than have aid agencies.[9] Such economic relationships are transnational in nature and therefore evade existing state-oriented regulatory mechanisms. Regional and other multilateral strategies may be developed for interrupting diaspora economic support for the perpetuation of conflicts, and encouraging their investment in reconstruction through such means as tax breaks, concessions, and low interest rates.

While we anticipate much forthcoming work on the interlinkages between the roles of "terrorist networks" and regional conflict complexes, other actors are underresearched, notably the roles of regional civil society groups and of multinational corporations. A particularly fruitful avenue of research as well would be in-depth investigations of the economic behavior of borderland communities, their relationship to wider war economies, and the challenges they pose for postconflict transformation.

Conclusion

Until recently, scholars overlooked the role of economic factors in causing and sustaining intrastate conflict, favoring instead explanations of conflict that emphasize ethnic enmity, religious fundamentalism, and the manipulation of identity by power-hungry politicians. In consequence, the role of economic agendas and external agents in both causing conflict and hindering peacebuilding has been obscured. As Sierra Leone demonstrates, however, even in cases where the economic dimensions of intrastate conflict have been recognized, too often they have been constructed in ways that emphasize the greed of vicious warlords, corrupt elites, or the whole society. The effect has been to minimize the contributing role of external economic actors, including international financial institutions and multinational corporations, in the descent to conflict.

The preceding analysis has endeavored to rectify this lacuna by highlighting the significance of the broader regional and global dimensions of the political economy of contemporary intrastate conflict and postconflict transformation. By placing the fragmented economies of war-torn societies in their wider, regional setting, this study has attempted to build upon a literature that generally focuses on the internal dynamics of territorially bounded economies and their global links. It may be the case that the emergence and persistence of shadow activity is integral to the process of state formation comparable to the activities of pirates, entrepreneurial explorers, and trading companies of Europe and the Americas in earlier centuries.[10] However, these wars of the late-twentieth and early-twenty-first centuries do not privilege strong central economic control and political independence, but manifest centripetal tendencies. In terms of both transnational linkages in war economies and ambitions for transformation, the immediate regional linkages have not hitherto been a major focus of research. There is clear merit, then, in considering regional solutions to regional challenges.

The shadow economies emerging from war have their own forms of regional transnationalism to cultivate and protect. Developing or rediscovering formal links with regional neighbors to protect and assert control over economic exchange, production, terms of trade, employment, and social welfare has the potential to change the current dynamics of transformation for the better. Placing the political economies of war-torn societies in their regional settings does not necessarily simplify the challenges of transformation, but it does present opportunities for those societies to consider alternatives to the narrow options currently presented to them by the outside world.

This study does not claim that regional approaches to peacebuilding and postconflict economic recovery are a panacea. There are limits, perhaps also disadvantages, to regional initiatives. For example, regionally dominant states, such as Nigeria in West Africa, may develop hegemonic ambitions that skew regional development to a particular advantage. Moreover, regionalism assumes interrelationships between territorial and predominantly statist units, forming an interface between the nation-state and the world order. However, nonstate entrepreneurs operate through nonterritorial networks to exert influence and establish "virtual communities" accessed by telecommunications and the Internet. Nevertheless, as the case studies have shown, established patterns of interregional economic exchange have not been forsaken, and to some extent the deterritorialized networks may simply represent the extension of preconflict mechanisms for old and new elites to process, organize, and confirm transactions.

None of this suggests that the political economies of peacebuilding are insulated from international developments, and certainly not from the technological dimensions of globalization. War-torn societies are caught between the modernizing agendas of international capitalism and a dependence on autochthonous clandestine activity for coping and survival. Both pressures have transnational dimensions that in a world of complex networks serve to reduce the role of states. In the case of structures and policies that conform to the requirements of the liberal peace, this amounts to the withdrawal of the state from economic and social functions in its reorientation toward the creation and maintenance of an environment favorable to the global networking of private capital and foreign investment. But neoliberal interventionists are not ultimately responsible for transformations and have no inalienable right to dictate economic norms. Their claim to nurse peripheral and war-torn societies into a partisan economic model derives from wealth and military power, not from discovering a golden rule of political economy or from an ethical or civilizational superiority.[11] Local communities have to acquire some control over their own future, including the authority to decide how they negotiate norms of political economy with the rest of the world. Indeed, a key lesson to be learned from this study is that the interventionists themselves—equipped with their exclusive model of peacebuilding—should examine their accountability to the societies that they attempt to engineer into peace.

Notes

1. R. Jeffrey Smith, "In Bosnia, Free Enterprise Has Gotten Way Out of Hand," *International Herald Tribune*, December 27, 1999, p. 5. Estimates of the contribution of the black economy to GDP are: Denmark and Sweden, 3–7 percent; France and Germany, 4–14 percent; Belgium, 12–21 percent; the UK, 7–13 percent; Italy, 20–26 percent; Greece, 29–35 percent. European Commission report cited by Martin Walker, "EU 'Victim of Growing Black Economy,'" *The Guardian,* April 6, 1998, p. 13. Political-business links and gross malpractice in advanced capitalist societies affecting the highest political levels have been the subject of legal and journalistic investigation. See Transparency International's website: www.transparency.de.

2. United Nations, *Report of the Panel on the United Nations Peace Operations,* UN Doc. A/55/305-S/2000/809, August 21, 2000.

3. See, for instance, Global Witness, *The Usual Suspects: Liberia's Weapons and Mercenaries in Côte d'Ivoire and Sierra Leone—Why It's Still Possible, How It Works, and How to Break the Trend,* March 2003, annex 2, pp. 44–45, www.globalwitness.org.

4. "Measures to Strengthen the Role of the United Nations in the Implementation of Targeted Sanctions" (Karen Ballentine, rapporteur), in Peter Wallensteen, Carina Staibano, and Mikael Eriksson, eds., *Making Targeted Sanctions Effective: Guidelines for the Implementation of UN Policy Options* (Uppsala, Sweden: Uppsala University, Department of Peace and Conflict Research, 2003), p. 28. *Final Report of the Stockholm Process on the Implementation of Targeted Sanctions,* www.%20smartsanctions.se.

5. *Final Report of the Stockholm Process on the Implementation of Targeted Sanctions.*

6. Ibid.

7. Béatrice Pouligny, "Acteurs et enjeux d'un processus équivoque: La Naissance d'une 'internationale civilie,'" *Critique Internationale* no. 13 (October 2001): 163–176.

8. International Crisis Group (ICG), *Tackling Liberia: The Eye of the Regional Storm,* ICG Africa Report no. 62 (Freetown: ICG, April 30, 2003), p. 34.

9. Michi Ebata, "Reconstructing War-Torn Societies in Africa," postdoctoral research project, King's College, London, 2002.

10. Francesco Strazzari, "Between Ethnic Collusion and Mafia Collusion: The 'Balkan Route' to State Making," in Dietrich Jung, ed., *Shadow Globalization, Ethnic Conflicts, and New Wars: A Political Economy of Intra-State War* (London: Routledge, 2003), pp. 140–162.

11. See Thomas Frank, *One Market Under God: Extreme Capitalism, Market Populism, and the End of Economic Democracy* (New York: Secker & Warburg, 2001).

Acronyms

AFRC	Armed Forces Revolutionary Council (Sierra Leone)
ATTA	Afghan Transit Trade Agreement
ATU	Antiterrorism Unit (Liberia)
BIB	Banque International du Burkina
BiH	Bosnia and Herzegovina
CAFAO	Customs and Fiscal Assistance Office (of the EU in BiH)
CARDS	Community Assistance for Reconstruction, Democratization, and Stabilization
CAS	country assistance strategy
CDF	Civil Defense Force (Sierra Leone)
CIA	Central Intelligence Agency (United States)
CFATF	Caribbean Financial Action Task Force
CTF	Consultative Task Force (of the EU in BiH)
DDR	disarmament, demobilization, and reintegration
DEA	Drug Enforcement Agency (United States)
DFID	Department for International Development (UK)
DRC	Democratic Republic of Congo
ECOMOG	Economic Community of West African States Cease-Fire Monitoring Group
ECOWAS	Economic Community of West African States
EITI	Extractive Industries Transparency Initiative (UK)
ESI	European Stability Initiative
EU	European Union
FATF	Financial Action Task Force (OECD)

FBiH	Federation (Bosniak-Croat) of Bosnia and Herzegovina
FDI	foreign direct investment
FRY	Federal Republic of Yugoslavia
FYROM	former Yugoslav Republic of Macedonia
GAO	General Accounting Office (United States)
GDP	gross domestic product
GTZ	Gesellschaft für Technische Zusammenarbeit (German Technical Cooperation)
HDZ	Croat Democratic Union
HIPC	highly indebted poor country
HPG	Humanitarian Practice Group (of ODI)
HVA	Helmand Valley Authority (Afghanistan)
HVO	Croat Defense Council
ICG	International Crisis Group
IDC	International Development Committee (UK)
IDM	illicit diamond miner/mining
IFI	international financial institution
IFOR	Implementation Force (in BiH)
IMF	International Monetary Fund
IMU	Islamic Movement for Uzbekistan
IPA	International Peace Academy
ISAF	International Security Assistance Force
ISI	Inter-Services Intelligence (Pakistan)
IWPR	Institute of War and Peace Reporting
KLA	Kosovo Liberation Army
KM	konvertibilna marka (BiH currency)
LURD	Liberians United for Reconciliation and Democracy
MJP	Mouvement pour Justice et Paix (Movement for Justice and Peace)
MNC	multinational corporation
MPIGO	Mouvement Populaire Ivoirien Grand Orient (Ivorian Popular Front Movement of the Great West)
MWPI	Maryland Wood-Processing Industries
NATO	North Atlantic Treaty Organization
NEPAD	New Partnership for African Development
NGO	nongovernmental organization
NPFL	National Patriotic Front of Liberia
NPRC	National Provisional Ruling Council (Sierra Leone)
ODI	Overseas Development Institute (UK)
OECD	Organization for Economic Cooperation and Development
OHR	Office of the High Representative (in BiH)

OSCE	Organization for Security and Cooperation in Europe
OTC	Oriental Timber Company (Liberia)
PRSP	poverty reduction strategy paper
PWYP	"publish what you pay"
RS	Republika Srpska
RTC	Royal Timber Company
RUF	Revolutionary United Front (Sierra Leone)
SALW	small arms and light weapons
SAM	Sanctions Assistance Mission
SAP	Stabilization and Association Process (EU)
SDA	Party of Democratic Action (BiH)
SDS	Serb Democratic Party
SFOR	Stabilization Force (in BiH)
SLST	Sierra Leone Selection Trust
SMEs	small and medium-sized enterprises
UF	United Front (Taliban)
UK	United Kingdom
UN	United Nations
UNAMA	United Nations Assistance Mission in Afghanistan
UNAMSIL	United Nations Mission in Sierra Leone
UNDCP	United Nations Drug Control Program
UNDP	United Nations Development Programme
UNHCR	United Nations High Commissioner for Refugees
UNITA	Union for the Total Independence of Angola
UNMIBH	United Nations Mission in Bosnia and Herzegovina
UNODC	United Nations Office on Drugs and Crime
UNOMSIL	United Nations Observer Mission in Sierra Leone
UNPROFOR	United Nations Protection Force
UNSC	United Nations Security Council
USAID	U.S. Agency for International Development
VAT	value-added tax
WTO	World Trade Organization

Selected Bibliography

Abdullah, Ibrahim, and Patrick Muana. "The Revolutionary United Front of Sierra Leone: A Revolt of the Lumpenproletariat." In Christopher Clapham, ed., *African Guerrilla*. Oxford: James Currey, 1998, pp. 172–193.

Abrahamsen, Rita. "Development Policy and the Democratic Peace in Sub-Saharan Africa." *Journal of Conflict, Security, and Development* 1, no. 3 (2001): 79–103.

Adebajo, Adekeye. *Building Peace in West Africa: Liberia, Sierra Leone, and Guinea-Bissau*. International Peace Academy Occasional Paper Series. Boulder, CO: Lynne Rienner, 2002.

Adebajo, Adekeye, and Chris Landsberg. "Back to the Future: UN Peacekeeping in Africa." *International Peacekeeping* 7, no. 4 (2000): 161–188.

Alao, Abiodun. "Diamonds Are Forever . . . But So Also Are Controversies: Diamonds and the Actors in Sierra Leone's Civil War." *Civil Wars* 2, no. 3 (1999): 43–64.

Alao, Abiodun, and 'Funmi Olonisakin. "Economic Fragility and Political Fluidity: Explaining Natural Resources and Conflicts." *International Peacekeeping* 7, no. 4 (2000): 23–36.

Arlacchi, Pino. "The Dynamics of Illegal Markets." *Transnational Organized Crime* 4, nos. 3–4 (Winter 1998): 7–12.

Ballentine, Karen, and Jake Sherman, eds. *The Political Economy of Armed Conflict: Beyond Greed and Grievance*. Boulder, CO: Lynne Rienner, 2003.

Bauman, Zygmunt. *Globalisation: The Human Consequences*. Cambridge: Polity, 1998.

Bennett, Christopher. *Yugoslavia's Bloody Collapse*. London: Hurst, 1995.

Berdal, Mats, and David Keen. "Violence and Economic Agendas in Civil Wars: Some Implications for Outside Intervention." *Millennium: Journal of International Studies* 26, no. 3 (1997): 795–818.

Berdal, Mats, and David M. Malone, eds. *Greed and Grievance: Economic Agendas in Civil Wars*. Boulder, CO: Lynne Rienner, 2000.

Berman, Eric G. *Re-Armament in Sierra Leone: One Year After the Lomé Peace Agreement*. Small Arms Survey Occasional Paper no. 1. Geneva: Small Arms, 2000.

Bhatia, Michael, and Jonathan Goodhand, with Haneef Atmar, Adam Pain, and Mohammed Suleman. "Profits and Poverty: Aid Livelihoods and Conflict in Afghanistan." In Sarah Collinson et al., *Power, Livelihoods, and Conflict: Case Studies in Political Economy Analysis for Humanitarian Action*, HPG Report 13 (February 2003).

Bjelakovic, N., and Francesco Strazzari. "The Sack of Mostar, 1992–1994: The Politico-Military Connection." *European Security* 8, no. 3 (1998): 73–102.

Bougarel, Xavier. *Bosnia and Herzegovina: Local Level Institutions and Social Capital Study*, vol. 1. Washington, DC: World Bank, ECSSD, June 2002.

— — —. *Bosnie: Anatomie d'un conflit*. Paris: La Découverte, 1996.

Boutwell, Jeffrey, and Michael T. Klare, eds. *Light Weapons and Civil Conflict: Controlling the Tools of Violence*. New York: Rowman and Littlefield, 1999.

Bradbury, Mark. "Living with Statelessness: The Somali Road to Development." *Journal of Conflict, Security and Development* 3, no. 1 (April 2003): 7–25.

Burawoy, Michael, and Katherine Verdery, eds. *Uncertain Transition: Ethnographies of Change in the Post-Socialist World*. Lanham, MD: Rowman and Littlefield, 1999.

Buzan, Barry, Øle Waever, and Jaap de Wilde, eds. *Security: A New Framework for Analysis*. Boulder, CO: Lynne Rienner, 1998.

Byrd, W. "Afghanistan's Reconstruction: Regional and Country Context." A World Bank discussion paper, revised draft (October 31, 2002).

Customs and Fiscal Assistance Office (CAFAO). *Revenue Loss from Tax and Customs Fraud in BiH Identified by CAFAO*. Internal document, u/eg/ CAFAOGeneral/revenue 260902. Sarajevo: CAFAO, December 13, 2002.

Cameron, Angus, and Ronen Palan. "The Imagined Economy: Mapping Transformations in the Contemporary State." *Millennium: Journal of International Studies* 28, no. 2 (1999): 267–288.

Campbell, David. *National Deconstruction: Violence, Identity, and Justice in Bosnia*. Minneapolis: University of Minnesota Press, 1998.

Campbell, Greg. *Blood Diamonds: Tracing the Deadly Path of the World's Most Precious Stones*. Boulder, CO: Westview Press, 2002.

Chandler, David. "*The Responsibility to Protect?* Imposing the Liberal Peace: A Critique." In Alex Bellamy and Paul Williams, eds., *Peacekeeping in Global Politics*. London: Frank Cass, 2004.

Chesterman, Simon. "Walking Softly in Afghanistan: The Future of UN State-Building." *Survival* 44, no. 3 (Autumn 2002): 37–46.

Chomsky, Noam. *Profit over People: Neo-liberalism and Global Order*. New York: Seven Stories Press, 1999.

Collier, Paul. "Doing Well Out of War: An Economic Perspective." In Mats Berdal and David M. Malone, eds., *Greed and Grievance: Economic Agendas in Civil Wars*, Project of the International Peace Academy. Boulder, CO: Lynne Rienner, 2000, pp. 91–111.

Hirsch, John L. *Sierra Leone: Diamonds and the Struggle for Democracy*. International Peace Academy Occasional Paper Series. Boulder, CO: Lynne Rienner, 2001.

Hirshleifer, J. *The Dark Side of the Force: Economic Foundations of Conflict Theory*. Cambridge: Cambridge University Press, 2001.

Holm, Hans-Henrik. "Failing Failed States: Who Forgets the Forgotten?" *Security Dialogue* 33, no. 4 (December 2002): 457–471.

Horvat, Branko. *Theory of International Trade: An Alternative Approach*. Basingstoke: Macmillan, 1999.

Howe, Herbert. "Lessons of Liberia: ECOMOG and Regional Peacekeeping." *International Security* 21, no. 3 (1996): 145–176.

Human Rights Watch. "Afghanistan: Crisis of Impunity—The Role of Pakistan, Russia, and Iran in Fueling the Civil War." Working Paper 13, no. 3 (July 2001).

Humphreys, Macartan. "Economics and Violent Conflict." (August 2002). www.preventconflict.org/portal/economics/portalhome.php.

Hyman, A. *Afghanistan Under Soviet Domination, 1964–1991*. 3rd ed. London: Macmillan, 1992.

Ignatieff, Michael. *The Warrior's Honour: Ethnic War and the Modern Conscience*. New York: Henry Holt, 1997.

Institute of War and Peace Reporting. *The Killing Fields of Afghanistan*. Afghan Recovery Report no. 16 (June 26, 2002).

International Advisory Group. *Functional Analysis and Strategic Implementation Plan: Transformation of the Payment Bureaus in Bosnia and Herzegovina*. Sarajevo: International Advisory Group, July 1999.

International Crisis Group (ICG). *Bosnia's Precarious Economy: Still Not Open for Business*. Report no. 115. Sarajevo: ICG, August 7, 2001.

———. *Liberia: Unravelling*. ICG Africa Briefing. Freetown: ICG, August 19, 2002.

———. *Sierra Leone: Managing Uncertainty*. ICG Africa Report no. 35. Freetown: ICG, October 24, 2001.

———. *Sierra Leone: Time for a New Military and Political Strategy*. ICG Africa Report no. 28. Freetown: ICG, April 11, 2001.

———. *Sierra Leone After Elections: Politics as Usual*. ICG Africa Report no. 49. Freetown: ICG, July 12, 2002.

———. *Why Will No One Invest in Bosnia-Herzegovina*. Report no. 64. Sarajevo: ICG, April 21, 1999.

International Monetary Fund (IMF). *Bosnia and Herzegovina: Selected Issues and Statistical Appendix*. Washington, DC: IMF, June 26, 2000.

Jean, François, and Jean-Christophe Rufin, eds. *Economie des guerres civiles*. Paris: Hachette, Collection Pluriel, 1996.

Johnson, C., W. Maley, A. Their, and A. Wardak. "Afghanistan's Political and Constitutional Development." HPG, ODI Report, January 2003.

Judah, Tim. *Kosovo: War and Revenge*. New Haven, CT: Yale University Press, 2000.

Jung, Dietrich, ed. *Shadow Globalization, Ethnic Conflicts, and New Wars: A Political Economy of Intra-State War*. London: Routledge, 2003.

———. *Economic Causes of Civil Conflict and Their Implications for Policy*. Washington, DC: World Bank, June 15, 2000. www.globalpolicy.org/security/issues/diamond/wb.htm.

Collier, Paul, and Anke Hoeffler. "Greed and Grievance in Civil War." October 21, 2001. www.worldbank.org/research/conflict/papers/greedandgrievance.htm.

Cooley, J. K. *Unholy Wars: Afghanistan, America, and International Terrorism*. London: Pluto Press, 1999.

Cooper, Neil. "Conflict Goods: The Challenges for Peacekeeping and Conflict Prevention." *International Peacekeeping* 8, no. 3 (Autumn 2001): 21–38.

———. "Dealing with War Economies: Control-lite as a Substitute for Real Reform." In Jurgen Brauer, Paul Dunne, David Gold, and John Tepper Marlin, eds. *ECAAR Review 2002*, New York: ECAAR, 2002, pp. 45–56.

———. "Raising the Cost of Conflict, Lowering the Price of Peace: Demilitarisation After Post-Modern Conflicts." In Michael Pugh, ed., *Regeneration of War-Torn Societies*. Basingstoke: Macmillan, 2000, pp. 54–73.

———. "Security Sector (Lack of) Transformation in Kosovo." In Keith Krause and Fred Tanner, eds. *Arms Control and Contemporary Conflicts: Challenges and Responses*. PSIS Special Studies no. 5. Geneva: Programme for Strategic and International Security Studies and Geneva Centre for Security Policy, 2001, pp. 65–127.

Cooper, Neil, and Michael Pugh. *Security-Sector Transformation in Post-Conflict Societies*. Conflict, Security, and Development Group Working Paper no. 5. London: Centre for Defence Studies, 2002.

Corpora, Christopher. "Boxing with Shadows: Understanding and Addressing the Global Asymmetric Threat Complex." Paper presented at the George C. Marshall Center conference "Countering Terrorism in Southeast Europe: Future Directions in SEDM Cooperation," Garmisch, December 7–12, 2002.

Cortright, David, and George A. Lopez. *Sanctions and the Search for Security: Challenges to UN Action*. Boulder, CO: Lynne Rienner, 2002.

Cousens, Elizabeth M., and Charles K. Cater. *Toward Peace in Bosnia: Implementing the Dayton Accords*. Boulder, CO: Lynne Rienner, 2002.

Cousens, Elisabeth M., and Chetan Kumar, with Karin Wermester. *Peacebuilding as Politics: Cultivating Peace in Fragile Societies*. International Peace Academy Occasional Paper Series. Boulder, CO: Lynne Rienner, 2001.

Cox, Robert W. *The Political Economy of a Plural World: Critical Reflections on Power, Morals, and Civilization*. RIPE Series. London: Routledge, 2002.

Cramer, C., and Jonathan Goodhand. "Try Again, Fail Again, Fail Better? War, the State, and the Post-Conflict Challenge in Afghanistan." *Development and Change* 33, no. 5 (2002): 885–909.

Crawford, Beverly, and Ronnie Lipschutz. "Discourses of War: Security and the Case of Yugoslavia." In Keith Krause and Michael Williams, eds., *Critical Security Studies*. Minneapolis: University of Minneapolis Press, 1997, pp. 149–185.

Crnobrnja, Mihailo. *The Yugoslav Drama*. London: I. B. Tauris, 1996.

Cullather, N. "Damming Afghanistan: Modernization in a Buffer State." *Journal of American History* (September 2002).

De Soto, Alvaro, and Graciana del Castillo. "Obstacles to Peacebuilding." *Foreign Policy* 94 (1994): 69–83.

"Development Strategy BiH: PRSP." *Poverty Reduction Strategy Paper,* draft for public discussion, Sarajevo, December 2002.

Dietrich, Christian. *Hard Currency: The Criminalized Diamond Economy of the Democratic Republic of the Congo and Its Neighbours.* Partnership Africa Canada, the Diamonds and Human Security Project, Occasional Paper no. 4, June 2003.

Donais, Timothy. "The Politics of Privatization in Post-Dayton Bosnia." *Southeast European Politics* 3, 1 (June 2002): 3–19.

Duffield, Mark. *Global Governance and the New Wars: The Merging of Development and Security.* London: Zed Books, 2001.

Duyvesteyn, Isabelle. "Contemporary War: Ethnic Conflict, Resource Conflict or Something Else?" *Civil Wars* 3, no. 1 (Spring 2000): 90–114.

Dyker, David A. *Yugoslavia: Socialism, Development, and Debt.* London: Routledge, 1990.

East-West Institute and European Stability Initiative. *Democracy, Security, and the Future of the Stability Pact for South Eastern Europe: A Political Framework.* Berlin: East-West Institute and European Stability Initiative, April 4, 2001.

Ero, Comfort. *Sierra Leone's Security Complex.* Security and Development Group Working Paper no. 3. London: Centre for Defence Studies, June 2000.

Ero, Comfort, Waheguru Pal Singh Sidhu, and Augustine Toure. *Towards a Pax West Africana: Building Peace in a Troubled Sub-Region.* Report on IPA-ECOWAS, September 27–29, 2001, Abuja Seminar. New York: International Peace Academy, 2001.

European Stability Initiative. "Taking on the Commanding Heights." Berlin: European Stability Initiative, May 3, 2000.

———. "Western Balkans 2004: Assistance, Cohesion, and the New Boundaries of Europe—A Call for Policy Reform." Berlin: European Stability Initiative, November 3, 2002.

Fatal Transactions. *Implementing Kimberley: Stopping the Blood Diamond Trade to Europe.* Report of the European Union Expert Meeting, March 7, 2002, Amsterdam: Fatal Transactions, April 2002.

Fielden, M., and J. Goodhand. "Beyond the Taliban? The Afghan Conflict and United Nations Peacemaking." *Conflict, Security and Development* 1, no. 3 (2001): 5–32.

Francis, David J. *The Politics of Economic Regionalism: Sierra Leone in ECOWAS.* Aldershot: Ashgate, 2001.

Garnett, John. "The Causes of War and the Conditions of Peace." In John Baylis, James Wirtz, Eliot Cohen, and Colin S. Gray, eds., *Strategy in the Contemporary World: An Introduction to Strategic Studies.* Oxford: Oxford University Press, 2002.

Gberie, Lansana. *War and Peace in Sierra Leone: Diamonds, Corruption, and the Lebanese Connection.* Occasional Paper no. 6. Ottawa: Partnership Africa Canada, November 2002.

Glenny, Misha. *The Fall of Yugoslavia: The Third Balkan War.* Harmondsworth: Penguin, 1993.

Global Witness. *All the President's Men: The Devastating Story of Oil and Banking in Angola's Privatised War.* March 2002. www.globalwitness.org.

———. *The Role of Liberia's Logging Industry on National and Reg[ional] [Se]curity: Briefing to the UN Security Council by Global Witness.* Jan[uary 2001]. www.globalwitness.org.

———. *A Rough Trade: The Role of Companies and Governments in th[e ...] Conflict.* December 1998. www.globalwitness.org/campaigns/d[...] reports.php.

———. *Taylor-Made: The Pivotal Role of Liberia's Forests in Regional [...].* September 2001. www.globalwitness.org.

———. *The Usual Suspects: Liberia's Weapons and Mercenaries in Côte [d'Ivoire] and Sierra Leone. Why It's Still Possible, How It Works, and How t[o Reverse] the Trend.* March 2003. www.globalwitness.org.

———. *Zimbabwe's Resource Colonialism in the DRC: A Briefing Docum[ent by] Global Witness.* August 26, 2001. www.globalwitness.org.

Goodhand, Jonathan. "Research in Conflict Zones: Ethics and Accountab[ility]." *Forced Migration Review* 8 (August 2000): 12–15.

———. "From Holy War to Opium War? A Case Study of the Opium Eco[nomy] in North Eastern Afghanistan." *Central Asian Survey* 19, no. 2 (2[000]): 265–280.

———. "Aiding Violence or Building Peace? The Role of International A[id in] Afghanistan." *Third World Quarterly* 23, no. 5 (2002): 837–859.

Gow, James. *Triumph of the Lack of Will: International Diplomacy and [the] Yugoslav War.* London: Hurst, 1997.

Gow, James, Richard Paterson, and Alison Preston, eds., *Bosnia by Televisi[on].* London: British Film Institute, 1996.

Granville, B. "Time for a Rescue: Balkans' Marshall Plan." *The World Today* 5[5], no. 7 (1999): 7–9.

Guaqueta, Alexandra (rapporteur). *Economic Agendas in Armed Conflict: Defin[ing] and Developing the Role of the UN.* New York: International Peace Acad[em]y and FAFO, 2002.

Hadžić, Miroslav. *The Yugoslav People's Agony: The Role of the Yugoslav People's Army.* Aldershot: Ashgate, 2002.

Hagman, Lotta (rapporteur). *Security and Development in Sierra Leone.* International Peace Academy Workshop Report. New York: International Peace Academy, June 2002.

Hansen, Lene. "Past as Preface: Civilizational Politics and the 'Third' Balkan War." *Journal of Peace Research* 37, no. 3 (2000): 345–362.

———. *Western Villains or Balkan Barbarism? Representations and Responsibility in the Debate over Bosnia.* Copenhagen: University of Copenhagen, Institute of Political Science, 1998.

Held, David, Anthony McGrew, David Goldblatt, and Jonathan Perraton. *Global Transformations: Politics, Economics, and Culture.* Cambridge: Polity Press, 1999.

Hentges, Harriet, and Jean-Marc Coicaud. "The Dividends of Peace: The Economics of Peacekeeping." *Journal of International Affairs* 55, no. 2 (2002): 351–367.

Herod, Andrew, Gearóid Ó'Tuathail, and Susan Roberts. *Unruly World? Geography, Globalization, and Governance.* London: Routledge, 1998.

Kaldor, Mary. *New and Old Wars: Organized Violence in a Global Era.* Cambridge: Polity Press, 1999.

Kaplan, Robert D. *Balkan Ghosts: A Journey Through History.* New York: Vintage Departures, 1993.

— — —. "The Coming Anarchy." *Atlantic Monthly,* February 1994, pp. 44–76.

Keen, David. *The Economic Functions of Violence in Civil Wars.* Adelphi Paper no. 320. Oxford: Oxford University Press for the International Institute of Strategic Studies, 1998.

Kreimer, Alcira, Robert Muscat, Ann Ewan, and Margaret Arnold. *Bosnia and Herzegovina: Post-Conflict Reconstruction.* World Bank Country Case Study Series. Washington, DC: World Bank Operations Evaluation Department, 2000. www.worldbank.org/html/oed.

Le Billon, Philippe. "The Political Ecology of War: Natural Resources and Armed Conflicts." *Political Geography* no. 20 (2001): 561–584.

— — —. "The Political Economy of War: What Relief Workers Need to Know." ODI, Humanitarian Practice Network Paper no. 33. July 2000.

Le Billon, Philippe, Jake Sherman, and Marcia Hartwell. *Controlling Resource Flows to Civil Wars: A Review and Analysis of Current Policies and Legal Instruments.* New York: International Peace Academy Policy Report, 2002.

Luke, Timothy, and Gearóid Ó'Tuathail. "On Videocameralists: The Geopolitics of Failed States, the CNN International, and (UN) Governmentality." *Review of International Political Economy* 4, no. 4 (1997): 709–733.

Macesich, George, ed., with Rikard Lang and Dragomir Vojnić. *Essays on the Yugoslav Economic Model.* New York: Praeger, 1989.

MacKinlay, John. *Globalisation and Insurgency.* Adelphi Paper no. 352. Oxford: Oxford University Press for the International Institute of Strategic Studies, 2002.

Magaš, Branka. *The Destruction of Yugoslavia: Tracking the Breakup, 1980–92.* London: Verso, 1993.

Magaš, Branka, and Ivo Zanić, eds. *The War in Croatia and Bosnia-Herzegovina, 1991–1995.* London: Cass, 2001.

Maley, W. "Talibanization and Pakistan." In *Talibanization: Extremism and Regional Instability in South and Central Asia.* Brussels: Conflict Prevention Network and Stiftung Wissenschaaft und Politik, 2001.

Maley, W., ed. *Fundamentalism Reborn? Afghanistan and the Taliban.* London: Hurst, 1998.

Mansfield, David. "Alternative Development in Afghanistan: The Failure of the Quid Pro Quo." Paper presented at the international conference on "Alternative Development in Drug Control and Cooperation." Feldafing, Germany (August 2001).

— — —. "The Economic Superiority of Illicit Drug Production: Myth and Reality." Paper presented at the international conference on "Alternative Development in Drug Control and Cooperation." Feldafing, Germany (August 2001).

Meagher, Kate. "Informal Integration or Economic Subversion? Parallel Trade in West Africa." In Réal Lavergne, ed., *Regional Integration and Cooperation in West Africa.* Trenton, NJ: Africa World Press with the International Development Research Centre, Ottawa, 1997, pp. 165–187.

Milinković, Brancko, ed. *Hate Speech*. Belgrade: Center for Antiwar Action, 1995.

Montague, Dena. "The Business of War and the Prospects for Peace in Sierra Leone." *Brown Journal of World Affairs* 9, no. 1 (2002): 229–238.

Mueller, John. "Thugs as Residual Combatants." Paper presented at the International Studies Association annual convention, New Orleans, March 24–27, 2002.

Musah, Abdel-Fatau. "A Country Under Siege: State Decay and Corporate Military Intervention in Sierra Leone." In Abdel-Fatau Musah and J. 'Kayode Fayemi, eds., *Mercenaries: An African Security Dilemma*. London: Pluto Press, 2000, pp. 76–116.

———. "Privatization of Security, Arms Proliferation, and the Process of State Collapse in Africa." *Development and Change* (Special Issue: "State Failure, Collapse, and Reconstruction") 33, no. 5 (November 2002): 911–933.

Nafziger, E. Wayne, and Juha Auvinen. "Economic Development, Inequality, War and State Violence." *World Development* 30, no. 2 (2002): 153–163.

Naqvi, Zareen F. *Afghanistan-Pakistan Trade Relations*. Islamabad: World Bank, 1999.

Naylor, R. T. "The Rise of the Modern Arms Black Market and the Fall of Supply-Side Control." *Transnational Organized Crime* 4, nos. 3 and 4 (Winter 1998): 211.

Noelle-Karimi, C., C. Schetter, and R. Schlagintweit, eds. *Afghanistan: A Country Without a State?* Frankfurt-am-Main: IKO-Verlag, Schriftenreihe der Mediothek für Afghanistan, 2002.

Nordstrom, C. "Shadows and Sovereigns." *Theory, Culture, and Society* 17, no. 4 (2000): 35–54.

O'Neill, William G. *Kosovo: An Unfinished Peace*. International Peace Academy Occasional Paper Series. Boulder, CO: Lynne Rienner, 2002.

Ottaway, Marina. "Rebuilding State Institutions in Collapsed States." *Development and Change* (Special Issue: "State Failure, Collapse, and Reconstruction") 33, no. 5 (2002): 1001–1023.

Oxfam. *Bitter Coffee: How the Poor Are Paying for the Slump in Coffee Prices*. Oxfam International Background Briefing, no. 5. Oxford: Oxfam, 2001. www.oxfam.org.uk/policy/papers/coffee.htm.

———. *Rigged Rules and Double Standards: Trade, Globalisation, and the Fight Against Poverty*. Oxford: Oxfam, 2002.

Pain, Adam, and Jonathan Goodhand. *Afghanistan: Current Employment and Socio-Economic Situation and Prospects*. Infocus program on crisis response and reconstruction, Working Paper no. 8. Geneva: International Labour Organization, March 2002.

Papić, Žarko, et al. *International Support Policies to SEE Countries: Lessons (Not) Learned in Bosnia-Herzegovina*. Sarajevo: Open Society Fund/Soros Foundation, 2001.

Paris, Roland. "Echoes of the *Mission Civiliatrice:* Peacekeeping in the Post–Cold War Era." In Edward Newman and Oliver P. Richmond, eds., *The United Nations and Human Security*. Basingstoke: Palgrave, 2001, pp. 100–118.

Peters, Ralph. "The New Warrior Class." *Parameters* 24, no. 2 (Summer 1994): 16–26.

Petras, James, and Steve Vieux. "Bosnia and the Revival of U.S. Hegemony." *New Left Review* no. 218 (July–August 1996): 3–25.

Pinnick, K., and J. Green, eds. *Central Asia and the Post-Conflict Stabilisation of Afghanistan.* London: International Institute for Strategic Studies, 2002.

Private Sector Development Task Force, Private Sector Development. "Progress Report of the Private Sector Development Task Force Secretariat," Sarajevo, September 1999.

Pugh, Michael. "Maintaining Peace and Security." In David Held and Anthony McGrew, eds. *Governing Globalization: Power, Authority, and Global Governance.* Cambridge: Polity Press, 2002, pp. 209–233.

— — —. "Postwar Political Economy in Bosnia and Herzegovina: The Spoils of Peace." *Global Governance* 8, no. 4 (October–December 2002): 467–482.

Pythian, Mark. "Intelligence and the Illicit Arms Trade: Problem or Solution?" Paper presented at the British International Studies Association conference, LSE, London, December 16–18, 2002.

Ramet, Sabrina Petra. *Balkan Babel: The Disintegration of Yugoslavia from the Death of Tito to Ethnic War.* 2nd ed. Boulder, CO: Westview Press, 1996.

Ramet, Sabrina Petra, and Ljubisa S. Adamovic, eds. *Beyond Yugoslavia: Politics, Economic, and Culture in a Shattered Community.* Boulder, CO: Westview Press, 1995.

Rashid, Ahmed. *Taliban: Islam, Oil, and the New Great Game in Central Asia.* London: I. B. Tauris, 2000.

Reno, William. "Clandestine Economies, Violence, and States in Africa." *Journal of International Affairs* 53, no. 2 (2000): 433–460.

— — —. "Resources and the Future of Violent Conflict in Sierra Leone." Paper presented at the British International Studies Association conference, LSE, London, December 16–18, 2002.

— — —. "War and the Failure of Peacekeeping in Sierra Leone." In Stockholm International Peace Research Institute, *SIPRI Yearbook 2001: Armaments, Disarmament, and International Security.* Oxford: Oxford University Press, 2001.

— — —. *Warlord Politics and African States.* Boulder, CO: Lynne Rienner, 1999.

Richards, Paul. *Fighting for the Rain Forest: War, Youth, and Resources in Sierra Leone.* London: James Currey, 1996.

Rogers, Paul. *Losing Control: Global Security in the Twenty-First Century.* London: Pluto Press, 2000.

Roy, O. *Islam and Resistance in Afghanistan.* Cambridge: Cambridge University Press, 1985.

— — —. "The Transnational Dimension of Radical Islamic Movements." In *Talibanization: Extremism and Regional Instability in South and Central Asia.* Brussels: Conflict Prevention Network and Stiftung Wissenschaaft und Politik, 2001.

Rubin, Barnett. *The Fragmentation of Afghanistan: State Formation and Collapse in the International System.* Lahore, Pakistan: Vanguard Books, 1996.

— — —. "The Political Economy of War and Peace in Afghanistan." *World Development* 28, no. 10 (2000): 1789–1803.

Rubin, Barnett J., A. Ghani, W. Maley, A. Rashid, and O. Roy. "Afghanistan: Reconstruction and Peacemaking in a Regional Framework." Swiss Center for

Peacebuilding (KOFF), Peacebuilding Reports no. 1, 2001. Bern (June 2001).

Schierup, Carl-Ulrik. *Migration, Socialism, and the International Division of Labour*. Aldershot: Avebury, 1990.

— — —. "Prelude to the Inferno: Economic Disintegration and Political Fragmentation of Socialist Yugoslavia." *Migration* no. 5 (1993): 5–40.

Schierup, Carl-Ulrik, ed. *Scramble for the Balkans: Nationalism, Globalism, and the Political Economy of Reconstruction*. Basingstoke: Macmillan, 1999.

Sen, Amartya. *Development as Freedom*. Oxford: Oxford University Press, 1999.

Shawcross, William. *Deliver Us from Evil: Warlords and Peacekeepers in a World of Endless Conflict*. London: Bloomsbury, 2000.

Sherman, Jake (rapporteur). *The Economics of War: The Intersection of Need, Creed, and Greed—A Conference Report*. Washington, DC: Woodrow Wilson International Center for Scholars, 2002.

Silber, Laura, and Allan Little. *The Death of Yugoslavia*. 2nd ed. London: Penguin, 1996.

Singer, M., and A. Wildavsky. *The Real World Order: Zones of Peace and Zones of Turmoil*. Chatham, NJ: Chatham House Publishers, 1993.

Smaldone, Joseph P. "Mali and the West African Light Weapons Moratorium." In Jeffrey Boutwell and Michael T. Klare, eds., *Light Weapons and Civil Conflict: Controlling the Tools of Violence*. Lanham, MD: Rowman and Littlefield, 1999, pp. 129–145.

Small Arms Survey. *Small Arms Survey 2002: Counting the Human Cost*. Oxford: Oxford University Press, 2002.

Smillie, Ian, Lansana Gberie, and Ralph Hazleton. *The Heart of the Matter: Sierra Leone, Diamonds, and Human Security*. Ottawa: Partnership Africa Canada, 2000.

Solioz, Christophe, and Svebor Dizdarević, eds. *Ownership Process in Bosnia and Herzegovina*. 2nd ed. Baden-Baden: Nomos Verl. Ges., 2003.

Sørensen, Jens Stilhoff. *The Threatening Precedent: Kosovo and the Remaking of Crisis*. MERGE Paper on Transcultural Studies, no. 2, 1999. Norrköping: University of Umeå, 1999.

Spear, Joanna. "The Security Sector: The Political Economy of Private Military Security: The Case of Sierra Leone." Paper presented at the British International Studies Association conference, LSE, London, December 16–18, 2002.

Stedman, Stephen John, Donald Rothchild, and Elizabeth M. Cousens, eds. *Ending Civil Wars: The Implementation of Peace Agreements*. Boulder, CO: Lynne Rienner, 2002.

Steil, B., and Susan Woodward. "A European New Deal for the Balkans?" *Foreign Affairs* 78, no. 6 (November–December 1999): 95–105.

Stewart, Francis. "Horizontal Inequalities as a Source of Conflict." In Fen Osler Hampson and David M. Malone, eds. *From Reaction to Conflict Prevention: Opportunities for the UN System*. Boulder, CO: Lynne Rienner, 2002, pp. 105–136.

Stiglitz, Joseph. *Globalization and Its Discontents*. London: Penguin, 2002.

Stojanov, Dragoljub. "International Financial Institutions and the Financial Stability in B&H (Federation of B&H)." Paper presented at the conference

"International Financial Institutions and Sustainable Development," Media Centre, Belgrade, December 2002.

———. "Understanding B&H Reform." Paper presented at the conference "Serbia and Monte Negro on the Way to EU," Belgrade, December 2002.

Strazzari, Francesco. "Between Ethnic Collusion and Mafia Collusion: The 'Balkan Route' to State Making." In Dietrich Jung, ed., *Shadow Globalization, Ethnic Conflicts, and New Wars: A Political Economy of Intra-State War*. London: Routledge, 2003, pp. 140–162.

Thomas, Caroline. *Global Governance, Development, and Human Security*. London: Pluto, 2000.

Tilly, Charles. *Coercion, Capital and European States, A.D. 900–1992*. Rev. ed. Oxford: Blackwell, 1990.

———. "War Making and State Making as Organised Crime." In P. Evans, D. Reuschemeyer, and T. Skocpol, eds., *Bringing the State Back In*. Cambridge: Cambridge University Press, 1995.

Titus, Paul, ed. *Marginality and Modernity: Ethnicity and Change in Post-Colonial Baluchistan*. Oxford: Oxford University Press, 1996.

Tomaš, Rajko. *Analysis of the Grey Economy in Republika Srpska*. Banja Luka: United Nations Development Programme, March 1998.

Turton, D., and P. Marsden, P. "Taking Refugees for a Ride? The Politics of Refugee Return to Afghanistan." Afghan Research and Evaluation Unit. Issues Paper Series, December 2002.

United Kingdom, House of Commons, International Development Committee. "Afghanistan: The Transition from Humanitarian Relief to Reconstruction and Development Assistance. First Report of Session 2002–3." Report together with the proceedings of the Committee, Minutes of Evidence, and Appendices, January 14, 2003.

United Nations. *United Nations Conference on the Least Developed Countries: Country Presentation by the Government of Sierra Leone*. Geneva: United Nations, 1990.

———. *Report of the Panel of Experts Appointed Pursuant to Security Council Resolution 1395 (2002), Paragraph 4, in Relation to Liberia*. S/2002/470. April 19, 2002.

———. *Report of the Panel of Experts Appointed Pursuant to UN Security Council Resolution 1306 (2000), Paragraph 19, in Relation to Sierra Leone*. S/2000/1195. December 20, 2000.

———. *Report of the Panel of Experts on Violations of Security Council Sanctions Against UNITA, Established by the Security Council Pursuant to Resolution 1237 (1999) Concerning the Situation in Angola*. S/2000/203. March 10, 2000.

———. *Report of the Panel of Experts Pursuant to Security Council Resolution 1343 (2001), Paragraph 19, Concerning Liberia*. S/2001/1015. October 26, 2001.

———. *Sixteenth Report of the Secretary General on the United Nations Mission in Sierra Leone*. S/2002/1417. December 24, 2002.

———. *United Nations Conference on the Least Developed Countries: Country Presentation by the Government of Sierra Leone*. Geneva: United Nations, 1990.

United Nations Development Programme (UNDP). *Early Warning System: Bosnia and Herzegovina*. Quarterly report, April–May 2002.

——— . *Human Development Report: Bosnia and Herzegovina, 2002*. Sarajevo: United Nations Development Programme, 2002.

United Nations Drug Control Program. "The Impact of the Taliban Prohibition on Opium Poppy Cultivation in Afghanistan." Islamabad, May 28, 2002.

U.S. General Accounting Office. *Drug Control: Efforts to Develop Alternatives to Cultivating Illicit Crops in Colombia Have Made Little Progress and Face Serious Obstacles*. GAO-02-291, Washington, DC: GAO, February 2002.

——— . *International Trade: Critical Issues Remain in Deterring Conflict Diamond Trade*. GA-02-678, Washington, DC: GAO, June 2002.

Uvin, Peter. *The Influence of Aid in Situations of Violent Conflict*. Report of the Informal Task Group on Conflict, Peace, and Development Co-operation, Development Assistance Committee. Paris: Organization for Economic Cooperation and Development, September 1999.

Van der Pijl, Kees. *Transnational Classes and International Relations*. London: Routledge, 1998.

Vaux, Tony, and Jonathan Goodhand. "Disturbing Connections: Aid and Conflict in Kyrgyzstan." *Conflict Assessments* 3, Centre for Defence Studies, King's College, London (July 2001).

Verdery, Katherine. *What Was Socialism and What Comes Next?* Princeton: Princeton University Press, 1996.

Vickers, Rhiannon. "Labour's Search for a Third Way in Foreign Policy." In Richard Little and Mark Wickham Jones, eds., *New Labour's Foreign Policy: A New Moral Crusade?* Manchester: Manchester University Press, 2000, pp. 33–45.

von der Schulenburg, M. "Illicit Opium Production in Afghanistan." In C. Noelle-Karimi, C. Schetter, and R. Schlagintweit, eds., *Afghanistan: A Country Without a State?* Frankfurt: IKO-Verlag für Interkulturelle Kommunikation, 2002.

Vucinich, Wayne S., ed. *Contemporary Yugoslavia: Twenty Years of Socialist Experiment*. Berkeley: University of Californian Press, 1969.

Vukadinović, Nebojsa. "Economies d'après-guerre entre reconstruction et transition." *Relations Internationales et Stratégiques* 28 (Winter 1997): 47–62.

Wallensteen, Peter. *Understanding Conflict Resolution. War, Peace and the Global System*. London: Sage, 2002.

Wallensteen, Peter, and Margareta Sollenberg. "Armed Conflict and Regional Conflict Complexes, 1989–97." *Journal of Peace Research* 35, no. 5 (September 1998): 621–634.

West Africa Network for Peace-building. *Crisis in Côte d'Ivoire*, WARN Policy Brief, November 6, 2002. www.wanep.org/aboutwanep.htm.

——— . *Côte d'Ivoire Crisis: WANEP Policy Briefs Update: December 3, 2002*. www.wanep.org/wanep_policy_briefs_update.htm.

Willett, Susan, ed. *Structural Conflict in the New Global Disorder: Insecurity and Development. IDS Bulletin* 32, no. 2 (April 2001).

Williams, John, Donald Sutherland, Kimberley Cartwright, and Martin Byrnes. *Sierra Leone: Diamond Policy Study*. January 2002. www.dfid.gov.uk.

Williams, Paul. "Fighting for Freetown: British Military Intervention in Sierra Leone." *Contemporary Security Policy* (Special Issue: "Dimensions of Western Military Intervention") 22, no. 3 (2001): 140–168.

Woodward, Susan L. *The Balkan Tragedy: Chaos and Dissolution After the Cold War.* Washington, DC: Brookings Institution, 1995.

— — —. "Economic Priorities for Successful Peace Implementation." In Stephen Stedman, Donald Rothchild, and Elizabeth Cousens, eds., *Ending Civil Wars: the Implementation of Peace Agreements.* Boulder, CO: Lynne Rienner, 2002, pp. 183–214.

— — —. *Economic Priorities for Peace Implementation.* International Peace Academy (IPA) Policy Paper Series on Peace Implementation. New York: IPA, October 2002.

World Bank. *Reconstruction and Development Program in Bosnia and Herzegovina: Progress Update.* Sarajevo: World Bank, June 2002.

— — —. *Transitional Support Strategy for the Republic of Sierra Leone.* March 3, 2002. www-wds.worldbank.org/servlet.

Zack-William, Alfred B. "Sierra Leone: The Political Economy of Civil War, 1991–1998." *Third World Quarterly* 20, no. 1 (1999): 143–162.

Index

About the Book

Confronting the corrosive influence that war economies typically have on the prospects for peace in war-torn societies, this study critically analyzes current policy responses and offers a thought-provoking foundation for the development of more effective peacebuilding strategies.

The authors focus on the role played by trade in precipitating and fueling conflict, with particular emphasis on the regional dynamics that are created by war economies. Their analysis highlights the darker side of the commitment to deregulation, open markets, and the expansion of trade routes that are key features of globalization. In each of these three case studies—Sierra Leone, Afghanistan, and Bosnia—they examine the nature of the war economy, the regional networks developed to support it, its legacies, and the impact of initiatives to transform it. That transformation, they argue, a process central to the transition from violent conflict to sustainable peace, can best be achieved through approaches that recognize critical regional factors.

Michael Pugh is director of the Plymouth International Studies Centre, University of Plymouth (UK). His publications include *Regeneration of War-Torn Societies* (editor) and *The United Nations and Regional Security: Europe and Beyond* (coeditor), and he is editor of the journal *International Peacekeeping*. **Neil Cooper** is principal lecturer in international relations at the University of Plymouth. He has published extensively on the arms trade and postconflict demilitarization and is coauthor of a forthcoming book on globalization, violence, and insecurity. **Jonathan Goodhand** is lecturer in development practice at the School of Oriental and African Studies, University of London. He has worked with numerous nongovernmental organizations, as well as the UK Department for International Development, in the areas of conflict analysis and prevention.